LOCKE

LOCKE

His Philosophical Thought

NICHOLAS JOLLEY

OXFORD
UNIVERSITY PRESS

*This book has been printed digitally and produced in a standard specification
in order to ensure its continuing availability*

OXFORD
UNIVERSITY PRESS

Great Clarendon Street, Oxford OX2 6DP

Oxford University Press is a department of the University of Oxford.
It furthers the University's objective of excellence in research, scholarship,
and education by publishing worldwide in

Oxford New York

Auckland Bangkok Buenos Aires Cape Town Chennai
Dar es Salaam Delhi Hong Kong Istanbul Karachi Kolkata
Kuala Lumpur Madrid Melbourne Mexico City Mumbai Nairobi
São Paulo Shanghai Taipei Tokyo Toronto

Oxford is a registered trade mark of Oxford University Press
in the UK and in certain other countries

Published in the United States
by Oxford University Press Inc., New York

© Nicholas Jolley 1999

ISBN 0-19-875200-8

Acknowledgements

During the course of writing this book I have incurred a number of debts to colleagues and fellow scholars. I am particularly indebted to two referees for Oxford University Press for their constructive and detailed criticisms of an earlier draft. I am also grateful to Michael Mendelson and Steven Yalowitz for reading various chapters and making helpful suggestions. Over the years I have benefited from many conversations about Locke with Henry Allison, Richard Arneson, Mark Collier, David Cunning, Michael LeBuffe, and Kyle Stanford.

I am very grateful to Tim Barton of Oxford University Press for inviting me to write this book and to his successor, Peter Momtchiloff, for his advice and encouragement. Finally, I should like to thank Angela Griffin and her colleagues for their expert assistance in overseeing the publication of the book.

Contents

Abbreviations

CL   *The Correspondence of John Locke*, ed. E. S. de Beer, 8 vols. (Oxford, 1976–89).

E   *John Locke: An Essay Concerning Human Understanding*, ed. P. H. Nidditch (Oxford, 1975). References are by book, chapter, and section.

ELN   *John Locke: Essays on the Law of Nature*, ed. W. von Leyden (Oxford, 1954).

ET   *John Locke: Epistola de Tolerantia / Letter on Toleration*, ed. R. Klibansky and J. W. Gough (Oxford, 1968).

LW   *The Works of John Locke*, 10 vols. (London, 1823; repr. Aalen, 1963).

T   *John Locke: Two Treatises of Government*, ed. P. Laslett (Cambridge, 1960). References are by treatise and paragraph.

In quotations from the *Essay* and the *Two Treatises* Locke's spelling and capitalization have been modernized; however, his punctuation and use of italics have been retained.

1

INTRODUCTION

SINCE it was first published in 1690 Locke's famous masterpiece, the *Essay Concerning Human Understanding,* has been many things to many people. To Locke's contemporary readers it was chiefly perhaps a subversive work which seemed to undermine such orthodoxies as the doctrines of innate ideas and the immateriality of the soul. During the age of Voltaire and the Enlightenment the *Essay* came to be seen as a liberating force; Locke's theory of knowledge not only sought to free people's minds from bondage to dogma and superstition, but it also provided the philosophical basis for religious toleration. With the advent of German idealism and the philosophical historiography which it inspired, the *Essay* began to assume what is still perhaps its most familiar aspect; it was the first major work in the tradition of British Empiricism, a school which was understood to lay the foundations for knowledge in sensory experience. Unlike his supposedly more innovative successors, however, Locke failed to draw the radical sceptical conclusions to which his empiricist premises entitled him.

These perspectives on Locke are not necessarily incompatible and none of them is wholly lacking in textual justification. But at best they are one-sided and at worst seriously misleading. The tradition which sees Locke as the first member of the school of British Empiricism has been especially unfortunate for a proper understanding of his philosophy; for it tends to offer a distorted account of his fundamental purposes. On this approach the concerns of the later 'Empiricists' such as Berkeley and Hume are read back into the *Essay;* by virtue of their supposed membership in a common school the three philosophers are taken to have a common agenda of philosophical problems. For example, it has been widely assumed that one of Locke's chief philosophical concerns arises from his commitment to the thesis that the immediate objects of perception are mental items, which Locke, following Descartes, calls ideas; Locke is supposed to be preoccupied with the problem of how, on these premisses, belief in the existence of an external physical world can be justified. Although they tackled it in very different ways, both Berkeley and Hume regarded the issue of our knowledge of bodies as a central one. But an unprejudiced reading of the *Essay* suggests that this problem was nowhere near the forefront of Locke's philosophical concerns. His *Essay* does contain a kind of response to scepticism about the existence of the external world, and it is one which is perhaps more intriguing than philosophers have often allowed it to be. But, as we shall see, Locke's interest in this problem is strictly subordinate to other interests concerning knowledge. It is obviously unfair of us to seek to impose on him a set of philosophical concerns by virtue of his supposed role in founding a school; he himself never acknowledged such a role for himself, and he never knew its other members. We must allow Locke to define his own philosophical agenda in his own way.

In recent years a number of scholars have sought to throw off the shackles of a historiography inspired by German idealism. Instead of imposing on Locke a role which he never acknowledged, they have taken their cue from one which he did accept for himself; in the Epistle to the Reader Locke famously claims that it is 'ambition enough to be employed as an under-labourer' to the great scientists of his time such as Boyle, Huygens, and Newton. Armed with passages like these, writers have insisted on Locke's role in explaining, clarifying, and defending the corpuscularian theory of matter which had gained currency in his age;[1] as we shall see, this is the theory according to which all bodies are composed of particles of the same fundamental type. On this approach a very different Locke emerges from the *Essay*; instead of a philosopher obsessed with the problem of breaking out of the circle of ideas, Locke steps forward in the

---

[1] For examples of this approach, see M. Mandelbaum, *Philosophy, Science and Sense Perception* (Baltimore, 1964), ch. 1; J. W. Yolton, *Locke and the Compass of Human Understanding* (Cambridge, 1970); R. S. Woolhouse, *Locke's Philosophy of Science and Knowledge* (Oxford, 1971); and P. Alexander, *Ideas, Qualities, and Corpuscles: Locke and Boyle on the External World* (Cambridge, 1985).

guise of a scientific realist. Locke is committed to the existence of a mind-independent realm of bodies whose properties are to be understood in corpuscularian terms. Although he is agreed to be pessimistic about our chances of success, he accepts that the task of science is to uncover as much of the truth as possible about the structure of this objective realm of bodies.

Unquestionably, such an approach has marked a real advance in our understanding of Locke's philosophy. We are now no longer tempted to see his discussions of such issues as primary and secondary qualities, substance, and essences as a series of analyses of discrete, unrelated philosophical topics; instead, it is clear that these discussions are contributions to a larger, integrated philosophy of matter. Yet, for all their merits, the proponents of this approach have painted only a one-sided portrait of Locke's achievement in the *Essay*, for there is much of substance in the work which has little directly to do with our knowledge of the physical world. On this approach it comes as something of a shock and a surprise to discover that the original impetus to the writing of the *Essay* came, not from the natural sciences, but from a discussion of the principles of morality and revealed religion.[2]

The Unity of the *Essay*

In this book I shall seek to argue for the fundamental unity of Locke's thought in the *Essay*. Locke may have no special interest in the problem of scepticism about the external world, but it is still correct to describe his project in the book in epistemological terms. Following Aristotle, Locke takes it for granted that the knowledge which is of greatest philosophical interest is both universal and necessary, and in the *Essay* he is chiefly concerned to advance a remarkable body of doctrine about the basis for such knowledge; indeed, there is little in the work that does not contribute to this goal. According to Locke, universal and necessary knowledge is possible for us if and only if it is conversant about essences which are

---

[2] Here we are dependent on the testimony of Locke's friend James Tyrrell. See M. Cranston, *John Locke: A Biography* (London, 1957), 140–1. See also J. Colman, *John Locke's Moral Philosophy* (Edinburgh, 1983), ch. 1, for an account of the significance of this remark.

transparent to the intellect. And Locke further argues, as we shall see, that there is only one remotely plausible explanation of how this condition might be satisfied: it is that the essences in question have been constructed by the human mind.

From these doctrines about the basis for knowledge Locke draws some controversial conclusions about its extent; in this way he is able to assess the prospects for knowledge in the various fields of human enquiry. We can achieve knowledge in mathematics and morals because in these areas the essences we need to know are indeed human constructions; as Locke puts it, they are archetypes of the mind's own making. But the situation is wholly different with regard to the natural sciences and what we might call the metaphysics of substances; in these cases the relevant essences are not human inventions or constructions at all, but rather the work of nature, and our cognitive faculties are such that they must remain for ever opaque to us. Although knowledge is in principle possible in these areas, there are thus conclusive reasons for believing that it is beyond the reach of human beings. We shall never know the internal constitutions of the various kinds of bodies or the ultimate natures of mind and matter. Here we must be satisfied with something less than knowledge, namely probability.

Locke develops his thesis about the prospects for knowledge in the sciences more fully than any previous philosopher, but the thesis itself is not wholly unprecedented; to some extent it finds a recognizable predecessor in a philosopher whose company he would not have welcomed. Some fifty years before, Hobbes had drawn a rather similar epistemological map; he had argued that demonstrative knowledge is attainable in geometry and civil (that is, political) philosophy but not in the natural sciences, where we must rest content with conjecture.[3] On the face of it, too, Hobbes's reasons are similar to those which Locke offers. The epistemological transparency of geometry and political philosophy derives from the fact that they are concerned with what we ourselves construct; geometrical figures and states or commonwealths are alike human artefacts. The epistemological opacity of the physical sciences, by contrast, derives from the fact that it is nature, not we, who makes

---

[3] See *The English Works of Thomas Hobbes*, ed. W. Molesworth, 11 vols. (London, 1839–45), vii. 184. Cf. J. W. N. Watkins, *Hobbes's System of Ideas*, 2nd edn. (London, 1973), 45.

bodies; here we can only conjecture about how natural phenomena came into being. Yet despite the superficial similarities, there is, I think, a difference in emphasis between the two thinkers. For Locke, the mathematical and moral essences which we construct are mental items; they are ideas whose logical consequences are perspicuous to us. It is this feature of such essences, rather than their status as human constructions, which is at least the immediate source of the certainty that we can attain in ethics and mathematics.

There is no doubt that Locke wishes to highlight his pessimism about the prospects for knowledge in the natural sciences and in the basic ontology of mind and matter; the theme is sounded on the very title-page of the *Essay* through a quotation from Ecclesiastes which seeks to invest it with the prestige of biblical authority: 'As thou knowest not what is the way of the spirit, nor how the bones do grow in the womb of her that is with child; even so thou knowest not the works of God, who maketh all things' (Eccles. 11: 5). Here Locke seeks to align himself with a tradition in philosophy which stressed the 'vanity of dogmatizing'.[4] But though Locke is committed to agnosticism about the ultimate natures of mind and matter, he none the less believes that it is possible and important to develop theoretical models in these areas. In the *Essay* he endorses the corpuscularian hypothesis about the structure of matter, but he devotes far more space and attention to developing a theory of mental contents (ideas) which appears to be modelled on the corpuscularian hypothesis. Both theories are guided by the intuition that we can offer intelligible explanations of the phenomena on the assumption that they are resolvable into simple elements which are homogeneous in nature. Locke thus believes that it is valuable and instructive to develop such models, but he is under no illusions about their ultimate epistemological status; the corpuscularian hypothesis, for instance, may be the most intelligible account of the structure of matter that has been offered, but, as we shall see, it does not meet the standards for genuine knowledge.

---

[4] *The Vanity of Dogmatizing* (1661) is the title of a book by Joseph Glanvill, who was closely associated with the early Royal Society. Although Glanvill charges the Aristotelian–Scholastic tradition with dogmatism, he never criticizes Descartes on these grounds.

The Metaphysics of Morals

Many people have paid at least lip-service to Locke's project of assessing the prospects for knowledge in the various fields of human enquiry. But the role which this project plays in organizing the *Essay* has not been fully appreciated. In particular, Locke's concern with the possibility of a demonstrative science of ethics has received somewhat less than its due; in fact, it has far-reaching ramifications for an understanding of the *Essay* as a whole. No one can reasonably complain that Locke has failed to prepare the ground for his interest in this topic; it is suggested by two well-known remarks in the Introduction: 'Our business here is not to know all things, but those which concern our conduct' (*E* 1. 1. 6); 'The candle, that is set up in us, shines bright enough for all our purposes' (*E* 1. 1. 5). It may be tempting to some readers to dismiss these remarks as conventionally pious asides, but I believe that this would be a mistake. Locke is preparing the reader for one of the central themes of the *Essay*; moral knowledge is of primary importance to us as God's creatures, and our natural faculties are such that we are capable of achieving it. Locke may stop short here of explicitly stating his commitment to a demonstrative science of ethics, but he certainly lays the basis for it.

More importantly, Locke seeks to underpin his commitment to such a science of ethics by outlining what we may call a 'metaphysics of morals'; he seems to see that he needs to offer a theoretical account of the conditions for moral responsibility. In order to be morally accountable for actions, it is necessary to be a person, and in a deservedly famous chapter Locke explains the nature of personhood and personal identity over time. In order to be a bearer of moral responsibility it is further necessary to be a free agent who in some sense could do otherwise, and in a long and only slightly less famous chapter Locke explains the nature of such freedom. In these chapters we can imagine Locke as implicitly answering a sceptic about the prospects for a science of ethics, for he seeks to show how we can at least know that these conditions for moral responsibility are satisfied. Locke's discussions of personal identity and free will conform to the same pattern and enforce the same moral; there are no relevant metaphysical facts which are hidden from our cognitive gaze. His development of this theme is particularly striking in connection with the topic of personal identity, for here, as he well recognizes, it is natural but mistaken to suppose that there are relevant metaphysical facts which are not available to us; we may be tempted to believe that we cannot know what it is to be a person unless we know the ultimate nature of the substance in which consciousness inheres. Locke argues that knowledge on this issue is indeed not to be had, but he strongly disputes its relevance for an understanding of personal identity and moral responsibility.

The Response to Descartes

To understand Locke's theory of knowledge, it is helpful to see that he self-consciously rejects two of the principal doctrines of his most influential predecessor in the seventeenth century. Descartes of course shared Locke's conviction that demonstrative knowledge is possible in mathematics, but he had also argued that metaphysics and the natural sciences were capable of emulating the achievements of mathematics; he had sought to show that we can achieve certainty concerning the ultimate natures of mind and matter and, at least on some readings, he believed that the most general laws of physics could be deduced from a priori metaphysical principles.[5] Descartes had combined his teachings about the prospects for human knowledge with a distinctive thesis about the basis of such knowledge; it is to be found in the 'clear and distinct' ideas and truths which a benevolent God has implanted in our minds from birth. The key to realizing our epistemological potential lies in uncovering, or, in computer jargon, 'accessing', these innate ideas and truths. As we have seen, Locke stakes out strikingly different positions on both these issues. Not merely does he offer a theory of the prospects for knowledge in the various disciplines which is in large measure more pessimistic than the Cartesian account, but he advances a very different theory of how the knowledge which we can hope to achieve is possible; for Locke, we realize our epistemological potential not by attending to God-given innate ideas, but

---

[5] For a balanced discussion of the issue of Descartes's commitment to a priori science, see B. Williams, *Descartes: The Project of Pure Enquiry* (Harmondsworth, 1978), ch. 9.

through perceiving the conceptual connections among ideas which we are forced to construct ourselves from the raw materials of sensation and introspection. One way of drawing the contrast between the two philosophers might be couched in theological terms. Descartes's God has done most of the work for us, whereas Locke's God confines his role to endowing us with natural faculties; he then leaves it up to us to complete the cognitive task.

Locke thus self-consciously opposes Descartes's central teachings concerning the extent and basis of human knowledge, and in the *Essay* he offers rival positive theories of his own in their place. But it would be quite wrong to suppose that Locke's attitude towards Descartes's epistemology is a wholly negative one. The mistake of characterizing Locke's attitude in these terms has been made many times in the past, and there is no excuse for repeating it; the weight of Lady Masham's testimony, as well as Locke's own, is against it.[6] Not merely does Locke tend to follow Descartes by subscribing to a strong conception of knowledge such that knowledge is paradigmatically a priori, but more importantly perhaps he approves of the strand of what we may call 'epistemological individualism' in Descartes's teachings. This strand in Descartes's thought is most famously and dramatically expressed in the programme of methodic doubt with which he opens the *Meditations*; none of our beliefs should be allowed to be exempt from rational scrutiny. But Descartes's epistemological individualism is also expressed, less dramatically, in a conceptual truth about the nature of knowledge to which he subscribes. For Descartes, if I genuinely know that p then I am in a position to justify my belief that p without reference to expert opinion or the authority of others; I must be able to see for myself that there is overwhelming evidence in favour of p.

This strand of epistemological individualism in Descartes's teaching was no doubt one of the attractions which his philosophy initially exerted on Locke. But the Locke of the *Essay* seems to

---

[6] According to Lady Masham, 'the first books (as Mr Locke himself has told me) which gave him a relish of philosophical studies were those of Descartes. He was rejoiced in reading of these because though he very often differed in opinion from this writer, yet he found that what he said was very intelligible; from whence he was encouraged to think that his not having understood others had, possibly, not proceeded altogether from a defect in his understanding.' Quoted in Cranston, *John Locke*, 100. In the last years of his life Locke was a paying guest of Lady Masham, who was the daughter of the Cambridge Platonist Ralph Cudworth. Cf. also *Letter to the Bishop of Worcester*, LW iv. 48.

believe that Descartes had not remained faithful to this programmatic commitment; in a sense Descartes's execution of his
philosophical project was an example of 'the revolution betrayed'.
Locke's dissatisfaction with Descartes on the grounds of betraying
his own principles is implicit in his response to the doctrine of innate
ideas. Locke argues explicitly that the defenders of this doctrine
had exploited it for the purposes of encouraging blind acceptance
of their opinions; they had removed various propositions from the
sphere of critical scrutiny by declaring that they were innate, and
thus unquestionably true and not to be challenged. Although Locke
does not mention Descartes or his disciples by name, it is reasonable to infer that they are the intended target of attack; through their
abuse of the doctrine of innate ideas, they had abandoned the spirit
of methodic doubt and returned to the very kind of epistemological authoritarianism which Descartes himself had earlier excoriated
(See *E* 1. 4. 24 and 4. 20. 8).

The Unity of Locke's Thought as a Whole

The principle of unity of the *Essay* is thus furnished by the systematic case which it offers for a striking combination of optimism and
pessimism about the prospects for human knowledge. Indeed, we
shall see how the *Essay* possesses a greater degree of unity than it
appears to do, for the famous discussions of personal identity and
free will play a crucial role in underpinning the optimistic side of
Locke's epistemological story. But though the *Essay Concerning
Human Understanding* is indisputably Locke's masterpiece, it is not
of course his only work; he is the author of a number of other
books, at least two of which—the Second Treatise of Government
and the *Letter on Toleration*—are also influential classics in their own
right. It is natural to ask, then, whether the thematic unity of the
Essay is complemented by a comparable unity in Locke's writings
as a whole.

The question is not easy to answer. It is true that a number of
these works—from the early *Essays on the Law of Nature* to the late
Reasonableness of Christianity—testify to Locke's lifelong interest in
the problems of moral epistemology; to this extent they are of a
piece with the project of the *Essay* in terms of the issues. But it is

not clear that a single consistent position is to be found in these writings. The problem of consistency is really twofold. First, even in a work such as the Second Treatise of Government, where Locke is optimistic about the possibility of achieving moral knowledge by means of reason, the grounds of his optimism do not appear to be the same as in the *Essay*: his treatment of moral epistemology in the Second Treatise is somewhat sketchy, but it seems to favour a theory of innate moral knowledge of precisely the kind which he had studiously rejected in the *Essay*. Secondly, in some of his works, especially the *Reasonableness of Christianity*, Locke appears to be much less optimistic about the prospects of rational moral knowledge than in either the *Essay* or the Second Treatise.[7] It is true that he does not officially withdraw his earlier claim that a demonstrative science of morality is possible in principle; none the less, as compared with the *Essay*, there is a clear shift of emphasis. What Locke now seeks to stress is the difficulties of knowing our moral duties through reason alone, and the consequent need for divine revelation; in Locke's rather attenuated version of Christianity, the chief aim of Jesus's mission to mankind is to confirm the content of our moral duties and to provide incentives for performing them in the shape of heavenly rewards.

A concern, amounting almost to an obsession, with the prospects for moral knowledge is thus a constant theme in Locke's writings from the academic disputations of his youth to the religious treatise of his old age; none the less, he seems to have changed his mind on a number of key issues. If we are to find a unifying theme in Locke's writings, we may locate it rather in his concern with promoting the cause of toleration and in his opposition to authoritarian societies which deny freedom of conscience to their citizens.[8] We have already seen that one reason why Locke became critical of Descartes was his belief that there were tendencies in Descartes's philosophy which encouraged a return to epistemological authoritarianism. When, in contrast to Descartes, Locke develops the agnostic, anti-dogmatic side of his theory of knowledge, he does so

---

[7] Both the Second Treatise of Government and the *Reasonableness of Christianity* were published anonymously.

[8] An exception must be made for two early tracts (1660–2) which argue against the case for religious toleration: see *John Locke: Two Tracts on Government*, ed. P. Abrams (Cambridge, 1967).

with a clear ulterior purpose. There is one place in particular in the *Essay* where Locke seeks to argue from the inevitability of our having opinions which are less than certain to the value of tolerating a diversity of views:

> Since therefore it is unavoidable to the greatest part of men, if not all, to have several *opinions*, without certain and indubitable proofs of their truths; and it carries too great an imputation of ignorance, lightness, or folly, for men to quit and renounce their former tenets, presently upon the offer of an argument, which they cannot immediately answer, and show the insufficiency of: it would, methinks, become all men to maintain *peace*, and the common offices of humanity, *and friendship, in the diversity of opinions*, since we cannot reasonably expect, that anyone should readily and obsequiously quit his own opinion, and embrace ours with a blind resignation to an authority, which the understanding of man acknowledges not. (*E* 4. 16. 4)

Now Locke is not explicit on the point here, but there is no mystery about the kinds of opinions which he has primarily in mind. Although the Locke of the *Essay* is optimistic about moral epistemology, he was never sanguine about the prospects for genuine knowledge in the sphere of religion. It is true that he agrees with the weight of the philosophical tradition in holding that the existence of God can be demonstrated, and he also acknowledges that there are precepts of natural religion which are plain and intelligible (*E* 3. 9. 23), but in general he is emphatic that religious enquiry is a sphere of great concern to us in which we must be content with belief, not knowledge.

It is not only in the *Essay* that Locke seeks to deploy epistemological considerations in the service of the cause of toleration. As we shall see in Chapter 9, in the *Letter on Toleration* Locke advances a very interesting argument from a non-Cartesian thesis about the nature of belief; in contrast to Descartes, it seems, Locke holds that belief is not a mental state which is under our voluntary control. But of course it would be foolish to pretend that in all his mature writings Locke is concerned to develop just such a case. Yet we can say that all his mature writings are contributions to a larger project of which the epistemological argument for toleration is a small but significant part; in their different ways, they all seek to make a case for an intellectually 'open society' in which citizens are free to think for themselves and to pursue their interest in salvation provided that they do not violate the rights of others.[9] By modern standards his conception of such a society may seem imperfect, and subject to qualifications which we now consider unjustified.[10] But the fact that the idea of an open society has become established in the West is in no small measure due to the writings of John Locke.

[9] For a similar emphasis, see the editor's introduction, G. A. J. Rogers (ed.), *Locke's Philosophy: Content and Context* (Oxford, 1994).

[10] Notoriously, in the *Letter on Toleration* (*Epistola de Tolerantia*), Locke argues that atheists and Roman Catholics should be excluded from toleration—the former because they cannot be trusted to keep promises, the latter because they owe allegiance to a foreign power. See *ET* 131–5.

2

THE PROJECT OF THE *ESSAY*

IN his quiet and unassuming way Locke proposes a revolution in philosophical method; the discipline should be reorientated towards what we now call epistemology or the theory of knowledge. In his view previous philosophers had been guilty of a serious mistake; they had simply assumed at the outset that the human mind is capable of achieving ultimate knowledge of the basic furniture of the universe. Instead, Locke believes that the very possibility of such metaphysical knowledge should be called into question. The proper method in philosophy is to examine the nature of knowledge itself and of our own cognitive faculties to see if they are adequate to the task.

Ever since his contemporaries there have been readers of Locke's *Essay* who have been tempted to play down or even ignore his statements of revolutionary intent. In the *New Essays on Human Understanding*, for instance, his commentary on the *Essay*, Leibniz simply passes over Locke's account of his project and effectively begins his critique by responding to Locke's polemic against innate ideas. The same absence of careful attention to Locke's account of his project is also characteristic of recent work which stresses his commitment to a form of scientific realism. On this view presumably there is so much metaphysics embedded in the *Essay* that Locke's stated resolve of questioning the possibility of such knowledge need not be taken very seriously; thus his claims on our attention must lie elsewhere. But this neglect of Locke's description of his project is a mistake. It is surely dangerous in general to ignore what a philosopher takes himself to be doing, and in Locke's case we thereby miss a central part of his importance and originality in the history of philosophy. By questioning the very possibility of metaphysical knowledge Locke inaugurates an 'epistemological turn' which was to launch philosophy on the road to Kant.

Locke's quiet revolution is important for understanding the unity of the *Essay*. One writer has said that the goal of Locke's project in his work is to save us needless intellectual effort and concentrate our minds on profitable enquiries instead.[1] But although this may be one of Locke's goals, it is not the only one or even the most important. We saw in the previous chapter that the pessimistic side of Locke's epistemology is in the service of his concern to promote the cause of toleration, and we can see here, in more specific terms, how his project of examining the prospects for knowledge is designed to contribute to that cause. In Locke's view the notorious heat and violence of seventeenth-century debates over metaphysical and religious issues had been fuelled by the assumption that certain and unrevisable knowledge was equally possible across the whole field of human enquiry; we could hope to achieve the same secure knowledge about the immortality of the soul as about the Pythagorean theorem in mathematics. Locke seeks to call such assumptions into question, and the conclusion at which he arrives is that they are indeed false. He is confident that establishing the falsity of such assumptions will contribute to a more temperate intellectual climate; once people are convinced by argument that they not merely do not, but cannot hope to, have certain knowledge in some areas of human enquiry they will be less inclined to be intolerant of other views; they will see that they are opposing belief, not in the name of knowledge, but in the name of simply other beliefs. Locke's confidence may perhaps be faulted as naive, for even if I concede that I necessarily lack knowledge on some topic, I might still defend my intolerance of other people's beliefs on the grounds that mine are strongly justified whereas theirs are not. But that he does feel such a confidence is suggested by some of his early statements:

If by this inquiry into the nature of the understanding, I can discover the powers thereof; *how far* they reach; to what things they are in any degree proportionate; and where they fail us, I suppose it may be of use, to prevail

[1] D. J. O'Connor, *John Locke* (London, 1952), 27. Cf. R. I. Aaron, *John Locke*, 3rd edn. (Oxford, 1971), 77.

with the busy mind of man, to be more cautious in meddling with things exceeding its comprehension; to stop, when it is at the utmost extent of its tether; and to sit down in a quiet ignorance of those things, which, upon examination, are found to be beyond the reach of our capacities. We should not then perhaps be so forward, out of an affectation of an universal knowledge, to raise questions, and perplex ourselves and others with disputes about things, to which our understandings are not suited; and of which we cannot frame in our minds any clear or distinct perceptions, or whereof (as it has perhaps too often happened) we have not any notions at all. (*E* 1. 1. 4)

And a little later Locke remarks that once we recognize the limits of our understandings, we shall 'not *peremptorily, or intemperately* require demonstration, and demand certainty, where probability only is to be had' (*E* 1. 1. 5; emphasis added). Locke's project may thus contribute not just to our own peace of mind, but to the peace of society as a whole. It is this noble aspiration which inspires the project of the *Essay* and not simply a desire to save ourselves needless intellectual effort.

Locke's Statements of Purpose

Locke seems to explain his fundamental purposes in two places in the *Essay* in rather different ways. In the Epistle to the Reader he describes his role in a way which famously combines handsome praise of his contemporaries with a remarkably self-deprecating account of his own contribution:

The commonwealth of learning, is not at this time without master builders, whose mighty designs, in advancing the sciences, will leave lasting monuments to the admiration of posterity; but everyone must not hope to be a Boyle, or a Sydenham; and in an age that produces such masters, as the great Huygenius and the incomparable Mr Newton, with some others of that strain; it is ambition enough to be employed as an under-labourer in clearing ground a little, and removing some of the rubbish, that lies in the way to knowledge.

In recent years it is this account of Locke's role which has received most attention, even at the expense of his statements in the

Introduction. Writers have seized on this passage as evidence that Locke sees himself as above all perhaps an apologist for the scientific assumptions and achievements of the newly founded Royal Society. The passage is certainly helpful by suggesting that he perceives a distinction between the enterprises of philosophy and science, as we now call them. In the *Essay* at least Locke does not himself seek to make a contribution to the advancement of science; he is engaged rather in a critical enterprise or enquiry which, in contemporary terms, is second-order in nature; that is, it aims to provide knowledge about knowledge. But despite its interest the passage in the Epistle can hardly be viewed as a complete or authoritative statement of Locke's purpose in the *Essay*.

In the first place, it is impossible to miss the conventional tone of Locke's statements in the passage; he is too obviously conforming to the literary customs of the period whereby an author assumes a pose of decorous modesty. On any natural interpretation, the role of an under-labourer who clears away rubbish is not merely modest, it is also menial; and at most only a small part of Locke's project could be captured in these terms. The word 'under-labourer' may perhaps be appropriate for describing Locke's demolition work in the *Essay*; as he himself goes on to say, he will mount an attack on insignificant and pretentious forms of speech which have indeed stood as obstacles in the way of scientific progress. The role of the under-labourer also encompasses his more substantive and carefully argued polemics against specific teachings of the Cartesians and the Scholastics. But even in relation to Locke's concern with the natural sciences of his time, the 'under-labourer' passage clearly does not tell the whole story; a term with such menial connotations cannot characterize Locke's systematic attempt to demonstrate why scientific enquiry cannot hope to achieve the status of genuine knowledge.

In the second place, the 'under-labourer' passage fails to do justice to the scope of Locke's project, which extends well beyond the scientific investigation of nature. In the Epistle to the Reader Locke tells us how the seed of the *Essay* was sown when 'five or six friends, meeting at my chamber and discoursing on a subject very remote from this found themselves quickly at a stand by the difficulties that rose on every side', and Locke's friend James Tyrrell glossed this passage by recalling the subject that was discussed on that occasion; Locke and his acquaintances were investigating the principles of morality and revealed religion.[2] It is true that, looking back on that occasion, Locke thinks of the topic of the conversation as very remote from the subject of the *Essay*, but this admission need not be taken to mean that the focus of the work is exclusively the prospects for the scientific knowledge of nature. His point is rather that the *Essay* is not a treatise on ethics or on revealed religion, but instead an attempt to assess our capacities for knowledge in these and other areas of human enquiry; in a sense it is our minds and their cognitive capacities rather than science or morality which is the subject of the *Essay*. The prospects for knowledge of morality and revealed religion are as close to the heart of the *Essay* as the prospects for knowledge of the physical world.

The fact that Locke is taking knowledge in general for his province emerges in the Introduction, which contains what is clearly his official statement of purpose; here for the first time he hints at the magnitude and originality of his enterprise. Locke explains that his purpose is to 'enquire into the original, certainty, and extent of human knowledge; together, with the grounds and degrees of belief, opinion, and assent' (*E* 1. 1. 2). And towards the end of the chapter Locke seeks to motivate this ambitious enquiry into knowledge by explaining his conviction that previous philosophers have been on the wrong track:

For I thought that the first step towards satisfying several enquiries, the mind of man was very apt to run into, was, to take a survey of our own understandings, examine our own powers, and see to what things they were adapted. Till that was done I suspected we began at the wrong end, and in vain sought for satisfaction in a quiet and secure possession of truths, that most concerned us, whilst we let loose our thoughts into the vast ocean of *Being*, as if all that boundless extent, were the natural, and undoubted possession of our understandings, wherein there was nothing exempt from its decisions, or that escaped its comprehension. (*E* 1. 1. 7)

Past philosophers have thus gone astray because they have embarked on the hazardous enterprise of speculative metaphysics without troubling to enquire whether they had the cognitive resources for such a task. Progress in philosophy requires a more circumspect approach; indeed, it dictates a reorientation of the

---

[2] See Cranston, *John Locke*, 140–1.

discipline away from the theory of being (metaphysics) to the theory of knowledge.

At *E* 1. 1. 2, then, Locke indicates that his aim is to enquire not just into the nature and extent of knowledge but also into its origin; here he clearly alludes to the project which he executes in book 2 of the *Essay*, namely, that of showing how all our ideas ultimately arise from the two sources of sensation and introspection. Philosophers have sometimes objected that Locke's enterprise, as he describes it, is a hybrid one; it combines, or even conflates, psychology, which seeks for genetic explanations, with the theory of knowledge, which is concerned with issues of justification and conceptual analysis. But this criticism seems misguided. Even if we agree that there are distinguishable strands in Locke's project, there is no doubt of their mutual relevance; the issue of the origin of knowledge is crucially important to the goal of assessing its extent. For Locke, our epistemological prospects are inevitably conditioned and limited by the sources of knowledge in the raw materials of sensation and introspection. The origins of knowledge are humble, and in a sense they are never wholly transcended.

Although Locke is pessimistic about the mind's capacity for metaphysical knowledge, his project should not by any means be seen as a sceptical one. Indeed, he is clear that his project provides an antidote to scepticism; those philosophers who deny that we can know anything have been able to make headway precisely by benefiting from the absence of such a critique of the mind's powers as Locke proposes. One of his aims in the *Essay* is to attack those sceptical philosophers who fallaciously infer from the fact that ultimate metaphysical knowledge is not to be had to the impossibility of knowledge in general:

Thus men, extending their enquiries beyond their capacities, and letting their thoughts wander into those depths, where they can find no sure footing; it is no wonder, that they raise questions, and multiply disputes, which never coming to any clear resolution, are proper only to continue and increase their doubts, and to confirm them at last in perfect [i.e. complete] scepticism. (*E* 1. 1. 7)

For Locke, the sceptic may be compared to someone who infers from the fact that no human being can jump twenty feet in the air to the conclusion that no human being can jump two feet. Knowledge of the powers and structure of the human body will cure us of the temptation to draw such a foolish inference. In the same way

THE PROJECT OF THE *ESSAY* 19

knowledge of the powers and structure of the human mind will
cure us of the temptation to draw the fallacious inference of the
sceptics.

Locke's Project in Relation to Descartes

Locke may propose a revolution in philosophy, but his own claims
to originality might be disputed. It is natural to object that the credit
for this revolution belongs properly rather with Descartes; it is
surely Descartes, the 'founder of modern philosophy', who made
the issue of knowledge fundamental in the discipline. Indeed, it has
been said that before Descartes knowledge was only one human
state or achievement among others in which philosophers were
interested; after Descartes it became the prime and almost only
focus of enquiry.[3]

It would be foolish to attempt to deny Descartes's claims to originality, but it can still be said that, as far as the *Meditations* is concerned, there are significant differences between the projects of the
two philosophers. The problem that confronts Descartes in the First
Meditation is the problem of universal or radical scepticism; by
advancing the strongest sceptical arguments he can think of, he
seeks to refute those who deny that we can know anything at all,
for even the sceptic must admit the indubitability of 'I think' and 'I
exist'. Now, as we have seen, Locke believes that it is an advantage
of his project that it can block the argument for 'perfect [complete]
scepticism', but though this is indeed an advantage, it is not what
his project is essentially about. Locke's real concern is to explain the
basis for universal and necessary knowledge, and to chart its limits;
he is not interested in demonstrating the possibility of knowledge
in general.

Descartes and Locke differ also in the place which they accord to
epistemology in their philosophical enterprise. Descartes begins his
project in the *Meditations* with questions about the possibility of
knowledge in general, but he certainly does not seek to end there;
the investigation of the possibility of knowledge is merely a
propaedeutic to metaphysics and a priori science; the ultimate goal
is to discover the essences of mind and matter and the laws of the

---

[3] See e.g. O'Connor, *John Locke*, 27.

physical world. Once Descartes has exorcised the malicious demon of the First Meditation, he feels no special doubts as to whether such metaphysical knowledge is possible.[4]

Curiously enough, the same moral can be drawn from a text which appears to point in a rather different direction. It is sometimes said that if we really seek a Cartesian precedent for the project of Locke's *Essay*, we shall find it not in the *Meditations*, but in the early work the *Rules for the Direction of the Mind*. At first sight the anticipations of Locke are striking:

The most useful enquiry we can make at this stage is to ask: what is human knowledge, and what is its scope? We are at present treating this as one single question . . . This is a task which everyone with the slightest love of truth ought to undertake at least once in his life, since the true instruments of knowledge and the entire method are involved in the investigation of the problem. There is, I think, nothing more foolish than presuming, as many do, to argue about the secrets of nature, the influence of the heavens on these lower regions, the prediction of future events and so on, without ever enquiring whether human reason is adequate for discovering matters such as these.[5]

Yet, as Gibson has observed, beneath the superficial similarities lie telling differences of emphasis.[6] For Descartes, the project in question should be undertaken once at least in one's life; for Locke, it is the focus of almost a lifetime's enquiry and labour. And this difference suggests a deeper point. Unlike Locke, Descartes does not expect that the results of his enquiry will seriously disturb his confidence in the possibility of speculative metaphysics.

The Coherence of Locke's Project

Some readers may concede that Locke intends to mount a revolution in philosophical method, but, as in the case of other revolu-

[4] See M. Wilson, *Descartes* (London, 1978), 221: 'The "possibility" of metaphysics does not seem to have been genuinely problematic for Descartes.'
[5] *Rules for the Direction of the Mind*, in *The Philosophical Writings of Descartes*, trans. J. Cottingham, R. Stoothoff, and D. Murdoch, 3 vols. (Cambridge, 1985), i. 31.
[6] J. Gibson, *Locke's Theory of Knowledge and its Historical Relations* (Cambridge, 1917), 209–10.

tions, they may be sceptical about its wisdom. Although some of his critics, such as Leibniz, have simply ignored his statements of intent, others have questioned the coherence of the project which Locke proposes to undertake. The situation with regard to Locke is not without intriguing historical parallels. When Kant proposed a 'Copernican revolution' in philosophy, he was similarly taken to task by Hegel for trying to do something which was fundamentally misguided. Locke's own revolutionary project has been criticized on two logically distinct grounds.

One traditional objection to his enterprise starts from the assumption that he wants to know whether the human intellect is a reliable instrument for achieving knowledge. But Locke then proposes to test the reliability of the instrument by turning it upon itself; we are to employ our intellect to determine whether its own deliverances can be trusted. But, the objection goes, if there is reason to doubt whether we can rely on the human intellect to give us knowledge, there will equally be reason to distrust its reports when it is turned upon itself.[7] Thus the conclusions of Locke's enquiry into the trustworthiness of the human understanding are bound to be epistemically worthless.

This objection is perhaps less powerful than it initially appears to be. In the first place, it does not follow from the fact that the human intellect is a possibly faulty source of information about the external world that it is a possibly faulty instrument for reporting on its own capacities; we might have good reason to believe that it is specially adapted to this task and to nothing else. Of course, in order to justify proceeding with his project, Locke would seem to have to show that we do have good reasons for believing this; otherwise, we shall still have grounds for doubting the results of the enquiry. But the more important point is that the objection seriously mistakes the nature of his project. Locke's worry is not the Cartesian one expressed in the First Meditation that the human intellect is systematically unreliable; he is not haunted by the fear of a malicious demon who endows us with only false beliefs. The concern that underlies Locke's project is rather that the human intellect is narrow and limited in its capacity for delivering knowledge.

---

[7] See e.g. Aaron, *John Locke*, 79, for a discussion of this objection. Aaron, however, does not endorse it. See also E. Craig, *The Mind of God and the Works of Man* (Oxford, 1988), 187, for discussion of a similar criticism of Kant.

A second traditional objection questions the coherence of Locke's project of charting the limits of human knowledge. Locke seeks to determine in advance of actual enquiry that there are epistemic boundaries that the human intellect will never be able to cross. But, the objection runs, in order to be able to stake out such limits, he would need to be able to have sight of what lies on both sides of the boundary; he would need to have knowledge of what he himself declares to be impossible for us to know.[8] Thus his project is in a way self-defeating. The force of the objection may be illustrated by means of an analogy with a familiar experience. We cannot even in principle date the exact moment at which we fall asleep precisely because we cannot see on the other side of the boundary; to do so, we would need to be awake, which is *ex hypothesi* impossible in this case.

This charge is at least more relevant to Locke's project than the first, but it seems equally unjustified; it appears forceful only because it construes the metaphorical talk of boundaries too literally. What is at issue in Locke's enquiry is not a situation where a line arbitrarily divides two regions that are qualitatively identical. Rather, what Locke does is to assume a certain strong model of knowledge and argue that in some areas of enquiry our beliefs, though perhaps in some degree rationally justifiable, can never conform to this model; in other words, the necessary and sufficient conditions for knowledge cannot be satisfied. Characteristically, his procedure is to support this claim by trying to show that the logical or conceptual links required for knowledge do not exist. It is not clear that there is anything incoherent about such a strategy.

It might still be objected that Locke assumes a contrast between our lack of knowledge in various domains and the knowledge which is available to God. And it might be questioned whether Locke can coherently talk of God's knowledge in some areas if the logical links required for such knowledge do not exist. But on Locke's behalf it can be replied that he certainly would not wish to say that God can perceive non-existent logical links; such a response may be available to Descartes, who, on some accounts, accepts God's ability to do absolutely anything, but it is not open to Locke. Nor would Locke argue that God has the power to achieve knowledge in areas denied

---

[8] See O'Connor, *John Locke*, 31; cf. Aaron, *John Locke*, 79–80.

to us in a way that somehow dispenses with logical connections altogether. Rather, he would surely adopt the strategy of arguing that in the relevant areas God has different ideas or concepts from those we have; and these ideas, being richer in terms of content than our own, do have the requisite entailments. But then the objection is simply pushed one stage further back; the focus of attention is now shifted to the question of whether Locke can provide compelling arguments for saying that we are debarred from having ideas which are as rich in content as God's ideas. How we judge Locke's success here depends in part on our estimate of his polemic against innate ideas, for the existence of such ideas would seem to be at least a necessary condition of our rivalling God in terms of our conceptual resources.

The Consistency of the Execution

Locke's project in the *Essay* is also subject to a rather different kind of challenge. Some readers may concede that the coherence of the project can be defended against such objections; none the less, they may be tempted to question whether his execution of the project is consistent. As we have seen, Locke insists that previous philosophers have been led astray because they simply assumed that the human mind could have metaphysical knowledge of the ultimate nature of reality; by contrast, Locke believes that the possibility of such knowledge should be called into question. Yet it may be objected that Locke himself is guilty of violating his self-imposed restraints; for in places he helps himself to metaphysical theories about the nature of mind and matter to which he is not entitled and which his own account declares to be beyond the reach of human knowledge. Some critics, such as Leibniz, for example, have felt not merely that a lot of metaphysics is smuggled into the *Essay* but even that Locke's primary pupose is metaphysical rather than epistemological; in the eyes of Leibniz, Locke's chief aim is to insinuate a materialist theory of mind by the back door.[9] But even if we do not go as far as this, with the example of Descartes in mind we may feel

---

[9] See N. Jolley, *Leibniz and Locke: A Study of the* New Essays on Human Understanding (Oxford, 1984), esp. chs. 1 and 6.

that Locke does not adhere strictly to the demands of his own
project. In the *Meditations*, for example, (at least on the surface)
Descartes never avails himself of principles to which he has not
earned a right. Locke, by contrast, may seem to fall short of
Descartes's austere standards of methodological rigour.

This line of objection is obviously important, but it needs
clarification. In fact there are at least three distinct charges which
might be brought against Locke here. I shall argue that Locke need
plead guilty only to the least serious of them, and that he can be
acquitted of the other two.

The first charge that might be brought against Locke is that he
clearly violates the rules of order or procedure which he has laid
down for himself. Book 2 of the *Essay*, for example, is entitled 'Of
Ideas', and Locke glosses this by saying that his intention in the book
is to confirm his attack on the innatist hypothesis by showing how
the mind may acquire all its ideas from experience; in other words,
the purpose of the second book is a genetic one. Yet the reader of
this important book can hardly fail to notice that Locke has other
fish to fry; in a number of places he is clearly interested in discussing
metaphysical issues. Indeed, sometimes his project of explaining
how various ideas originate in experience seems to be little more
than a pretext for such discussions: chapters 21 and 27 begin by
explaining how we acquire the ideas of power and identity respectively, but their real concerns lie elsewhere; they seek to advocate
and defend theories of human freedom and personal identity. Somewhat similarly, chapter 1 is entitled 'Of Ideas in General and their
Original', but Locke soon switches away from explaining and
defending his empiricist hypothesis of idea-acquisition to mounting
a sustained polemic against the Cartesian doctrine that the soul
always thinks.

It must be admitted that in places Locke departs from the rules
of order which he has established for himself, and that he entitles
chapters in a way that sometimes masks their real contents. It is
perhaps this lack of honesty in advertising which helped to form
Leibniz's conviction that Locke has a secret agenda in the *Essay*. Yet
even if Locke should plead guilty to the charge of procedural inconsistency, it is not clear that it is a very grave crime; certainly it is not
on a par with claiming certainty for metaphysical doctrines which
his own epistemology declares to be unknowable. In some cases
what is at issue is not the assertion of metaphysical claims, but

rather the discussion of metaphysical issues in a way that leads to no dogmatic resolution. It is true that there are cases where Locke does assert doctrines that would normally be classified as metaphysical; as we have seen, he propounds theories of the nature of personal identity and human freedom. But although these doctrines are metaphysical, they are metaphysical in an epistemologically innocent way, as it were; Locke believes that all the facts we need to know are open to our cognitive gaze. In this manner Locke remains faithful to his thesis that the nature of the fundamental furniture of the world is opaque to us. Particularly in the case of personal identity he is at pains to argue that its nature can be established despite our ignorance of the essences of the basic substances. In the case of human freedom Locke has less argument to offer, but he may well believe that the epistemic transparency of the issue is a necessary condition of the justice and benevolence of a God whose existence can be proved.

Locke might further be accused of helping himself in many places to metaphysical theories of a more suspect nature; in other words, he smuggles in positive theories about the fundamental furniture of the world which he has not earned the right to assert. Here a distinction must be made between two kinds of objection. In the first place Locke might be charged with assuming such theories without argument; secondly, he might be charged with claiming certainty for metaphysical theories in defiance of the fundamental tenets of his epistemology. Clearly, if our concern is with the consistency with which he executes his project, then it is the latter charge which is the more serious of the two. But although the two charges are thus logically distinct, one kind of defence will serve against both; a vindication of Locke on the first indictment will also serve to show how he can be acquitted on the second.

A defence of Locke should begin by conceding what can hardly be gainsaid; in the *Essay* he advances positive theories with respect to mind and matter which are in some sense metaphysical. The corpuscularian hypothesis, for example, is a theory not just about the structure of individual bodies or particular kinds of matter, but about the structure of matter in general. And like many metaphysical theories it claims that the way physical things really are is unlike the way they appear to be. Clearly, since such a theory is concerned with nature's workmanship, it is not open to Locke to defend the hypothesis on the ground that it is epistemologically innocent; the kind of strategy which works in the case of human freedom and personal identity is not available to him here.

The corpuscularian hypothesis is thus in some sense a metaphysical theory, but is it true that Locke asserts it without argument? Some readers have felt that as early as his discussion of primary and secondary qualities (in book 2 chapter 8) he simply assumes the truth of the corpuscularian hypothesis, to which, along with Boyle and others, he is committed. But though there may be places like this in the *Essay*, it does not follow that Locke has no justification for his corpuscularian claims. Here it is helpful to treat the corpuscularian hypothesis in tandem with Locke's theory of ideas. As we shall see in the next chapter, the latter may be modelled on the former, and there is certainly reason to believe that they are intended to enjoy the same kind of epistemic status. Locke justifies his theory that all our ideas originate in experience on the grounds of its explanatory virtues; the theory is simpler and more intelligible than its rivals, such as the Cartesian doctrine of innate ideas. In a key passage Locke suggests that he would seek to justify the corpuscularian hypothesis in the same terms:

I have here instanced in the corpuscularian hypothesis, as that which is thought to go farthest in an intelligible explication of the qualities of bodies; and I fear the weakness of human understanding is scarce able to substitute another, which will afford us a fuller and clearer discovery of the necessary connection, and *coexistence*, of the powers, which are to be observed united in several sorts of them. (*E* 4. 3. 16)

The corpuscularian hypothesis, like the theory of ideas, is thus defended on the grounds that it is the best available explanation of the phenomena; though in places Locke may assume the truth of the hypothesis, he is clear as to how it is to be justified. And once we see how Locke would justify availing himself of such theories, we realize that he is in no danger of running foul of his most cherished epistemological commitments. The corpuscularian hypothesis, like the theory of ideas, is not an ungrounded assumption; it is a theory which there is good reason to accept. But to say this is not to say that it satisfies Locke's stringent standards for knowledge. In order to achieve knowledge of the corpuscularian hypothesis something else would be required; we should need to have adequate ideas of the essence of matter which would allow us to perceive that its structure has to be corpuscularian. But just such a necessary condition is unsatisfied for Locke, and will remain so. Thus there is no reason to suspect that Locke's commitment to the corpuscularian hypothesis, or to the theory of ideas, is inconsistent with his strictures about the limits of human knowledge.

Few readers of the *Essay* have doubted its philosophical importance, but some critics have felt that its greatness owes little to its announced aims. As we have seen, Locke's conception of his project has been dismissed as incoherent, and his execution of it has been criticized as faltering and inconsistent. In this chapter I have sought to show how Locke can be largely defended against these charges; in general, the *Essay* is a work which is powerfully conceived and powerfully executed. Almost everything in the *Essay* helps to further the stated purpose of discovering those areas in which knowledge is possible for us. As we shall see in the next chapter, the first stage in Locke's undertaking is to give an account of the raw materials of knowledge.

3

THE ORIGIN AND NATURE OF IDEAS

O NE of the most curious misconceptions about Locke is that he regards the mind as essentially passive. The origin of this misconception is no doubt to be found in his reference to the mind as a *tabula rasa*; the mind is at first 'white paper void of all characters' (*E* 2. 1. 2) on which the finger of experience subsequently writes. Perhaps Locke has been the victim of his own choice of a striking if unhappy metaphor which does not do justice to his model of mind. Although Locke regards the mind as passive with respect to simple ideas, the raw materials for knowledge, he is much more concerned to emphasize its active role in processing these materials; the mind is active not only in constructing other ideas from the simples, but also in combining ideas into propositions which can be items of knowledge. Indeed, this emphasis on the constructive activity of the mind is central to Locke's assessment of our cognitive prospects; it plays a vital part in his theory of the areas in which knowledge in a strong sense is possible. It is true, as we have seen, that the ultimate origins of human knowledge are humble, and there is a sense in which knowledge can never fully transcend its origins. But to say this is not to imply that we are condemned to be passive spectators of what we take in from sensation and introspection.

Locke's project in the first two books of the *Essay* has often been the target of severe criticism. His positive theory of ideas has been faulted for failing to draw basic distinctions between types of mental content; at least since Kant, for example, philosophers have charged that Locke has no understanding of the nature of concepts. Indeed, from Leibniz to the present Locke's whole theory of ideas has been typically regarded as a series of muddles. Equally, philosophers have complained that Locke's attack on the theory of innate ideas and knowledge is directed against a straw man. I believe that neither of these main charges can be sustained. In particular, I shall argue that in his positive genetic theory of ideas Locke is advancing a programme which he knows to be controversial; the programme may be flawed and unsuccessful, but it is not a muddle. Instead of supposing that Locke has fallen victim to a series of obvious errors and conflations, we shall find it both more fruitful and historically more accurate to see him as a philosopher who knows exactly what he is trying to do.

The Question of Strategy

It is clear that in some sense books 1 and 2 of the *Essay* tell a negative and a positive story respectively, but beyond that the relation between them has not been well understood. The difficulty which some readers find in understanding Locke's project here might be put in the form of an objection. In book 1 of the *Essay* he sets his sights on attacking primarily, if not exclusively, a doctrine of innate principles; that is, the entities whose innateness is in question are supposed to be propositions with a truth-value. Now in book 2 Locke advances a positive genetic theory according to which all ideas derive from experience; if they are not simply given in sensation or introspection, they result from the mind's variously processing the data which are given through these channels. But the positive theory is a theory about ideas, and ideas are not themselves propositions but (at most) rather elements of propositions. It is thus natural to wonder how the first two books hang together. For even if we suppose that Locke's polemic in the first book is successful, it does not follow from the fact that there are no innate principles that there are no innate ideas; there might be innate ideas, even though, by means of its natural faculties, the mind needed to work these up into propositionally structured items of knowledge.[1] Now, in book 1 chapter 4 Locke does incidentally select a few ideas and try

[1] By contrast, the entailment does hold in the other direction; that is, if there are no innate ideas, there are no innate principles.

to show that they are not innate, but he does not undertake a systematic investigation of ideas in this respect. It is tempting to object, then, that at the end of book 1 Locke's demolition work is left substantially incomplete, since he has failed to argue that no ideas are innate.

The response to this objection is twofold. In the first place, Locke is clear that his positive theory of the origin of ideas is supposed to be self-sufficient; it is not intended to require the assistance of the polemic against the nativist hypothesis. There are two passages in which he indicates that it is the positive theory which supports the polemic, and not, as one might imagine, the other way round:

> It would be sufficient to convince unprejudiced readers of the falseness of this supposition [of innate principles], if I should only show ... how men, barely by the use of their natural faculties, may attain to all the knowledge they have, without the help of any innate impressions; and may arrive at certainty, without any such original notions or principles (E 1. 2. 1)

> I suppose, what I have said in the foregoing book, will be much more easily admitted, when I have shown, whence the understanding may get all the *ideas* it has, and by what ways and degrees they may come into the mind. (E 2. 1. 1)

But to indicate the direction of support in this way is not to say that Locke regards the positive theory as demonstratively certain; he regards it, rather, as the best explanation by virtue of its simplicity and intelligibility. By contrast, the nativist hypothesis is treated as a hypothesis of last resort which has appealed to philosophers because they have failed to see the power of the Lockean positive theory in explaining all mental content.[2]

But there is a second way of responding on Locke's behalf to the objection concerning the adequacy of his strategy. It is true that in book 1 he concentrates his big guns on innate principles rather than ideas, but he does attack claims for the innateness of various ideas such as those of identity, God, and substance. And these examples are carefully picked, for they are all highly abstract metaphysical ideas which were supposed by the champions of the nativist hypothesis to be paradigmatically innate. Locke's strategy of argument is thus clear; he seeks to show that the ideas of substance, identity, and

---

[2] Cf. E. J. Lowe, *Locke on Human Understanding* (London, 1995), 23–4.

God are not innate, and since they have a paradigmatic status, *a fortiori* no ideas are innate.

Locke thus takes the paradigmatic status of these ideas to be common ground between him and his opponents. He also believes that he is relieved from the need to examine the innatist credentials of one class of ideas, namely sensations; he tells the reader that no one will maintain that colour sensations, for example, are innate in creatures to whom God has given a power of receiving ideas through the eyes (*E* 1. 2. 1). Here Locke may be a little hasty, for in the *Comments on a Certain Broadsheet* Descartes seems to assert just this; although elsewhere he seems to share with Locke the view that it is abstract metaphysical concepts which are supposed to be paradigmatically innate, in this work he reverses himself and accords that status to sensations:

Nothing reaches our mind from external objects through the sense organs except certain corporeal motions ... But neither the motions themselves nor the figures arising from them are conceived by us exactly as they occur in the sense organs ... Hence it follows that the very ideas of the motions themselves and of the figures are innate in us. The ideas of pain, colours, sounds and the like *must be all the more innate* if, on the occasions of certain corporeal motions, our mind is to be capable of representing them to itself, for there is no similarity between these ideas and the corporeal motions.[3]

It has to be said, however, that intriguing as it is, the doctrine of the *Comments* is motivated by outdated Scholastic assumptions concerning causality; the argument crucially relies on the premiss that there must be a likeness between an effect and its cause. An argument of this kind need give Locke little pause.

If Locke's positive case for idea-acquisition is indeed self-sufficient, one may wonder why he troubles to devote the first book of the *Essay* to a polemic against the innatist hypothesis. Why could he not simply have begun the *Essay* with what is now book 2? The prominent position of the polemic against nativism makes the issue particularly pressing. The answer, I think, lies in Locke's belief that the doctrine of innate knowledge is a serious threat to the epistemological individualism which I examined in the Introduction. For one thing, the nativist hypothesis licenses the attribution of

---

[3] R. Descartes, *Comments on a Certain Broadsheet*, in *The Philosophical Writings of Descartes*, trans. J. Cottingham, R. Stoothoff, and D. Murdoch, 3 vols. (Cambridge, 1985), i. 304; emphasis added.

knowledge to the minds of infants, and such minds are incapable of assessing evidence for themselves. The doctrine of innate principles thus rests on a faulty conception of knowledge. Further, as deployed by some of its proponents it serves as an excuse for removing classes of propositions from the sphere of rational scrutiny; it plays into the hands of those of an authoritarian cast of mind: 'Nor is it a small power it gives one man over another, to have the authority to be the dictator of principles, and teacher of unquestionable truths; and to make a man swallow that for an innate principle, which may serve to his purpose, who teacheth them' (E 1. 4. 24). Unlike the first criticism Locke's second objection voices a political concern about the uses to which the doctrine may be put. It seems, then, that his decision to accord the polemic pride of place in the *Essay* is motivated not just by a wish to expose philosophical error but also by a desire to expose a threat to the open society.

The Polemic against Innate Principles

One of the striking, if little-remarked, features of Locke's polemic is the way in which it foreshadows his own positive theory of knowledge. His central conviction that knowledge is possible in the very different areas of mathematics and morality is largely mirrored in the structure of the polemic; separate chapters are devoted to challenging the innatist credentials of the 'speculative' principles of logic and mathematics on the one hand and the 'practical' principles of morality on the other. Locke himself hints forward to his rival positive theory of knowledge when he reminds the reader that it does not follow from the fact that there are no innate practical principles that morality is not capable of demonstration; thus his polemic is in no danger of undermining one of his own principal commitments. In view of Locke's preoccupation with moral epistemology, the chapter attacking innate practical principles thus plays a structurally important role in the *Essay*, and some of its arguments will be discussed in Chapter 10, below. Here I shall follow convention in concentrating on Locke's attack on speculative principles, since it is in this attack that his overall strategy is clearest.

Locke's case against innate knowledge has been criticized on the ground that it attacks a straw man; it is often said that some versions of the doctrine which he attacks are so crude that no serious philosopher could possibly have entertained them. But this criticism is unfair. Although, for reasons that which are historically intelligible, Locke omits one telling objection to the innatist hypothesis, his argument is in many ways a model of philosophical stategy; he employs one of his own favourite techniques, namely, that of arguing through a dilemma. According to Locke, the doctrine of his opponents can be interpreted in two ways. On one interpretation it asserts the existence of actual innate knowledge of speculative principles such as the law of non-contradiction; but so understood, it is empirically false, for children and idiots do not assent to these principles. On the other interpretation, it asserts merely that potential knowledge of such principles is innate in every mind. But understood in this way, the theory of innate knowledge is trivialized, for every proposition which we ever come to know will be innate in this sense. Thus either the innatist hypothesis is empirically false or it is trivially true; that is the basic dilemma for its defendants.

Locke's polemic shows more dialectical sophistication in the details of its arguments than is sometimes allowed. For example, he reinforces his case against the first horn of the dilemma by means of a *reductio ad absurdum*. His opponents may be tempted to say that while mathematical and logical principles are innate, they are not discovered until people reach the age of reason. But Locke thinks that his opponents will agree in defining reason as simply 'the faculty of deducing unknown truths from principles or propositions that are already known' (E 1. 2. 9). Thus they are involved in a contradiction; the truths which reason discovers are both known and not known before the age of reason (E 1. 2. 9). Locke's opponents might seek to evade the conclusion of this *reductio* by making a distinction: the truths in question are actually known only at the age of reason, but they are potentially known at least since birth; indeed, it is in this latter sense that they are innate. But in that case Locke can reply that the victory of his opponents is a hollow one; for they have escaped from the contradiction only at the price of impaling themselves on the second horn of the dilemma.

Locke's polemic against innate principles shows how effective he can be in his role of the under-labourer; the doctrine of innate principles is precisely the kind of pretentious rubbish which has impeded our progress towards knowledge. At a minimum estimate his polemic challenges his opponents to clarify and defend their thesis in such a way that it is no longer vulnerable to his objections.

Some defenders of the innatist hypothesis have risen to his challenge.

One way of responding to Locke is to seek to go through the horns of his dilemma. In other words, there is a defensible third way of construing the doctrine which Locke overlooks and which is not vulnerable to his strictures. This is the strategy of defence which Leibniz adopts in the *New Essays* when he argues that truths are innate in us not in a merely potential way, but as 'inclinations, dispositions, tendencies, or natural virtualities'.[4] Leibniz famously illustrates the distinction by means of a picturesque analogy. We are invited to contrast a homogeneous block of marble which is indifferent as to how it is sculpted with one in which the figure of Hercules is already marked out by the veins; it is in terms of this latter analogy that we should think of innate ideas and truths. Leibniz's defence of innate knowledge in turn clearly echoes a famous passage where Descartes tells a renegade former disciple that ideas are innate in us 'in the same sense as that in which we say that generosity is "innate" in certain families, or that certain diseases such as gout or stones are innate in others; it is not so much that the babies of such families suffer from these diseases in their mother's womb as that they are born with a certain faculty or disposition to contract them'.[5] Unlike Leibniz, Descartes is exclusively concerned here with the innateness of ideas or concepts rather than certain principles, and unfortunately for Leibniz this dispositional model seems to make more sense in connection with items of the former sort. Descartes's analogy with disease is clearly intended to suggest that we are differentially predisposed to employ some ideas rather than others, and when ideas are at issue this claim has some plausibility; we might say that the idea of substance is innate in the sense that we are innately predisposed to carve up the world in terms of things or substances, rather than clusters of features; it is more natural to us, for example, to respond to cats rather than furriness-instances. In this sense, then, the mind has a certain grain to it. But it is not similarly clear how we are to unpack such claims regarding differential predispositions when logical or mathematical principles are at issue, for it is obscure what the

[4] *Leibniz: New Essays on Human Understanding*, trans. P. Remnant and J. Bennett (Cambridge, 1981), preface, 52; trans. modified.

[5] Descartes, *Comments on a Certain Broadsheet*, in *Philosophical Writings of Descartes*, i. 304.

terms of the contrast are supposed to be. If, for example, Leibniz claims that the rules of the propositional calculus in logic work with the grain of the mind, as it were, it is open to Locke to reply that most people's reasoning is fallacious much of the time. And it will be no answer to Locke to say that at least some minds are born with an aptitude for learning the rules of the propositional calculus. Although such a claim succeeds in finding some kind of contrast, it is clearly of the wrong kind for Leibniz's purposes; for it locates a difference between knowing minds rather than between the objects of knowledge. It is Leibniz's thesis that all human minds are equally predisposed in favour of the laws of logic and mathematics.

Another way of responding to Locke's polemic would be to challenge one of the unexamined assumptions on which it rests. He seems to assume that if there were any principles which were innately known they would be few in number; indeed, he even appears to hold that it is sufficient to show the absurdity of the doctrine if he can argue that it implies that all propositions we come to know are innate. Now it may be that some of Locke's opponents would share this assumption; that is, they would presumably say that the class of innately known propositions is restricted to those which have the status of self-evident axioms which are foundational for a discipline such as logic or mathematics. But not all of Locke's opponents share this assumption. Leibniz, for instance, regards even the theorems of logic and mathematics as innate, and he is further prepared to deny that the fact that a proposition needs to be learned disqualifies it from counting as innate. Of course, if Leibniz is not to be impaled on the triviality horn of the dilemma, then he must find a means of showing how he can expand the class of innate truths in this way while still maintaining that the mind has a disposition to know them; talk of dispositions, propensities, and aptitudes cannot be allowed simply to collapse into talk of a bare potential for knowledge. And, as we have seen, Leibniz faces a difficulty in cashing out his dispositional thesis in such a way that a plausible contrast is specified.

Locke's polemic is also subject to the very different kind of objection that it is seriously incomplete: it overlooks what is perhaps the most damaging weakness in the doctrine of innate propositional knowledge. Locke's contemporary Samuel Parker acutely put his finger on the issue here when he observed that even if there were innate propositions, the epistemological issue of their truth-value would still be open; he makes the point by means of a horticultural analogy:

But suppose that we were born with these congenite anticipations and that they take Root in our very Faculties, yet how can I be certain of their Truth and Veracity? For 'tis not impossible but the seeds of Error might have been the natural Results of my Faculties, as Weeds are the first and natural Issues of the best Soyles, how then shall we be sure that these spontaneous Notions are not false and spurious?[6]

Parker's objection could be elaborated by saying that the defenders of innate knowledge often appear to be in danger of conflating two distinct kinds of issue. Since Plato philosophers have been puzzled by the problem of explaining how we can have knowledge of a priori truths, as in logic and mathematics, but they have not always seen that the psychological question of how certain beliefs are acquired is logically distinct from the epistemological question of how they are to be justified. Plato and others may be tempted to answer the psychological question by saying that such beliefs can only be explained on the assumption that they are innate, but even if they are right on that score, it would not settle the question of justification. As Parker says, we might have come into the world with our heads stuffed full of rubbish which we would then need systematically to unlearn.

Parker's objection is indeed a powerful one, and it is true that it finds no place in Locke's polemic. The explanation of this lacuna is suggested by the nature of Locke's target. Among those whom he is opposing are Descartes and his disciples, who held that our innate beliefs have been implanted by a benevolent God; the epistemic credentials of the beliefs are therefore beyond reproach. For reasons of piety Locke would not wish to dispute the Cartesian thesis that whatever is implanted by God is true; he agrees with Descartes that God is not a deceiver. It is of course still open to Locke to challenge the premiss that if there are any innate beliefs they have been implanted by God, but here too he would need to tread with care, for the divine origin of any innate endowments may seem to be guaranteed by the fact that God created us.

---

[6] Samuel Parker, A Free and Impartial Censure of the Platonick Philosophie (1666) quoted in J. W. Yolton, John Locke and the Way of Ideas (Oxford, 1956), 44.

Moreover, it would not be philosophically effective to accuse the Cartesians of conflating psychological and epistemological questions. For the Cartesians would reply that they are indeed aware of the logical distinctness of the two types of issue; however, the fact that our innate beliefs have their source in God makes it appropriate to appeal to their psychological origin in connection with issues of justification.

The Theory of Ideas (1): Locke and Descartes

Although the parallel is not exact, the concept of an idea is as important in Locke's theory of mind as the concept of a particle is on the corpuscularian hypothesis. The term 'idea' is not of course new with Locke, nor even is his definition of the word as 'whatsoever is the object of the understanding when a man thinks' (*E* 1. 1. 8). The term had been reintroduced into philosophy by Descartes to denote the contents of the human mind, whether of thought or sense-perception. Descartes himself had not succeeded in freeing his own use of the term from ambiguity; for sometimes he uses 'idea' to mean the object of a mental act and sometimes to mean the mental act itself.[7] None the less, in both cases Descartes's use of the term 'idea' is designed to draw attention to what philosophers call the intentionality of mental states; it is of the nature of thought and perception to have objects or content even if nothing exists in the world which corresponds to such content. Thus I have thoughts of unicorns and of centaurs, and these thoughts clearly differ in terms of what they are about, although the classes of both unicorns and centaurs are likewise empty.

In using the term 'idea' for the contents of the human mind, Descartes was departing from philosophical tradition; before Descartes the word had been a term of art which referred to archetypes or blueprints in the divine mind in accordance with which things were created. Revealingly, however, even while domesticating ideas in this way, Descartes does not seek to suppress the traditional divine associations of the term; he tells Hobbes, for

[7] See N. Jolley, *The Light of the Soul: Theories of Ideas in Leibniz, Malebranche, and Descartes* (Oxford, 1990), ch. 2.

example, that he has used the term *because* it was the standard one for referring to the forms of perception belonging to the divine mind.[8] In speaking of our mental contents as ideas, Descartes thus seems to wish to draw attention to the fact that on his philosophy the human mind is in a way godlike. It is not difficult to see how this is so. Considered in terms of his cognitive capacities, God of course is supposed to be a pure intellect, and paradigmatically, for Descartes, our ideas are wholly intellectual items; they are thoughts of mathematical and metaphysical objects such as triangles and God.

Locke agrees with Descartes about the mind-dependent nature of ideas; he resists the attempts of Malebranche to revive the Augustinian theory that the objects of human thought are ideas in the mind of God. But in other respects Locke differs markedly from Descartes, though the extent of the disagreement is controversial. For one thing, although Descartes had been prepared to speak of sensory ideas (for example, the sensory perception of the sun), he had tended to regard such items as ideas only in a courtesy sense. By contrast, for Locke, it is precisely such sensory ideas which enjoy paradigmatic status. Secondly, although Descartes had recognized a class of what he termed 'factitious' ideas which the mind invents from the sensory data it receives, he had tended to write as if such a class were small and of little epistemological significance; it was rather the class of innate ideas to which he had appealed to explain how our a priori knowledge is possible. By contrast, in Locke's theory it is the class of 'factitious' ideas which bears the weight of his positive account of knowledge and which plays a role in his theory analogous to that of innate ideas for Descartes.

The contrast between the two theories of ideas might be summarized by saying that Locke, unlike Descartes, wishes wholly to suppress the divine associations of the term 'idea'. For Locke, the human mind not only receives no direct assistance from God in the form of ideas implanted at least at birth; it enjoys no form of thinking which is directly godlike. The progress towards knowledge is a painful one whereby we must pull ourselves up by our own bootstraps. In the next section we shall see that Locke goes out of his way to emphasize the humble origins of our knowledge.

[8] Third Replies, in *Philosophical Writings of Descartes*, ii. 127–8.

The Theory of Ideas (2): Imagism

Towards the end of the first chapter in book 2 Locke reviews his project of deriving all ideas ultimately from experience with an eloquence which is rare in his writings: 'All those sublime thoughts, which tower above the clouds, and reach as high as heaven itself, take their rise and footing here: in all that great extent wherein the mind wanders, in those remote speculations, it may seem to be elevated with, it stirs not one jot beyond those *ideas*, which *sense* or *reflection*, have offered for its contemplation' (E 2. 1. 24). This passage conveys the excitement of a thinker who believes that he is embarking on a new and challenging project. Although the claim is controversial, I believe that it is most fruitful to suppose that in book 2 Locke is engaged in a research project, as we now call it, which is self-consciously modelled on the corpuscularian theory of matter. Such an approach has the merit of solving some otherwise vexing problems of interpretation.

One of the standard objections against the corpuscularians was that the resources of their hypothesis were too meagre to explain all the variety of physical phenomena. Boyle himself alludes to the objection and seeks to rebut it:

And this puts me in mind to add that the multiplicity of qualities that are sometimes to be met with in the same natural bodies needs not make men reject the opinion we have been proposing, by persuading them that so many differing attributes as may be sometimes found in one and the same natural body cannot proceed from the bare texture and other mechanical affections of its matter.[9]

Boyle goes on to indicate ways in which the explanatory resources of the theory are richer than they appear to be. In a rather similar way Locke's programmatic statements implicitly concede that by dispensing with innate content the resources of his theory may appear to be meagre; none the less, he seeks to persuade the reader

---

[9] *Origin of Forms and Qualities*, in *Selected Philosophical Papers of Robert Boyle*, ed. M. A. Stewart (Manchester, 1979), 26. Boyle uses the analogy of the letters of the alphabet to illustrate the power of the corpuscularian hypothesis; see *About the Excellency and Grounds of the Mechanical Hypothesis*, ibid. 142. Significantly Locke uses the same analogy to illustrate the power of his theory of ideas (E 2. 7. 10).

that this is not really the case. In the course of book 2 it becomes clear that Locke rests his confidence in the power of the theory on his account of what he calls our 'natural faculties'; in other words, although the only raw materials with which it has to work are the data of sensation and reflection, the mind is endowed with a rich array of machinery for processing these raw materials. In book 2 Locke devotes considerable space to describing the ways in which the mind can operate on the raw materials with which it is presented; the mind has the power to abstract, combine, and enlarge its ideas, for example. Such an inventory of the range of our mental faculties enables us to appreciate the full power of the theory; it puts us in a position to see that the content of 'all those sublime thoughts' can be explained on the assumption that they take 'their rise and footing' in experience. The moral, then, is that it is simply superfluous to postulate innate content in order to explain the rich variety of our mental life. The appeal to innate ideas is as idle as the Scholastic appeal to substantial forms and occult qualities.

Some philosophers who are not necessarily friends of innate content have none the less objected that Locke's theory is fatally flawed; it fails to do justice to the facts about mental content which it seeks to explain. Such philosophers typically start from Locke's umbrella use of the term 'idea' to denote all the contents of the human mind; it is said that he uses the term in an extraordinarily wide way to cover sense-perceptions, bodily sensations (such as pains and tickles), mental images, and thought and concepts.[10] Now clearly there can be no real objection to Locke's using a term to denote a genus provided he recognizes that there are distinct species within the genus; the substance of the objection, then, must be that he fails to do just this. Even here, though, the objection needs to be refined further, for no one can fairly complain that Locke fails to recognize different kinds of ideas; the titles of later chapters of book 2 advertise a whole host of distinctions; ideas can be simple or complex, clear or obscure, adequate or inadequate, real or fantastical, and so on. The objection, then, is not that Locke fails to make any distinctions among ideas—for this is palpably false—but rather that he fails to make some much-needed distinctions. In particular, he employs the term 'idea' to mask the important difference between the intellectual and the sensory sides of the human cogni-

[10] Editor's Introduction, *Berkeley's Philosophical Writings*, ed. D. Armstrong (London, 1965), 8.

tive condition; he fails to see any fundamental distinction between thinking of x and having a sense-perception of x. Some philosophers would add that there is a further contrast to which Locke is insensitive; this is the distinction between episodic and occurrent thoughts on the one hand and the possession of concepts on the other. Just what is involved in possessing a concept is controversial, but on one analysis it consists in the possession of a kind of skill; to have the concept of a triangle is to have the ability to pick out triangles in a rule-governed way.

Since Kant at least, philosophers have tended to see Locke's failure to make these sorts of distinction as something more than accidental; rather, they have charged that the inadequacies of his theory of mental content spring from fundamental weaknesses in the empiricist programme of deriving all ideas from sensation and reflection. Locke failed to recognize that there is a whole domain of mental representations for which the empiricist programme could not account; the programme is inherently condemned to give an impoverished account of our mental states and skills. In Kant's famous words, 'Locke sensualized the pure concepts of the understanding.'[11] The diagnosis of course could take the form of maintaining that Locke was unduly optimistic about the empiricist programme because he was insensitive to the distinction between sense-perception and thoughts or concepts.

The proper way of responding to this line of objection is, I think, clear. Locke may be over-optimistic about the resources of his programme, but he is not guilty of any sort of muddle; as we have said, he is self-consciously proposing a theory about the nature of mental content. To appreciate Locke's position, we can again consider an analogous objection that might be made to the corpuscularian hypothesis. It is easy to imagine a conservative, Scholastic critic of the hypothesis who charges that the programme is inevitably doomed, for the corpuscularians fail to recognize that matter comes in fundamentally different types; celestial bodies, for instance, are quite unlike in nature to the terrestrial bodies that we see around us. Any hypothesis which fails to take account of such a distinction can have no hope of explaining the phenomena. The corpuscularians of course will reply that they are indeed committed to the supposition that matter is homogeneous; none the less,

---

[11] I. Kant, *Critique of Pure Reason*, A 271 / B 327.

their theory has the resources to explain the phenomena. In a structurally similar way Locke will reply that he too holds, as a matter of theory, that ideas are fundamentally homogeneous. None the less, we should explain the complexity of the phenomena through the variety of the mental operations by which the mental data are processed. There is no need to postulate irreducibly different types of mental content.

If this approach to Locke is correct, then he may be in some sense an imagist; in other words, he may hold that the homogeneity of ideas consists in the fact that they are all of the nature of mental images. This reading of Locke's theory of ideas has recently beeen revived by Michael Ayers, who states that the 'grounds for holding him an imagist are conclusive',[12] and it has a long and distinguished pedigree; in the *New Essays on Human Understanding*, for instance, Leibniz complains of Locke's tendency to confuse ideas with images. In the *New Essays*, Leibniz's spokesman Theophilus makes his charge in response to Philalethes, who defends the Lockean thesis that our idea of a thousand-sided figure is a confused one:

PHILALETHES. In a man who speaks of a body of a thousand sides the idea of the figure may be very obscure though that of the number may be very distinct.

THEOPHILUS. That is not an apt example. A regular thousand-sided polygon is known just as distinctly as is the number one thousand, because in it one can discover and demonstrate all sorts of truths.

PHIL. But one has no precise idea of a thousand-sided figure, such that one could distinguish it from one that has only nine hundred and ninety nine sides.

THEO. That example shows that the idea is being confounded with the image.[13]

Now the case of the idea of the thousand-sided figure is precisely one which Descartes had exploited in the Sixth Meditation to underline the point that mathematical ideas could not in general be identified with images; like Leibniz here, Descartes had observed that chiliagons can be demonstrated to have all sorts of properties which are not possessed by nine-hundred-and-ninety-nine-sided figures; thus we do have distinct ideas of the figures in question despite our inability to distinguish the two figures in imagination. It is

[12] M. R. Ayers, *Locke*, 2 vols. (London, 1991), i. 44.
[13] *New Essays on Human Understanding*, 2. 29, p. 261.

impossible to believe that Locke was unaware of how Descartes had used this very example to argue that ideas are not in general images; it makes sense to suppose that Locke is self-consciously availing himself of Descartes's example to point a very different moral in the theory of ideas.[14] Whether we feel that Locke's discussion of the geometrical ideas compels the imagist reading may be disputed. But there is one approach that can be summarily dismissed; it cannot be right to suppose that he simply conflates ideas and images, if this means that he has fallen into a careless muddle. If Locke holds that all ideas are images, it is as self-conscious theory on his part, not as a silly mistake.

One obvious group of ideas which poses problems for the imagist interpretation is the class of ideas of reflection, namely those ideas which the mind acquires by turning its attention back on itself and its own operations:

The other fountain, from which experience furnisheth the understanding with *ideas*, is the *perception of the operations of our own minds* within us, as it is employed about the *ideas* it has got; which operations, when the soul comes to reflect on, and consider, do furnish the understanding with another set of *ideas*, which could not be had from things without: and such are *perception, thinking, doubting, believing, reasoning, knowing, willing*, and all the different actings of our own minds. (*E* 2. 1. 4)[15]

It is not impossible to think of ways of accommodating ideas of reflection within the imagist framework. We might be tempted to suppose that my idea of thinking, for example, consists of having an image of Rodin's 'Thinker' before my mind; your idea might consist in the image of some other suitably contemplative figure you have experienced. Such an interpretation runs into no difficulty on one score; although Locke holds that reflection is a distinct source of ideas, he seems to think that ideas from this source typically—perhaps necessarily—come later than ideas of sensation (*E* 2. 1. 8); acquiring ideas of sensation may even be a causally necessary condition for having ideas of reflection. Thus it is not an objection to this reading that it assumes the possession of sensory ideas. But to

[14] Cf. Ayers, *Locke*, i. 49. It is interesting to note that Locke's account of the chiliagon example seems inconsistent with a theory of ideas (concepts) as abilities to pick things out. Unless I am subject to certain time constraints, I certainly do have the ability to distinguish thousand-sided figures from 999-sided figures.
[15] Some ideas come from both sensation and reflection. See book 2 ch. 7.

read Locke in this way encounters other kinds of difficulty, both textual and philosophical. For one thing, the interpretation is hard to reconcile with Locke's claims that 'this source of ideas everyone has wholly within himself', and that ideas of reflection have 'nothing to do with external objects' (*E* 2. 1. 4). Moreover, if we ask what makes my image of Rodin's sculpture an idea of thinking rather than an idea of sitting, the answer can only be in terms of how I take the image; I consider the image in a certain respect, namely thinking. But then either my idea of thinking is not a mental image after all, or if we still insist on this claim, we seem forced to postulate a further image of the 'Thinker', and so on; we thus incur an infinite regress.

Locke is not very forthcoming in his own attempts to explain the nature of ideas of reflection; he tells us that though reflection is not sense, it is none the less very like sense (*E* 2. 1. 4), but he does little to fix the shape of the likeness. Perhaps we should conclude that while he is indeed an imagist, he interprets the programme with some latitude. But even if Locke's adherence to the imagist programme is not very strict, one thing is clear; his theory makes no provision whatever for an irreducibly distinct class of intellectual representations. Perhaps he believed that such representations stand or fall with innate ideas; having demolished the latter, he could be taken to have put paid to the claims of the former. But even if the details of Locke's theory are sometimes unclear, there can be no doubt about its general character or motivation. Like more recent philosophers who seek to advance an ambitious programme, he may at times issue promissory notes; but making promises is not the same thing as making mistakes.

The Theory of Ideas (3): Compositionalism

Whether Locke's theory of ideas is a form of imagism is a controversial issue, but no one, I think, has denied its compositionalist character. This feature of the Lockean theory is a clear point of parallel with the corpuscularian hypothesis, though to say this is not of course to say that the one was self-consciously modelled on the other. As we shall see, Locke's compositionalism has some obvious explanatory advantages for a philosopher who denies the existence of innate mental content, and there is no doubt that he is well aware of them. Even here, however, there are some thorny issues of interpretation on which opinion is still divided. Fortunately, the parallel with the corpuscularian hypothesis has the power to illuminate at least some of them.

Although Locke is in some sense a compositionalist, it is not clear how thoroughgoing is his commitment to this doctrine. A strong form of compositionalism would hold not merely that there are simple ideas and complex ideas which are somehow built up out of simples, but that all ideas are either simple or complex; in other words, this classification is both exclusive and exhaustive. In the early editions of the *Essay* Locke is indeed committed to compositionalism in this strong sense, but in the fourth edition he abandons it; he seems to have come to feel that the category of complex ideas could not carry the weight which it had originally been made to bear. Although, as Aaron recognizes, Locke failed to tidy up the text completely, he now comes to revise his official scheme of classification so that there are ideas which are neither simple nor complex;[16] the ideas of relation and abstract ideas which had formerly been subsumed under the heading of complex ideas now constitute two distinct categories. But Locke's final theory of ideas may still be called compositionalist in a weak sense; for all ideas are either simple or products of the mind's power over such ideas. And of course he still recognizes a category of complex ideas which are composed from the simples.

At different points in the *Essay* Locke suggests various conditions which all and only simple ideas satisfy. But when he introduces the notion of a simple idea, the criterion he proposes is an experiential or phenomenological one: simple ideas contain in themselves nothing but one uniform appearance or conception in the mind (*E* 2. 2. 1); by this criterion the patch of red which I perceive when I look at a certain book would qualify as a simple idea if I could not distinguish any variety in it. Some readers of the *Essay*, however, have been impressed by a linguistic criterion which Locke proposes; simple ideas are those whose names are indefinable (*E* 3. 4. 4). But it seems unlikely that Locke would wish to make our understanding of simple ideas parasitic on the role which their names play in a language. If it is not to be merely ostensive, a definition of course

---

[16] Aaron, *John Locke*, 113.

must be couched in linguistic terms, but to say this is not to say that the definition itself must appeal to a linguistic criterion.

Locke thus defines a simple idea in terms of its phenomenological character, but if this is so he may seem vulnerable to the objection that his examples do not satisfy the definition; indeed, perhaps nothing in our experience strictly does so. O'Connor states a standard criticism:

> The examples Locke offers here of simple ideas of sensation are the coldness and hardness of a piece of ice, the whiteness of a lily, the smell of a lily, the smell of a rose, or the taste of sugar. But even simple sense data such as these, as they occur in everyday experience, rarely present one uniform character indistinguishable into parts which differ sensibly one from another, be it ever so slightly. And even if we take a coloured patch in which no part is sensibly different in hue from any other part, such a sense datum is clearly not 'uncompounded' in an unqualified sense. It is, for example, made up of smaller patches, i.e. it is spatially compounded.[17]

That this criticism is misguided is suggested by the parallel with the corpuscularian hypothesis. Not all of those scientists who called themselves corpuscularians were committed to the existence of truly simple or indivisible bodies, namely atoms. None the less, they did believe in the existence of bodies which were simple relative to others. The more familiar example of a pile of bricks may make this clear. There is a perfectly good sense in which each individual brick may be called simple with respect to the pile; the pile itself can be called complex with respect to the individual bricks which make it up. The distinction is still a valid and useful one even if someone says that the individual bricks are not truly simple because each is further divisible into smaller units. In the same way Locke's simple ideas may not be absolutely simple, but they are at least relatively simple with respect to the complex ones.[18] And this standard of relative simplicity may be all he needs.

Simple ideas are not merely uniform in appearance; they are also given in experience. As Locke puts it, the mind is wholly passive in respect of its simple ideas. And though he does not intend to define simplicity in these terms, he clearly means to state an equivalence here; the mind is passive with respect to all and only its simple ideas.

[17] O'Connor, *John Locke*, 47.

[18] Cf. M. A. Stewart, 'Locke's Mental Atomism and the Classification of Ideas (I)', *Locke Newsletter*, 10 (1979), 53–82.

It may be wondered whether he sticks consistently to this equivalence. Indeed it has seemed to some readers that Locke contradicts himself on the same page by implying that there are complex ideas in respect of which the mind is entirely passive; thus he writes of simple ideas that are observed to exist in several combinations united together (*E* 2. 12. 1). This might suggest that when I experience the colour, scent, and tactual sensations of a rose petal, I am simply presented with a complex idea to which my mind contributes nothing.[19] But though Locke's phrasing may be imprecise, this reading is, I believe, mistaken. It is true that he appears to contrast such complex ideas of 'sensory manifolds' with other complex ideas which more strikingly involve the activity of the mind; examples of the latter kind are ideas composed of wholly discrete elements. But there is no need to read him as denying that my mind is active even in respect of the bundle of sensations I have in experiencing the scent, colour, and feel to the touch of a rose. For to speak of a complex idea is to speak of a single, unified idea, and Locke is clear that it is the mind which imposes the unity on elements which are given in experience; it is the mind, so to speak, which ties them together into a bundle. As Locke puts it, 'the mind has a power to consider several of them united together as one idea' (*E* 2. 12. 1). Once again an analogy may be helpful. It is a fact, independent of my mind, that certain stars are physically contiguous, but there is none the less a perfectly good sense in which constellations are products of mental activity. It is the mind that determines which stars to include and which to omit; indeed, it imposes the particular pattern implied by such names as The Plough and Orion. In the same way there is a sense in which certain simple ideas are contiguous by virtue of their causal link to a physical object; the ideas of colour, scent, and touch are causally anchored in the rose. But it is still my mind alone which combines them into a single complex idea. To say that I have such a complex idea is not necessarily to say that I take myself to be experiencing a single thing. For instance, on the table in front of me there is a desk calendar which contains reproductions of details of paintings by Monet; in looking at such reproductions I experience a complex idea composed of a number of bounded patches of colour, but I am not experiencing a thing, as the rose is. But in so far as I do have a complex idea of a thing or substance

---

[19] V. Chappell, 'Locke's Theory of Ideas', in V. Chappell (ed.), *The Cambridge Companion to Locke* (Cambridge, 1994), 37.

there is a role for a further act of the mind; as we shall see, to experience a thing as a thing, I must add the idea of a substratum in which the qualities of which I have ideas inhere. Thus in respect of ideas of things my mind is, as it were, doubly active.

Locke's compositionalism, even in its modified form, is clearly a powerful theoretical resource. In terms of this theory he can explain how the mind is not limited to receiving what is given in experience, or even to simply unifying the experiential data; it can frame radically new content by combining or otherwise processing its simple ideas. With his eye on the strictly complex ideas in particular, Locke shows himself to be well aware of the theory's advantages: 'In this faculty of repeating and joining together its *ideas*, the mind has great power in varying and multiplying the objects of its thoughts, infinitely beyond what *sensation* or *reflection* furnished it with' (E 2. 12. 2). Locke of course is not the first philosopher to appreciate the advantages of compositionalism; Hobbes had somewhat similarly explained how the mind could create ideas of fictional creatures such as unicorns by combining the sensory data of experience.[20] Locke also discusses 'fantastical ideas' of mythical beings, in their due place, but he shows little interest in them. Of far greater interest to him are two other classes of non-simple ideas which play a central role in his theory of knowledge. One such class—ideas of 'mixed modes' as he calls them—are complex in the strict sense; that is, they result from the mind's power of combining simple ideas of different sensory modalities into compounds. This category includes ideas such as those of adultery and incest that are particularly important for Locke's theory of the possibility of strict moral knowledge, and will be discussed below (Chapter 8). The other class is constituted by abstract ideas which are not strictly complex, but none the less result from the mind's power over its simple ideas. Locke's theory of abstract ideas has not merely been highly influential; it has also been thought to be vulnerable to criticism. It therefore receives special attention below.

Before we conclude this section it is worth noting one theoretical advantage of Locke's insistence that only simple ideas are given in experience; it enables him to offer a more economical explanation of how the mind produces radically new combinations of ideas. If Locke held that complex ideas came ready-made to the mind, he

---

[20] T. Hobbes, *Leviathan*, 1. 2.

would need to postulate a two-stage process for framing the idea of a centaur, for example; the mind must first break down experienced complex ideas into simple elements before it could produce the new complex idea. By contrast, his actual theory allows him to dispense with the supposition that there is a prior stage of decomposition; the mind need only combine the simple ideas which are given in experience. It is true that in explaining abstract ideas Locke does seem to think that the mind has something like a power of decomposition; thus perhaps he cannot simplify his model of the mind by dispensing with this piece of machinery altogether. But he does not need to suppose that this power is exercised in the formation of new compound ideas, such as ideas of centaurs or unicorns. To this extent Locke's actual theory has the advantage of explanatory simplicity.

Abstract Ideas

Abstract ideas, Locke's second class of non-simple ideas, play a major role in his anti-Aristotelian theory of classification, as we shall see below, in Chapter 8. But more important for our present purposes is the role they play in his other main polemic; it is in terms of abstract ideas in large measure that Locke outlines a distinctively anti-Cartesian theory of the basis of universal knowledge, especially in mathematics and science.

It is tempting to say that whereas Locke recognizes a great many abstract ideas, Descartes accepts the existence of none, or at least relatively few. But this way of contrasting the two philosophers is potentially misleading. If an abstract idea is defined in terms of content, that is, as a general idea under which particulars can fall, then Descartes of course accepts the existence of abstract ideas in this sense. But for Locke, to say that an idea is abstract is not just to talk about its role in organizing our thought about particulars; it is to say something about its genesis: abstract ideas essentially result from the mind's exercising its power of processing the data in a certain way. The concept of an abstract idea is thus to be defined in causal terms. Now those ideas, such as the general idea of a triangle, which for Locke are paradigmatically abstract are certainly not abstract for Descartes in this sense; on the contrary, they have been implanted in our minds by the finger of God himself. Thus the origins of such mathematical concepts are more humble in the philosophy of Locke than they are in the philosophy of Descartes; they have a less distinguished pedigree. Locke seeks to drive home this anti-Cartesian moral when he says (in a passage that may help to explain Berkeley's antipathy, which we shall discuss below) that abstract ideas are a mark of our imperfection (E 4. 7. 9). For Descartes, by contrast, the ideas which Locke regards as formed by abstraction are precisely those which most display our perfection; not merely do they have a divine pedigree, but they are stored in that faculty of the human mind which (with the exception of the will) is most nearly godlike—the pure intellect.

To speak of abstract ideas, for Locke, is thus to say that they result from a certain mental process. Unfortunately, however, it is less than clear whether he offers a single consistent account of this mental process whereby abstract ideas are formed. To some readers it has seemed that Locke offers one account in the chapter 'Of Discerning' (2. 11) and a rather different account in the chapter 'Of General Terms' (3. 3). In 2. 11. 9 Locke offers what might be called a 'selective attention' account;[21] on this view I have a particular experience of white in snow, for example, and I attend to that image only in respect of that feature in terms of which it resembles my ideas of chalk and milk. By contrast, in 3. 3. 7 Locke seems to offer what might be called an 'elimination' account of how my abstract ideas are formed. In terms of the example he gives there, we experience ideas of a number of individuals such as John, Paul, and Mary, and we eliminate everything except that which is common to them all; what is left is the abstract idea of human being.

Since Locke emphasizes that the essence of abstraction is the separation of an idea from those with which it is conjoined in experience, we should be cautious in attributing to him more than one account of the matter. The difficulty in deciding whether we are faced by two non-equivalent accounts is compounded by the fact that in the two discussions Locke offers examples from different categories; my particular experiences of white are simple ideas, my particular experiences of John, Paul, and Mary are complex ideas. On the face of it, however, there is a certain difference between the two discussions. It is true that even selective attention will involve

---

[21] This phrase is used by J. L. Mackie, Problems from Locke (Oxford, 1976), 110.

a kind of elimination; it will involve the rejection of certain features of the experience as objects of attention. But in the first discussion it is a particular idea which functions as an abstract general idea by being made to bound the species; in the second, my abstract idea seems to be a residue, or perhaps a product, of a number of various particular ideas.

Although the two accounts thus seem non-equivalent, there is one argument for this conclusion which should be viewed with scepticism. It might be said that the discussion in 2. 11. 9 is consistent with—perhaps even requires—a theory of ideas as images; my abstract idea of white is a particular image which is supposed to be representative of the whole class of white things, and is made to bound it. By contrast, it might be objected that in 3. 3. 7 Locke's account of abstraction is inconsistent with a theory of ideas as images. Here the abstract idea of a human being is what is common to my particular complex ideas of certain individuals, and this common element cannot be an image or even a set of images; it is rather that set of properties which are individually necessary and jointly sufficient for being a human being. The difficulty with this argument is that the elimination account is not in fact so clearly inconsistent with the imagist theory of ideas which, as we have seen, he appears to hold. For Locke may be thinking of the common element as an indeterminate image; my abstract idea of a human being is thus an image which is indeterminate in respect of height, eye-colour, and even sex. Such a theory of abstract ideas may be unfamiliar, but it is not obviously incoherent.[22]

The objection that an idea, that is, an image, cannot be indeterminate plays a central role in Berkeley's famous polemic against the doctrine of abstract ideas. But Berkeley's objection turns not so much on an appeal to the phenomenology of images as on a general principle or 'received maxim': whatever is impossible in reality is impossible in thought or idea.[23] Now it is obviously impossible that there should exist a particular human being who had no determinate height or eye-colour. Hence it is impossible to form such an idea or image of a human being.

---

[22] Cf. J. Bennett, *Locke, Berkeley, Hume: Central Themes* (Oxford, 1971), 41. Bennett is here following a suggestion made by Michael Tanner.

[23] G. Berkeley, *Principles of Human Knowledge*, introd., para. 10. Cf. B. Belfrage, *George Berkeley's Manuscript Introduction* (Oxford, 1987), 74.

The same general principle underlies Berkeley's second objection to the Lockean theory. With obvious relish Berkeley seizes on a passage in which Locke explains that abstract ideas are difficult to form:

For example, does it not require some pains and skill to form the *general idea* of a *triangle*, (which is yet none of the most abstract, comprehensive, and difficult,) for it must be neither oblique, nor rectangle, neither equilateral, equicrural, nor scalenon; but all and none of these at once. In effect, it is something imperfect, that cannot exist; an *idea* wherein some parts of several different and inconsistent *ideas* are put together. (E 4. 7. 9)

Berkeley believes that he is in a position to deliver a 'killing blow' against Locke's theory.[24] He takes Locke to be saying that the abstract idea of a triangle combines inconsistent features; it is the idea of a triangle which is simultaneously scalene, isosceles, and equilateral. Now it is obviously impossible that such an inconsistent triangle should really exist; hence, by Berkeley's general principle, it is impossible as an object of thought.

But this objection is totally misguided. It is true that, for Locke, the abstract idea is something imperfect that cannot exist; by this he means that there cannot be a triangle instantiating only those properties contained in the general abstract idea. But the reason for this claim is not that the idea combines inconsistent features, but that it is indeterminate; by contrast, any existing triangle would have to be scalene or isosceles or equilateral etc. Despite the impression that Berkeley conveys, what Locke actually says is not that the idea of a triangle combines inconsistent parts of different ideas, but that it combines 'some parts of several different and inconsistent ideas', and this is a very different matter. Locke's phrasing may be in one place incautious; it is perhaps unwise of him to say that the triangle, in idea, is all and none of these at once. But the meaning is clear to any reader who is prepared to exercise a little charity. What Locke is doing is to shift without warning from the extensional to the intensional perspective. The idea, considered extensionally (that is, in terms of the figures which fall under it), is all of these; that is, all triangular figures, whether scalene or equilateral, fall under the abstract idea. But considered intensionally, the idea is none of these; that is, being scalene, for example, is not part of the content of our

---

[24] G. Berkeley, *Philosophical Commentaries*, Notebook A, entry 687.

abstract general idea of a triangle. So Berkeley is quite wrong to suppose that the idea itself combines inconsistent features. Of course, it is still open to Berkeley to pounce on Locke's admission that the intentional object of our thought is something imperfect by virtue of its indeterminacy; in other words, as we have seen, no existing triangle could instantiate only those properties contained in the idea. Berkeley can then appeal to what he calls his received maxim that whatever is impossible in reality is impossible in thought or idea. But in that case what Berkeley is opposing is not a muddle at all; for arguably Locke holds as a matter of theory that our ideas—the objects of our thought—can be indeterminate. Locke simply does not accept the received maxim to which Berkeley appeals.

Berkeley's objections to Locke's theory of abstract ideas are not very powerful; one of them depends on a straightforward misreading of Locke's text. To say this is not of course to say that Locke's theory faces no difficulties; indeed, the theory at least seems to be seriously inconsistent with some of his other commitments. Consider Locke's explanation, in terms of the elimination account, of how we ascend to higher levels of abstraction:

Leave out of the *idea* of *animal*, sense and spontaneous motion, and the remaining complex *idea*, made up of the remaining simple ones of body, life, and nourishment, becomes a more general one, under the more comprehensive term, *vivens*. And not to dwell longer upon this particular, so evident in itself, by the same way the mind proceeds to *body*, *substance*, and at last to *being*, *thing*, and such universal terms, which stand for any of our *ideas* whatsoever. (*E* 3. 3. 9)

The implication of Locke's account seems to be that at the highest level of abstraction the ideas are all simple. Now in one way this harmonizes well with Locke's theory of simple ideas. For, as we have seen, one criterion for simple ideas is that they are those 'the names of which are not capable of any definitions' (*E* 3. 4. 4); and it is at least plausible to suppose that the abstract idea of thing or being, like the idea of red, is not further analysable; hence the term 'thing', like the word 'red', is indeed indefinable. But of course Locke also has another criterion of simplicity; simple ideas are supposed to be those which are uniform in appearance, and this criterion makes no sense in relation to abstract ideas. Indeed, this incoherence points us to the general problem of consistency;

the categories of simple and abstract ideas are supposed to be mutually exclusive, yet he appears to hold that one and the same idea may fall into both classes.

Perhaps Locke might seek to remove or palliate the difficulty in the following way. He might concede that the general ideas of being and thing cannot be truly simple since they are abstract ideas and, as such, result from the mind's exercise of its power over the data of sensation and reflection. None the less, the ideas at the highest level of abstraction have something in common with simple ideas; they are free from complexity, that is, they are not strictly compounded from simpler elements. But he could then remind us that, according to his final system of classification, lack of complexity does not entail simplicity. But we can only guess at whether this is the form his defence would take.

Whether the overall coherence of Locke's theory of ideas can be defended in this way may be disputed, but there is one idea which seems to raise a further problem of internal consistency. Near the highest level of abstraction he places the idea of substance (E 3. 3. 9). Yet to many readers it seems that in his main discussion of substance Locke plainly denies that we acquire the idea of it by abstraction from experience. Indeed, ever since Bishop Stillingfleet attacked his philosophy, what Locke says about substance has seemed to raise all sorts of difficulties. How far these difficulties can be overcome we shall see in the next chapter.

4

THE PHILOSOPHY OF
MATTER

L OCKE'S philosophy of matter is an intriguing marriage of two
tendencies which reflect rather different sides of his intellectual
inheritance. On the one hand, his thought about the physical world
exhibits an admiration for the explanatory virtues of the corpuscularian hypothesis which Boyle had championed; indeed, the
Essay has even been regarded as a defence of this hypothesis. On the
other hand, Locke's thought about the ultimate nature of matter is
also subject to the pull of a deep agnosticism which finds a precedent in Gassendi; this latter tendency is obviously in line with the
Essay's insistence that little, or no, strict scientific knowledge of the
physical world is possible. To some extent which of these tendencies is in the ascendant at any point in the *Essay* is a function of
Locke's polemical concerns of the moment. When he has the
Scholastic tradition fixed in his sights he tends to appear as an advocate of the corpuscularian hypothesis; when, by contrast, he is
attacking the dogmatism of the Cartesians, he tends to emphasize
the necessary limits on our knowledge. Yet though there may be
tensions in Locke's thought, it would be wrong to suggest that his
philosophy of the physical world is simply incoherent. Locke may
be an enthusiast for the corpuscularian theory, but his enthusiasm
is always tempered by the qualification that we have, and perhaps
can have, no knowledge in the strict sense of the truth of this
hypothesis.

   In response to even friendly criticism Locke likes to remind his
reader to reflect on what issue he is addressing at some particular

point in the *Essay*.[1] For all its virtues recent work on Locke's thought about the physical world has been in some danger of ignoring his advice. In the search for a unitary Lockean philosophy of matter readers have been tempted to ignore the immediate context of his discussions of the physical world. This failing may help to explain why, despite advances in our understanding, on some topics there has been no tendency to move towards a consensus; on Locke's theory of substance and its relation to his doctrine of real essences, for instance, positions are as far apart and as deeply entrenched as ever they were. Perhaps we can make progress in resolving some of these controversies by remembering the lesson which Locke himself taught his readers.

The Under-Labourer Role (1): Anti-Cartesianism

As we have seen, Locke's philosophy of matter parallels in some degree his theory of ideas, for which it may well have furnished the model. Once again there is both a negative and a positive dimension to his thought. As an under-labourer to the best physical scientists of his time Locke must clear ground a little and remove some of the rubbish that lies in the way to knowledge of the physical world. The 'rubbish' comes in two distinct varieties, old and new; Locke's task is to help to remove both.

One obstacle to the advancement of scientific knowledge which must be removed is the Cartesian thesis that extension is the essence of matter; in other words, space void of matter is a logical or conceptual impossibility. Locke deploys a battery of arguments against this thesis, and as in the case of his polemic against Cartesian nativism, he tends to argue through a dilemma; he reinforces this strategy through his equally favourite technique of the thought-experiment. Suppose, he says, that 'God placed a man at the extremity of corporeal beings' (*E* 2. 13. 21); could he not stretch out his hand beyond his body? If he could, then the Cartesians must recognize the existence of empty space; if he could not, then they must give some account of what it is that impedes him, which Locke believes they are unable to do without conceding the infinity of

---

[1] See e.g. Locke to Molyneux, 19 Jan. 1694, *CL* iv. 785.

matter. Thus 'the truth is, these men must either own, that they think body infinite, though they are loth to speak it out, or else affirm that space is not body' (E 2. 13. 21). Locke is right to say that the Cartesians are 'loth' to concede the first disjunct: Descartes officially denies that matter is infinitely extended. But he does assert that matter is indefinite, and his reasons for refusing to go further have more to do with theological caution than philosophy. Thus it seems that at most Locke scores only a technical victory against Descartes.

A second dilemmatic argument against the Cartesians also takes the form of a thought-experiment. Suppose, says Locke, that God were to put an end to all motion in the universe. Then if God were to annihilate just one part of matter (say, this book) a vacuum would result; for on the supposition in question, we cannot say that neighbouring portions of matter would rush in to fill the empty space. Thus the Cartesians must either hold that God cannot bring off this particular feat of annihilation or admit the logical possibility of a vacuum. Once again Locke reveals his knowledge of his Cartesian opponents and the range of weapons in their armoury; for Descartes, of all philosophers, is the least willing to set limits to God's power.

Even if successful, neither of these arguments of course establishes the reality of empty space against the Cartesians. Even the first argument establishes only the conditional thesis that if there is no such space, then matter is infinite. But we should not infer from this that Locke regards the Cartesian thesis concerning the essence of matter as simply unjustified dogmatism. Certainly Locke believes that it is not possible for us to know the real essence of matter, but it is also clear that he regards the Cartesian thesis as demonstrably false. For, as he realizes, to prove the falsity of the doctrine he does not need to show that there is in fact empty space in our universe; he needs to establish only the logical possibility of such a supposition, for this is what the Cartesian thesis denies. And Locke believes that the ideas of matter and space are evidently distinct, that is, not equivalent; any analysis of the concept of body or matter must include the concept of solidity. Hence, it must be admitted that there could be space void of matter. Descartes's thesis about the essence of matter thus involves conceptual and even linguistic absurdities; it is part of the rubbish that must be cleared away.

The Under-Labourer Role (2): Anti-Scholasticism and the Status of Sensible Qualities

In attacking the Cartesian thesis that extension is the essence of matter Locke is thus clearly engaged in his role of under-labourer. But the attack on Descartes is of course part of a quarrel within the ranks of the moderns; that is, it is part of a debate among those who share the central assumption of the scientific revolution that the manifest image—the way the world presents itself to our senses—is not a reliable guide to the nature of physical reality. But in the *Essay* Locke plays his most prominent role as under-labourer in attacking those philosophers who deny precisely this assumption; in his day these philosophers were the Scholastics, the heirs to the Aristotelian legacy. Locke shares the general hostility of many seventeenth-century philosophers to Scholastic teaching about bodies; he ridicules its alleged commitment to empty or circular explanations in terms of dormitive powers and substantial forms. Much of this hostility will resurface in a later chapter (Chapter 8) when we examine Locke's theory of language and classification; there we shall see how he rejects the Scholastic thesis that the world comes to us neatly packaged into hard-edged natural kinds. Here we are concerned with Locke's attack on what is perhaps a more inviting aspect of Scholastic teaching. The famous chapter 8 of book 2, modestly entitled 'Some Farther Considerations Concerning our Simple Ideas', is important, as we shall see, for expounding and defending the corpuscularian hypothesis, and in recent years it has been customary to stress its positive teachings. But the chapter is no less important for mounting a sustained polemic against the Scholastic doctrine of sensible qualities.

The Scholastic body of doctrine which is the target of Locke's attack consists of two claims which are natural to the pre-scientific mind. First, the Scholastics suppose that the sensible qualities—colour, taste, odour, and sound—are perfectly genuine and straight-forward properties of bodies; the redness of an English pillar box enjoys the same kind of ontological status as its size and cylindrical shape. Secondly, the Scholastics hold that when I look at a pillar box, my sensation of red resembles a sensible quality in the box itself. In radical opposition to the first claim Locke insists, with clear deflationary intent, that colours, sounds, odours, and tastes are not real or primary qualities, but only secondary qualities; they are powers in bodies to produce ideas (sensations) in our minds. From the thesis that sensible qualities are only powers, Locke infers to the falsity of the second Scholastic claim. This inference has troubled some readers, but it is in reality straightforward. There is a crude, if intuitive, sense in which there is no similarity between a power and a sensation of red.

Locke tells the reader that the terms 'real quality' and 'primary quality' pick out the same property, but in the negative side of this chapter it is the first term which he prefers; he characteristically expresses his opposition to the Scholastic theory by saying that sensible qualities are not 'real qualities' of bodies. Unfortunately, Locke's conception of a real quality is not altogether clear. Sometimes he appears to suggest that being really in bodies 'whether anyone's senses perceive them or no' is a logically sufficient condition for being a real quality (E 2. 8. 17); by this criterion the size, shape, and motion of a body, which number among the primary qualities, do indeed qualify as real. But if Locke wishes to contrast sensible qualities with real qualities, then this criterion is ill suited to his purpose, for even if colour, taste, and odour are demoted to the level of powers, they still seem to satisfy this condition. Even if no one's senses are perceiving the colour of the Pacific Ocean, it is still true that the relevant power is in the body of water: that is, if a normally sighted person were to perceive the Pacific Ocean in sunlit conditions, he or she would have the sensation of blue.

One approach to this problem is suggested by a curious view of the nature of powers which was current in Locke's day. In the *Origin of Forms and Qualities* Boyle seems to hold that a power is not present in a body in a world which lacks the stimuli to activate it:

When Tubal Cain, or whoever else were the smith that invented locks and keys, had made his first lock . . . that was only a piece of iron contrived into such a shape; and when afterwards he made a key to that lock that also in itself considered was nothing but a piece of iron of such a determinate figure. But in regard that these two pieces of iron might now be applied to one another after a certain manner, and that there was a congruity betwixt the wards of the lock and those of the key, the lock and the key did each of them now obtain a *new capacity*; and it became a main part of the notion and description of a lock that it was capable of being made to lock or unlock by that other piece of iron we call a key.[2]

If we adapt the story slightly by reversing the presumed order of invention, we can say that, for Boyle, keys do not have the power to open locks in a lockless world. By parity of reasoning, the Pacific Ocean does not have the power to cause ideas (sensations) of blue in a world which lacks human observers; in such a world, then, the ocean is not blue. Now it is only a short step from here to saying that the ocean does not have the power to cause such sensations unless it is actually perceived by human observers. If this were Locke's view of powers, then he could consistently block the argument for conceding to sensible qualities the status of real qualities; for no power, and *a fortiori* no sensible qualities, would satisfy the condition of being really in bodies, whether anyone's senses perceive them or no. But the problem of interpretation is solved at the high price of saddling Locke with a theory of powers which seems most unattractive.

An equally draconian approach to the problem of coherence goes back to Berkeley. Berkeley's goal of course was not to save Locke from himself but rather to exploit the alleged incoherence of Locke's distinction between primary and secondary qualities in the service of immaterialism. None the less, in spite of himself, as it were, Berkeley pioneered a reading of Locke's theory of secondary qualities which showed why they would not qualify as real qualities of bodies. For Berkeley's Locke, secondary qualities are not in bodies at all; they are simply ideas or sensations in the human mind.[3] Clearly, if secondary qualities are not in bodies at all, they do not satisfy Locke's apparent sufficient condition for a real quality, that is, of being in a body whether anyone's senses perceive them or no. Berkeley's reading is not wholly gratuitous; it can claim support from a passage which neighbours on Locke's statement of his troublesome sufficient condition for a real quality: 'Take away the sensation of them [light, heat, whiteness, or coldness]; let not the eyes see light, or colours, nor the ears hear sounds; let the palate not taste, nor the nose smell, and all colours, tastes, odours, and sounds, as they are such particular *ideas*, vanish, and cease, and are reduced

---

[2] Boyle, *Origin of Forms and Qualities*, in *Selected Philosophical Papers of Robert Boyle*, ed. M. A. Stewart (Manchester, 1979), 23; emphasis added.

[3] Berkeley, *Principles of Human Knowledge*, part I, para. 10.

to their causes' (*E* 2. 8. 17). But Berkeley's reading conflicts with Locke's repeated official insistence that secondary qualities are not ideas but rather powers to produce ideas in us. And it also runs into trouble from Locke's own admission that he is sometimes careless about the distinction between ideas and qualities.

Faced with these difficulties, some readers may be tempted to question whether Locke does mean to deny that secondary qualities are real qualities. Indeed, there is one place where he may seem to concede that they do have this status. In 2. 8. 10 Locke introduces the reader to a third kind of quality:

> To these [secondary qualities] might be added a third sort which are allowed to be barely powers though they are as much real qualities in the subject, as those which I to comply with the common way of speaking call *qualities*, but for distinction *secondary qualities*. For the power in fire to produce a new colour, or consistency in wax or clay by its primary qualities, is as much a quality in fire, as the power it has to produce in me a new *idea* or sensation of warmth or burning. (*E* 2. 8. 10)

Clearly Locke wishes the reader here to concede that secondary and tertiary qualities are on the same metaphysical footing. And superficially it may seem that the equal status which they enjoy is that of being real qualities. But a closer inspection suggests that nothing in the passage compels this reading. Locke's central point is surely a negative one: secondary qualities have no better claim than tertiary qualities to be regarded as real, and everyone (Scholastics included) is supposed to concede that tertiary qualities are barely powers in bodies (*E* 2. 8. 24–5).

If secondary qualities are clearly properties of bodies yet not real qualities, we may seem to have reached an impasse. We may feel tempted to throw up our hands and admit that there is an incoherence at the very heart of Locke's attack on the Scholastic theory of sensible qualities. But such pessimism or despair would be premature. The most promising strategy, I believe, is to recall what Locke really opposes in the Scholastic theory of sensible qualities; it is surely not the assumption that they are in bodies, but an account of how they are in bodies; in other words, for the Scholastics, as for pre-scientific common sense, the redness of an English pillar box is just as much a manifest or non-dispositional property of the box as its cylindrical shape. A real quality, then, is not just a property of a body; it is a manifest property of a body. It follows that in 2. 8. 17

Locke is not strictly formulating a sufficient condition for being a real quality, but only a necessary condition; to get a sufficient condition we must add the word 'manifest'. Such an interpretation concedes that Locke expressed himself with less than complete precision, but it does rescue his case against Scholasticism from the charge of incoherence on a central issue.

The coherence of Locke's opposition to the Scholastic theory of sensible qualities can thus be defended. But there is still a question of his strategy in opposing the Scholastic account which has not so far been addressed. As an under-labourer to the best science of his time Locke could surely be expected to offer arguments against the Scholastic theory which do not presuppose the truth of the corpuscularian hypothesis. Such a condition is certainly satisfied, *mutatis mutandis*, in his other performances of the under-labourer role which we have examined. Locke does not merely clarify the nature of his opposition to the theory of innate ideas; he offers arguments to show that the nativist hypothesis is false. Again, Locke does not merely state, following Boyle, that solidity must be part of the essence of matter; he offers arguments to show that the Cartesian theory is false. Whether Locke does indeed adopt this kind of strategy in the present case has become an issue of some controversy.

The traditional answer to this question, following Berkeley, is a resounding 'yes'. Berkeley, for instance, thought that Locke offered at least two arguments which were designed to show that the qualities which Locke identifies as secondary are less than real properties of bodies. The first such argument depends on the premiss that we are subject to illusion and perceptual variation with regard to the so-called secondary qualities alone; whereas the same water, for example, may produce the sensation of heat in one hand and cold in another, it is never the case that a figure feels square to one hand and spherical to another. The second argument starts from the premiss that whereas a body loses its secondary qualities in the process of division, it none the less retains its primary qualities throughout; no matter how far it is divided up, it will always be found to possess size and shape and motion. Berkeley then had no trouble in dispatching these arguments which he supposed Locke to advance.[4] The first argument depends on a premiss which is obvi-

---

[4] Berkeley, *Principles of Human Knowledge*, part 1, para. 14.

ously false; no less an advocate of the distinction than Descartes observed that towers which at a distance look round appear square when observed close at hand. The second argument depends on an equally egregious mistake; it slides back and forth between determinate and determinable qualities. It is true that an almond loses its original whiteness when it is pounded by a pestle; but it is no less true that it loses its original particular size and shape as a result of this process. Again, it is true that a grain of wheat retains some size and shape when it goes through the mill, but it is no less true that it retains some colour or other throughout this process. When determinates are compared with determinates, and determinables with determinables, primary and secondary qualities are clearly on an equal footing.

The obvious weakness of such arguments has led some readers to re-evaluate the question of Locke's strategy. It has been plausibly suggested that he does not seek to advance the arguments which Berkeley purported to find in the text of the *Essay*; indeed, Locke does not seek to advance any arguments for the distinction, and thus against Scholastic doctrine, which are independent of the corpuscularian hypothesis itself.[5] Rather, where Berkeley thought he found (bad) arguments for a (bogus) distinction, Locke is simply trying to show how the corpuscularian hypothesis can explain phenomena for which the Scholastics offer only pseudo-explanations; the hypothesis, for instance, suggests an explanation of why the same water may appear cold to one hand and warm to the other. On this view, then, there is indeed a disanalogy between Locke's strategy in opposing the Scholastic doctrine of sensible qualities and the kind of strategy he adopts elsewhere. We may bring out the difference with respect to the theory of ideas; it is as if Locke were to begin the *Essay* with book 2 and deprive himself of the polemic in book 1. Perhaps it is an exaggeration to say that he has no negative arguments against the Scholastic theory of sensible qualities; for instance, he does appear to seek to refute the resemblance thesis with regard to sensible qualities by appealing to the fact of perceptual variation (*E* 2. 8. 16). But in general Locke seems more interested in diagnosing how belief in the Scholastic thesis

---

[5] P. Alexander, 'Boyle and Locke on Primary and Secondary Qualities', *Ratio*, 16 (1974), 51–67; repr. in I. C. Tipton (ed.), *Locke on Human Understanding* (Oxford, 1977), 62–76.

gains a foothold than in offering analogues to the kind of negative arguments which he deployed against the doctrine of innate ideas. For Locke, the best reasons for supposing the Scholastics are wrong are furnished by the superior explanatory virtues of the corpuscularian hypothesis.

Qualities and the Corpuscularian Hypothesis

Locke's main argument for his distinction between primary and secondary qualities thus depends on the corpuscularian hypothesis to which, with Boyle, he is committed. Reduced to its bare essentials, this is the theory that the physical world is ultimately composed of tiny, imperceptible corpuscles whose only primary (intrinsic and manifest) qualities are size, shape, position, solidity, and motion; such corpuscles can differ in size and shape, but they are all of the same basic type. A further component of the theory is what was called mechanism; the only way in which bodies can interact with one another is by impulse or contact action. There is no such thing as action at a distance. As we shall see, this last assumption was to give Locke pause for thought after he had read Newton.

The logical relationship between the corpuscularian hypothesis and Locke's doctrine of sensible qualities may seem to be straightforward, but, strictly speaking, it is not. The issue is complicated by the fact that it is not only corpuscles but compound bodies which have primary qualities; indeed, it is essential to bodies to have such qualities (E 2. 8. 9). With his eye on the latter class of bodies Locke sometimes numbers texture among the primary qualities (E 2. 8. 10); by texture, he means the arrangement of the corpuscles along the surface of a compound body. But if texture is allowed to count as a primary quality, then there is nothing in the corpuscularian hypothesis itself to show that sensible qualities are not primary; for the corpuscularian hypothesis is powerless to rule out a reductive analysis of sensible qualities in terms of textures. Indeed, Locke himself seems at points to flirt with such an analysis (E 2. 8. 19). One way of excluding such a surprising and undesirable result is to supplement the corpuscularian hypothesis with a further principle to the effect that compound bodies have no determinable primary qualities which are not also common to the corpuscles. On this principle, then, texture will not count as a primary quality, for texture arises only at the level of compound bodies. Locke does not always avoid this trap, but the proposed solution to the problem is consistent with most of what he says.

Locke has the resources to show, then, that sensible qualities are not primary, but their status is still undetermined by the corpuscularian hypothesis; consistently with this hypothesis, as we have seen, such qualities might be textures of bodies, or they might be powers, or they might be purely mind-dependent sensations which we project onto the physical world. Locke in fact endorses the second option, and he elaborates it by saying that sensible qualities are powers to produce sensations in us by virtue of the primary qualities; in other words, such powers are causally dependent on the texture of the particles along a body's surface. But in opting for this account Locke is taking a step beyond what is entailed by the corpuscularian hypothesis. It is only a small step, but it is a step nevertheless.

The route from the corpuscularian hypothesis to Locke's version of the distinction between primary and secondary qualities is thus not a very direct one, but it is the route which he none the less prefers; it is the corpuscularian hypothesis which bears the weight of his case against the Scholastic theory of sensible qualities. But if Locke's Scholastic opponents are referred to the hypothesis, they will wish to know of course what recommends it. Locke answers the Scholastics here, as Boyle did, by appealing to its explanatory advantages. Compared with its rivals (especially Scholastic theories), the hypothesis possesses key virtues: (1) explanatory power: it explains a wide range of phenomena; (2) simplicity: it employs a small number of concepts in its explanations; and (3) intelligibility.

It is the intelligibility of corpuscularian explanations which seems to impress Locke most. In 4. 3. 16 for instance (a passage which is otherwise pessimistic in tone) Locke instances the corpuscularian hypothesis as 'that which is thought to go furthest in an intelligible explication of the qualities of bodies'; in the chapter on primary and secondary qualities itself he gives a concrete example: the corpuscularian hypothesis offers an intelligible explanation of how it is possible that 'the same water, at the same time, may produce the idea of cold by one hand, and of heat by the other' (E 2. 8. 21). But in what exactly is the intelligibility of such explanations supposed to consist? In the seventeenth century the quest for intelligible explanations often meant the quest for explanations in terms of necessary causal laws which could be known a priori, and were therefore transparent to the intellect; and it may be tempting to suppose that this is what is at issue here. Now Locke surely does not think that the truth of the corpuscularian hypothesis—or its specific account of heat in terms of molecular motion—can be known in this way; indeed, he is explicit that the corpuscularian hypothesis is less than certain for us. In any case what is supposed to be easy to understand, a paradigm of intelligibility, is not this but something else: 'it is easy to be understood, that if that motion be greater in one hand, than in the other; if a body be applied to the two hands, which has in its minute particles a greater motion, than in those of one of the hands, and a less, than in those of the other, it will increase the motion of the one hand, and lessen it in the other' (*E* 2. 8. 21). But today, following Hume, we would be inclined to say that even this conditional is not a truth which we can know a priori; it seems conceivable to us that the application of the water to the two hands might produce a very different result.

Perhaps Locke would not disagree with the Humean view. As we shall see, Locke does seem to hold that there are bridge laws (between the microscopic and the macroscopic levels) whose necessity can in principle be known a priori, but he does not believe that they can be known by human minds; all may be ultimately intelligible, but not to us. Thus there is no need to suppose that such intelligible explanations as we do have involve necessary laws whose necessity we can perceive. Perhaps all that he means is that the corpuscularian style of explanation appeals to models which are familiar to us from the world of everyday experience; although these explanations (of heat, for example) invoke hidden structures, we are invited to conceive of such structures in terms of the behaviour of macroscopic bodies in motion. In this way corpuscularianism is far removed from, and superior to, the Scholastic style of explanation which appeals to occult qualities of which we have no experience.

Real Essences and Qualities

Locke's emphasis on the intelligible nature of corpuscularian explanations is perhaps most prominent in his discussion of primary and secondary qualities; it is here that he appears most like an enthusiastic advocate of a promising and relatively new research programme. But even in this chapter he sounds a rather pessimistic note on occasions; he suggests there are limits to what is intelligible in the physical world. In 2. 8. 25, for instance, he remarks that it is a mystery how bodies produce sensations in our minds: 'nor can reason show how bodies by their bulk, figure, and motion should produce in the mind the *ideas* of blue, or yellow' (*E* 2. 8. 25). With these words in mind we may notice a remarkable feature of those earlier passages where Locke parades the strengths of the corpuscularian hypothesis; he tends to pass over the problem of the relation between mental and physical properties. Locke may even appear to dissolve the problem by simply identifying sensations with physical properties; in one place sensations of heat and cold are even said to be nothing but the increase or diminution in the minute parts of our bodies (*E* 2. 8. 21). Taken at face value this claim suggests a reductive materialist account of sensations which would be inconsistent with Locke's overall commitment to property dualism, but it is perhaps more natural to suppose that, for his present purpose of explaining the corpuscularian hypothesis, he is simply bracketing the mind–body problem until he draws our attention to it later in the chapter.

The issue of the limits of intelligibility is complicated by Locke's theory of real essences, which is remarkable for its agnostic tone. The notion of an essence is of course part of the Aristotelian legacy, and here as elsewhere Locke is breaking with that tradition while deploying some of its vocabulary. Broadly, in the Aristotelian tradition, essences were supposed to play two key roles: they classified the physical world into natural kinds (such as gold and lead and horses) and they explained the observable, superficial properties and behaviour of things. One of Locke's major anti-Aristotelian innovations is to deny that one and the same item plays these two distinct roles. Against the Aristotelians Locke insists that the role of classification is performed by what he calls a nominal essence; the role of explanation is played by what he calls a real essence. We shall discuss Locke's influential account of nominal essence in Chapter 8 when we look at his theory of the basis of classification; here we are concerned with his notion of a real essence.

It is natural to claim that the idea of a real essence is closely connected with the corpuscularian hypothesis, and in one way this is correct; they are both integral to Locke's anti-Aristotelian theory of the physical world. But it is important to note that his definition of a real essence is broad enough to apply to entities other than substances: a real essence is 'the being of anything, whereby it is what it is' (E 3. 3. 15). In other words, it is that about a substance or mode which explains those superficial properties in terms of which we pick out something as a human being or a triangle. In the case of bodies a real essence is perhaps by definition an internal constitution, but for Locke it is a contingent a posteriori fact that it is a corpuscularian structure that satisfies the criterion. There is nothing in the definition of a real essence which logically guarantees that this internal constitution is what the corpuscularians say it is.

Locke is famously pessimistic about the prospects for knowing the real essences of bodies, and it is sometimes said that his pessimism is unwarranted. According to Locke, although we have good, though not conclusive, grounds for believing the corpuscularian hypothesis in general, we do not and perhaps never shall know the particular corpuscular structures of gold and lead, for example. In response to this, writers have observed that Locke's dispiriting forecast has been belied by the development of the natural sciences since his time; physicists have succeeded in discovering just those structures which he thought were unknowable for us. Moreover, they have in general made such discoveries not by devising more and more powerful microscopes but by adopting the hypothetico-deductive method; in other words, they have imagined models of the internal structures and deduced empirical consequences from them which have been confirmed by the observable data.[6]

This objection to Locke's theory of real essences may be misguided. It seems that, for Locke, the real essence of gold, for example, is not just a certain internal constitution; it is a constitution on which the observable properties depend.[7] And the model of dependence here is geometrical; the properties are supposed to follow from the internal structure with the same kind of necessity as the properties of a triangle follow from the axioms and definitions

---

[6] Mackie, *Problems from Locke*, 101.

[7] Here I am indebted to an unpublished paper by Kyle Stanford, 'Reference and Natural Kind Terms: The Real Essence of Locke's View'.

of Euclidian geometry. By definition, then, a real essence explains properties in what we might call a rationalistic way:

Had we such *ideas* of substances, as to know what real constitutions produce those sensible qualities we find in them, and how those qualities flowed from thence, we could, by the specific *ideas* of their real essences in our own minds, more certainly find out their properties, and discover what qualities they had, or had not, than we can now by our senses: and to know the properties of *gold*, it would be no more necessary, that *gold* should exist and that we should make experiments upon it, than it is necessary, for the knowing the properties of a triangle, that a triangle should exist in any matter. (*E* 4. 6. 11; cf. 4. 3. 25)

If the rationalistic model indeed captures Locke's view, then he would be right in his belief that real essences are yet to be discovered. But most contemporary philosophers would be quick to respond that in that case his victory is very much a Pyrrhic one; for on a standard philosophy of science, there are no real essences of bodies in this sense, since the bridge principles for which Locke is looking are contingent and a posteriori, not necessary and a priori.

With regard to the microstructure of bodies Locke preaches a twofold ignorance. Not merely are we (perhaps incurably) ignorant of real essences, but also we can never discover how secondary qualities depend on primary qualities; we can discover no necessary connections in this case:

And if we knew these primary qualities of bodies, we might have reason to hope, we might be able to know a great deal more of those operations of them one upon another: but our minds not being able to discover any *connection* betwixt these primary qualities of bodies, and the sensations that are produced in us by them, we can never be able to establish certain and undoubted rules, of the consequence or *coexistence* of any secondary qualities, though we could discover the size, figure, or motion of those invisible parts, which immediately produce them. (*E* 4. 3. 13)

Here Locke argues from the fact that we cannot understand how bodies by their primary qualities produce sensations to the conclusion that we cannot understand how secondary qualities depend on primary qualities. Locke is of course relying on the principle that secondary qualities are by their nature mind-involving: a secondary quality is not just a power, but a power to produce ideas or sensations in our minds. In modern terminology we might say that, for

Locke, secondary qualities appear to be emergent properties; from a specification of gold's internal structure, together with the laws of physics, we cannot deduce that it will be yellow, for example.

Curiously perhaps, Locke's two strands of agnosticism are in tension with one another. His case for agnosticism about real essences depends, as we have seen, on the assumption that observable properties follow with geometrical necessity from the internal constitutions. But with regard to the relationship of primary and secondary qualities Locke seems to hold that there is no such necessary connection. On the face of it, then, Locke is committed to the following inconsistent triad of propositions:

(1) All observable (macroscopic) properties follow with geometrical necessity from internal constitutions.
(2) Secondary qualities are observable properties.
(3) Secondary qualities do not follow with geometrical necessity from primary qualities (i.e. the primary qualities at the microscopic level).

It may be objected that Locke is not really committed to (1) as it stands, for it is only those observable properties which serve to distinguish kinds of substance which follow from the internal constitutions (E 3. 3. 17). This may be true, but it will not remove the inconsistency, for he certainly thinks that secondary qualities are to be numbered among those properties; yellowness, for example, is one of the properties by which we distinguish gold from other sorts of substances. But there are still at least two possible ways in which we might seek to free Locke from this inconsistency. We could opt for a weak version of (1) so that secondary qualities are explicitly excluded; or we could take the path of denying that Locke is committed to (3). In favour of this last strategy we may notice that he characteristically makes his claim in epistemic terms; what he denies is not so much the existence of a necessary connection as our capacity to discover it.

Substance and Real Essence

Apart from a few minor complications Locke's agnosticism about real essences is relatively easy to understand. By contrast, his agnosticism about substance is much more difficult to grasp, and its interpretation remains highly controversial. In particular, readers of the *Essay* have found it hard to decide whether in his chapter entitled 'Of our Complex Ideas of Substances' (2. 23) Locke is preaching a radically new form of ignorance about a kind of entity which is on a different ontological level from real essences.

The problem of Locke's intentions arises in the following way. For a corpuscularian such as Locke the basic items in the ontology of the physical world seem to be clear: they are singly insensible particles endowed with the primary qualities of size, shape, solidity, and the like. Such a picture of the world may involve puzzles which the human understanding cannot resolve; we may not be able to determine whether these corpuscles are truly indivisible atoms and we may be mystified by the relationship between primary and secondary qualities. It is of course important for us to recognize these problems, but it would seem that there is nothing that needs to be added to the ontology of the physical world.

In book 2 chapter 23, however, Locke appears to disagree; he develops a train of thought about the world which strikes many readers as surprising. He begins by remarking how we notice that certain qualities tend to cluster; we observe, for instance, that furriness, purring, and a certain size and shape go constantly together. But since we cannot imagine how qualities can exist on their own, 'we accustom ourselves, to suppose some *substratum*, wherein they do subsist' (E 2. 23. 1). As we shall see, Locke is famously ironic in some of his remarks about substance, but he seems to be quite serious in his two main claims. On the one hand, in order to make sense of our experience we are forced to postulate the existence of a substratum, or substance in general, which supports qualities, both observable and unobservable; on the other hand, nothing can be known of this substratum except that it has the relational function of supporting these qualities. The problem, then, is to see not just why Locke finds it necessary to talk of substrata at all but also whether his various claims about them can be integrated into a single coherent account. This is a challenge which can, I believe, be met.

Some philosophers, such as Michael Ayers, have supposed that Locke cannot possibly admit such 'bare particulars' or naked substrata into his corpuscularian ontology.[8] In their eyes such a

[8] M. R. Ayers, 'The Ideas of Power and Substance in Locke's Philosophy', *Philosophical Quarterly*, 25 (1975), 1–27; repr. in Tipton (ed.), *Locke on Human Understanding*, 77–104.

commitment would be radically inconsistent with his assault on the Aristotelian tradition, from which the concept of substance derives, and with his associated reluctance to countenance bogus entities such as 'occult qualities' and 'prime matter'. They therefore seek to find a way of reconciling Locke's claims about substance with the overall tenor of his philosophy of matter; the preferred way of doing this is to show that these claims must be understood in the light of his doctrine of real essence. On this view, Locke is not preaching agnosticism at two distinct metaphysical levels; our ignorance of substance is not something over and above our ignorance of real essence. To say this does not imply that the terms 'substance' and 'real essence' express the same concept; on the contrary 'substance in general' means 'whatever it is that unites qualities', whereas 'real essence' means 'that inner constitution, whatever it may be, which explains the observable qualities'. But what is being claimed is that the concepts of substance and real essence pick out the same thing; in logical terms, they are extensionally equivalent.[9]

This approach to Locke's theory of substance in general is far from gratuitous, but it is almost certainly misguided; it faces serious difficulties of various kinds. For one thing, as several writers have noticed, there is no direct textual evidence in its favour; Locke passes up opportunity after opportunity to explain to the reader the close relationship between the concepts of real essence and substance in general.[10] More seriously, there is damaging textual evidence against such an equivalence in a little-regarded corner of the Essay. In a chapter on the inadequacy of our ideas (E 2. 31. 13) Locke does something altogether rare for him; he discusses the concepts of real essence and substance in tandem. What he says is revealing:

And, after all, if we could have, and actually had, in our complex *idea*, an exact collection of all the secondary qualities, or powers of any substance, we should not yet thereby have an *idea* of the [real] essence of that thing. For since the powers, or qualities, that are observable by us, are not the real essence of that substance but depend on it, and flow from it, any collection whatsoever of these qualities, cannot be the real essence of that thing. Whereby it is plain, that our *ideas* of substances are not *adequate*; are

---

[9] The point is well made by E. McCann, 'Locke's Philosophy of Body', in Chappell (ed.), *Cambridge Companion to Locke*, 81.
[10] Cf. ibid. 82.

not what the mind intends them to be. Besides, a man has no *idea* of substance in general, nor knows what substance is in itself. (*E* 2. 31. 13)

Consider just how difficult it is to reconcile Locke's thought here with the view that makes 'substance' and 'real essence' extensionally equivalent. It is as if Locke were to say: we do not know real essences; we do know that the terms 'real essence' and 'substance in general' pick out the same thing. And besides, we do not know substance in general. We can see how little sense this makes by means of an analogy with someone who says: I have an obscure idea of the nature of the morning star. I know, however, that the terms 'morning star' and 'evening star' pick out one and the same planet. And besides (as if introducing a new thought), I have an obscure idea of the nature of the evening star. Clearly a person who talks in these terms is guilty of an inconsequential redundancy. Everything that Locke says here naturally suggests that he is preaching agnosticism at two distinct metaphysical levels.

This view of Locke's meaning is powerfully supported by the fact that the concepts of substance and real essence are invoked to address different philosophical problems. Locke appeals to the notion of a real essence when he is addressing the question of the nature of scientific explanation; against the Scholastics, as we have seen, he argues that what causally explains the yellowness and malleability of the gold ring on his finger is a certain corpuscularian constitution. By contrast, he regularly invokes the concept of substratum, or substance in general, to address a problem which goes back to Aristotle; it is the issue of giving a philosophical analysis of our concept of a thing, or a thing of a certain kind, as opposed to a property or even a collection of properties. Locke characteristically approaches this issue by means of a genetic investigation into the origin of an idea, but he is recognizably interested in analysing a concept.

It may be objected that Locke is not well positioned to distinguish these two issues. Today it is natural for us to say that the relation between the real essence and observable properties is not at all like the relation between a thing and its properties in general; observable properties depend causally on real essences, but properties in general depend logically on things or substances. Locke, by contrast, tends to assimilate the two relations of causal and logical dependence. As Bennett says of another philosopher, 'it is not that he sees logical relations as weaker than they are, but rather that he sees causal relations as stronger'.[11] This objection is important, but it is not, I think, fatal. Even if we allow that, for Locke, observable properties flow with geometrical necessity from the real essence, we can still prevent the two relations from collapsing into one another; the key point is that the relation of dependence is different in the two cases. Real essences are supposed to be logically sufficient conditions for the observable properties which they explain; it is supposed to be impossible in a strong sense that a body should have real essence x and not have observable properties y. By contrast, Locke is surely not committed to the view that properties derive from the substratum; the substratum is not a sufficient condition for such-and-such individual properties, but only a necessary condition. It is true that in one place Locke speaks of qualities as resulting from the substratum (E 2. 23. 1), and this claim may seem troublesome. But what he means is not that the substratum somehow produces individual qualities, but that it is responsible for the 'union' of the qualities in a single substance (E 2. 23. 6); it is one and the same thing which is miaowing, purring, and chasing a mouse.[12]

When Locke invokes the notion of a substratum, then, he is not interested in the correct form of scientific explanation; he is interested in our thought about what it is to be a thing. Locke's own analysis has been judged to be highly vulnerable, but it would be wrong to exaggerate the weakness of his account; indeed, much of what he says can be defended. He is clearly right, for instance, to say that we cannot conceive how a quality can exist on its own; it is this conceptual impossibility which Lewis Carroll captured brilliantly with his story of the Cheshire cat, which gradually disap-

[11] J. Bennett, A Study of Spinoza's Ethics (Cambridge, 1984), 30.

[12] One further factor which may seem to establish or support the present thesis is Locke's employment of what has been called a 'logico-linguistic' argument for a substratum. Locke observes that our ways of speaking of substances as things which have such-and-such qualities intimate that substance 'is supposed always something besides the extension, figure, solidity, motion, thinking, or other observable ideas' (E 2. 23. 3). But it is natural to say that we should still speak in the same way even if we did know the real essence in question; therefore, our ignorance of substance seems to be of a different order from our ignorance of real essence. Ayers (Locke, ii. 55–64) has a long, subtle, but not entirely convincing reply to this objection.

peared until only its grin was left.[13] The idea of a grin which is not the grin of anything strikes us as absurd. (The word 'grin', though grammatically substantival, clearly does not denote a thing or substance.) But Locke's critics may object that while a grin standing alone is indeed an absurdity, we do not need to postulate a substratum in order to capture our concept of a thing or substance. We may even be tempted to say, with Berkeley, that a thing is nothing over and above a bundle of qualities: to say that a grin requires a grinner (something which grins) is simply to say that a quality is necessarily the member of some bundle or other.

This approach is attractive, but a little reflection shows that it is unsatisfactory. For there are many bundles of qualities which are intuitively not things or substances, even if these qualities are spatially contiguous. For instance, when my hand rests on the paper, the pinkness and fleshiness of my hand and the firmness of the paper constitute a bundle of contiguous qualities, but they do not constitute a thing. It may be objected that the contiguity in question is only temporary, but even if my hand never left the paper, we should still not be inclined to think of the bundle as a genuine thing. It is clear, then, that something needs to be added to the notion of a bundle of qualities in order to capture our conception of a thing or substance.

Critics may concede that the Berkeleian approach is unsatisfactory, while still objecting that the appeal to a substratum is a solution of last resort. It is gratuitous to suppose that qualities are attached to substrata by a sort of metaphysical glue; no philosopher with any empiricist bones in his body should be tempted by such a hypothesis. Indeed, the notion of a substratum is simply the product of a tendency to project on to the world the grammatical difference between subject and predicate. But perhaps Locke would not disagree with these strictures; as we have mentioned, his comments on the notion of a substratum are frequently tinged with irony. The irony is perhaps nowhere more visible than in the following passage:

If anyone should be asked, what is the subject wherein colour or weight inheres, he would have nothing to say, but the solid extended parts: and if he were demanded, what is it, that solidity and extension inhere in, he

---

[13] Carroll's philosophical point is perhaps obscured by Tenniel's famous illustration which shows, not a grin, but a grinning mouth—i.e. a substantial item.

would not be in a much better case, than the *Indian* . . . who, saying that
the world was supported by a great elephant, was asked, what the elephant
rested on; to which his answer was, a great tortoise; but being again pressed
to know what gave support to the broad-backed tortoise, replied, something, he knew not what. (*E* 2. 23. 2)[14]

Locke's main concern in 2. 23 is thus not to endorse the appeal
to a substratum, but to lay bare and expose our thinking about
these matters. It may be said that Locke is wrong in his account
of our thinking; our concept of a substantial entity does not
include the hypothesis of an unknown substratum in which qualities inhere. But he would still be right that the Berkeleian approach
overlooks important features of our judgements about what counts
as a thing.

   Much of Locke's discussion of substance in general can be
defended, but it may still seem that there is an obvious incoherence
in his thought. For, on the one hand, he appears to say that there is
something that can in principle be known about substance of which
we are ignorant; substance in general is supposed to have 'a secret
and abstract nature' (*E* 2. 23. 6). Yet, on the other hand, our idea of
a substratum is simply that of a bare particular whose only characteristic is the relational one of supporting accidents. But if our
concept of a substratum is empty of content in this way, then
Locke's agnosticism becomes untenable. It is simply misguided to
complain that the nature of substance in general cannot be known,
for there is nothing which could in principle be known. The relevant objection was brilliantly stated by Leibniz: 'If you distinguish
two things in a substance, the attributes or predicates, and their
common subject, it is no wonder that you cannot conceive anything
[specific] in this subject. That is inevitable, because you have already
set aside all the attributes through which details could be conceived.'[15] In other words, if substance has an abstract nature that is
hidden from us ('secret'), that would mean that substance in general
has intrinsic properties. But *ex hypothesi*, that cannot be the case, for

---

[14] Locke's first mention of the Indian occurs in connection with his discussion
of the issue whether space is a substance (*E* 2. 13. 18). For a good discussion of this
passage, see McCann, 'Locke's Philosophy of Body', in Chappell (ed.), *Cambridge
Companion to Locke*, 77–8.

[15] *Leibniz: New Essays on Human Understanding*, trans. P. Remnant and J. Bennett
(Cambridge, 1981), 2. 23, p. 218.

the substratum, or substance in general, is opposed to all non-relational properties whatever. Thus Locke's agnosticism about substance may seem simply incoherent.

One helpful way of responding to this problem is to recall how Locke introduces his famous account of substance in general. Here, as elsewhere, he begins with a genetic investigation of our ideas. Locke must of course provide an alternative account to the nativist hypothesis which holds that the idea of substance is innate. That Locke's own positive account is dubiously consistent with his empiricist programme of idea-acquisition may be true, but this is not our present concern; the important point is that it is *our* idea of substance whose origin he investigates and whose content he seeks to analyse. Locke can concede that, as the concept of a bare particular, our idea of substance in general is empty. But to concede this much is not to concede that there are no grounds for agnosticism. Locke can reply to the criticism by saying that he intends an implicit contrast between our idea of substance and that of an omniscient being. In comparison with, say, God's idea, our idea of substance is indeed obscure; there is something that God knows and we do not. To say this is not to return to the view that the substance of things is simply their real essence picked out under a different description, for what is at issue is not the causal explanation of observable properties, but rather the different question of what it is to be a thing.

Locke's agnosticism about substance in general can thus be rescued by supposing an implicit contrast between our idea and that of an omniscient being. But this suggestion seems subject to a further difficulty; it appears that we have paid a high price for this result. For if the idea of an omniscient being is richer and more perfect than ours, it must have some content which ours lacks; but it seems that it can have such content only by including intrinsic properties, and in that case it cannot be the idea of substance in general, for, as we have seen, this is opposed to all (non-relational) properties whatever. But this objection is misguided; it falsely assumes that God's idea of substance in general is, like ours, the idea of a bare particular or substratum. Rather, God's idea would be whatever enables him to see what it is for properties to be coinstantiated, that is, to be properties of a single thing. Here, I think, the weaknesses of the substratum theory actually work in Locke's favour. If we agree that this theory is unsatisfactory, yet still hold that what it is to be a thing is a real philosophical problem, then we implicitly concede that there is something more to be known; and this is all that Locke needs. God's perfect idea of substance enables him to solve the problem that baffles us. And, as we shall see in the next chapter, it also enables him to solve the mind–body problem.

Mechanism and Action at a Distance

There is one further strand in Locke's agnosticism which is relevant to the mind–body problem, and that is the apparent weakening of his commitment to mechanism in the wake of Newton's *Principia*. According to strict mechanism, as we have seen, all interaction between bodies takes place by way of impulse or contact action; action at a distance is thus impossible. In the early editions of the *Essay* Locke accepted the doctrine as an integral part of the corpuscularian hypothesis. But in the course of his controversy with Stillingfleet Locke tells his opponent that Newton's theory of universal gravitation has caused him to have second thoughts:

It is true, I say, 'that bodies operate by impulse and nothing else.' And so I thought when I writ it and can yet conceive no other way of their operation. But I am since convinced by the judicious Mr Newton's incomparable book, that it is too bold a presumption to limit God's power, in this point, by my narrow conceptions. The gravitation of matter towards matter, by ways inconceivable to me, is not only a demonstration that God can, if he pleases, put into bodies, powers, and ways of operation, above what can be derived from our idea of body, or can be explained by what we know of matter, but also an unquestionable and everywhere visible instance, that he has done so. And therefore in the next edition of my book, I shall take care to have that passage rectified. (*LW* iv. 467–8)

Locke did indeed rectify the passage (*E* 2. 8. 11) for the fourth edition, but he revised it in a manner which did not draw attention to his change of view; for instance, he continued to say that impulse is the only way in which we can conceive bodies to operate. But in the light of his exchange with Stillingfleet we can see that he now means to suggest that our ideas or conceptions may not be an adequate measure of God's way of working in the world.

At least one of Locke's early critics took a sinister view of his motives for abandoning mechanistic orthodoxy in the wake of Newton. Leibniz believed that Locke had sought to prepare the ground for acceptance of the hypothesis that matter might think.[16] Whether or not Leibniz was right about Locke's motives, he was clearly right on one score; in controversy with Stillingfleet Locke abandons a key premiss in a negative argument against a non-reductive form of materialism which does not simply identify thought with a body's mechanical actions: in other words, he crucially gives up the thesis that the only powers and properties which bodies can possess are those countenanced by Boylean mechanism. What Locke had to say about the thinking-matter hypothesis we shall see in the next chapter.

There is an irony in the story of Locke's response to the Newtonian theory of universal gravitation. Locke presumably believed that he was simply following Newton in drawing the moral that, in the wake of the *Principia*, unrestricted mechanism should no longer be accepted. But Newton himself drew a different moral. He was at pains to dissociate himself from those of his disciples (and enemies) who believed that the theory of universal gravitation required the reintroduction of action at a distance; on his part, at least, there is no weakening in his commitment to mechanistic orthodoxy.[17] That Locke reacted in the way he did serves as a reminder that it did not take Newton to lead him in the direction of agnosticism; agnosticism about the physical world is a pervasive strand in Locke's thought from the beginning. It can of course be readily agreed that this strand is in tension with his tendency to champion the explanatory virtues of the corpuscularian hypothesis. But tension is not inconsistency or incoherence, and that Locke's position is free from incoherence is clear from the fact that he never regards the corpuscularian hypothesis as other than the best theory we have. But agnosticism is the deeper tendency in Locke's thought, for, as we shall see, it is the one which is closer in spirit to the overall thrust of his theory of knowledge.

[16] Leibniz to Hugony, n.d. (1714?); quoted in Jolley, *Leibniz and Locke*, 64–5.
[17] See Newton to Bentley, 25 Feb. 1692/3, in *The Correspondence of Isaac Newton*, ed. H. W. Turnbull (Cambridge, 1961), 253–4.

5

THE MIND–BODY PROBLEM

LOCKE'S contemporary readers tended to believe that the mind–body problem, as we call it today, was near the forefront of his concerns; that is, he was exercised by the problem of giving a philosophical account of the nature of the mind and its relationship to the body.[1] By contrast, modern books on Locke rarely devote much space to this issue. One reason for this neglect is superficial: Locke's discussions of the mind–body problem are not concentrated in one single place in the *Essay*. The other reason goes deeper: it is to be found in the habit of reading Locke's philosophical agenda in the light of Berkeley and Hume, his two major empiricist successors, neither of whom showed much interest in this problem. But though Locke's discussions of the topic may be scattered, there is no doubt that his contemporaries were right in sensing the importance which it had for him. As we have seen, one of his main objectives in writing the *Essay* was to assess the prospects for metaphysical knowledge, and for Locke, the mind–body problem raises this issue in a singularly acute form.

In the seventeenth century the stage for all subsequent discussions of the problem had been set by Descartes, who famously argued that the mind is a thing which is really distinct from the body. Descartes had further argued that the natures of these two substances are completely heterogeneous: whereas body is a substance whose whole essence is constituted by extension, mind is a substance whose whole essence is constituted by thought. In a charac-

---

[1] Leibniz and Bishop Stillingfleet were both prominent among Locke's critics in this respect.

teristically agnostic vein Locke argues that such metaphysical dog-matism is unjustified: the ultimate natures of mind and matter are beyond our knowledge. But here, as elsewhere, there are tensions in his thought between the vein of agnosticism and a more positive thesis. The existence of such tensions is often conceded, but it is generally traced to his residual sympathy for Descartes's dualism. There is no need to deny that in places Locke feels the pull of the Cartesian doctrine; in the wake of his controversy with Stillingfleet he even revises his text to make it sound more dualistic. But I shall argue that nowhere in the *Essay* is Locke unequivocally committed to the truth of substantial dualism about the created world; that is, nowhere does he proclaim it as certain that the mind is a substance of a nature distinct from body. Most of the passages which have been read in dualistic terms in fact commit Locke to less than is usually supposed and are consistent with a form of agnosticism. I shall also argue that for Locke the main positive competitor to an agnostic stance is not substance dualism but a form of materialism. However, the form of materialism towards which he sometimes seems to lean is of a weak sort which is consistent with the truth of property dualism. That is, Locke may not be certain that the mind is a non-material substance, but he is certain that mental states, such as thinking and willing, are not physical states.

Substance, Substratum, and the Issue of Dualism

Those who believe that Locke is in places committed to the truth of Cartesian substance dualism tend to point to the chapter 'Of our Complex Ideas of Substances' (2. 23). Now, as we have seen, it is in this chapter that Locke develops his famous, or notorious, analysis of our idea of substance in general as a 'something, I know not what'. And, as we have also seen, to make sense of this analysis we must be able to explain how Locke can simultaneously declare the idea empty and obscure, implying by the latter term that there is something more to be known. Due attention to this interpretative constraint will help us to see that Locke is not engaged in a straight-forward defence of substance dualism; rather, he is developing a complex approach to the mind–body problem whose interest and originality have gone largely unnoticed.

Perhaps the main reason for scepticism about Locke's dualist intentions is a contextual one. The chapter in question ('Of our Complex Ideas of Substances') is of course a contribution to the natural history of our ideas; in conformity with his overall programme in book 2, Locke must explain how we acquire the idea of mind. As we would expect, he impresses on the reader that our idea of substance in general is a component of this complex idea. Having explained how we acquire the idea of sorts of corporeal substances, Locke informs us that there is a similar story to be told about our idea of mind:

The same happens concerning the operations of the mind, *viz.* thinking, reasoning, fearing, *etc.* which we concluding not to subsist of themselves, nor apprehending how they can belong to body, or be produced by it, we are apt to think these the actions of some other *substance*, which we call *spirit*; whereby yet it is evident that, having no other *idea* or notion, of matter, but *something* wherein those many sensible qualities, which affect our senses, do subsist; by supposing a substance wherein *thinking, knowing, doubting,* and a power of moving, *etc.* do subsist, *we have as clear a notion of the substance of spirit, as we have of body.* (E 2. 23. 5)

Locke's purpose here is not a metaphysical one. He is not engaged in making an inventory of the basic furniture of reality; rather, he is taking stock of the contents of our mind. To say that we have the idea of a spiritual substance, and to explain how we come by it, is not to say that there is anything in the world that falls under the concept. Locke could similarly explain how we acquire the concept of a unicorn and add that a component of this concept is the idea of substance in general, but such an explanation would obviously not commit him to the existence of unicorns.

It may be objected that in places Locke seems to go beyond taking stock of our ideas; he seems to say that there are key respects in which we can be certain about the furniture of the world. One thing we can be sure about is that the world contains spiritual substances of which our own minds are examples:

It is for want of reflection, that we are apt to think, that our senses show us nothing but material things. Every act of sensation, when duly considered, gives us an equal view of both parts of nature, the corporeal and spiritual. For whilst I know, by seeing or hearing, *etc.* that there is some corporeal being without me, the object of that sensation, I do more

certainly know, that there is some spiritual being within me, that sees
and hears. This I must be convinced cannot be the action of bare insensible matter; nor ever could be, without an immaterial thinking being.
(E 2. 23. 15)

In view of the unmistakable echoes of Descartes's *Meditations*, it is
tempting to suppose that Locke commits himself here to an immaterialist theory of the human mind.[2] But such a temptation should
be resisted. In controversy with Bishop Stillingfleet Locke explains
that his concept of a spiritual substance is weaker than one might
imagine. To say that *x* is a spiritual substance is simply to say that *x*
is a thinking substance; it does not imply that the bearer of mental
properties is not also the bearer of physical properties (*LW* iv. 33).
Even at the end of the paragraph Locke is careful to keep his metaphysical options open. It is true that he is clear that bare matter
cannot think, but it does not follow from this concession that matter
might not be made to think by an act of God (who may well be the
'immaterial thinking being' in question).

At no point in 2. 23, then, does Locke commit himself to substantial dualism, with regard to the created world, and a closer look
at passages which seem to lean in this direction suggests instead
that something more interesting is going on. Philosophers from
Descartes to the present day have often tended to assume that there
is a fact of the matter over the right answer to the mind–body
problem; dualists and their materialist opponents can at least agree
that there is an objective truth to be discovered, independently of
human decisions. By contrast, in places Locke seems to be suggesting that just this assumption needs to be called into question. In
other words, he hints at what we might call a deflationary approach
to the mind–body problem, at least at one level. To attribute such
a stance to Locke is by no means intrinsically implausible. As we
shall see in a later chapter, he adopts just this kind of approach to
debates over classification. To questions of the form: 'Is *x* really a
human being?' Locke replies that there is no fact of the matter to
be discovered. What is at issue is simply whether a given individual
falls under a concept which we have decided to adopt.

The deflationary approach is thus a cap which fits Locke, but is

---

[2] See Descartes, Second Meditation, in *The Philosophical Writings of Descartes*,
trans. J. Cottingham, R. Stoothoff, and D. Murdoch, 3 vols. (Cambridge, 1985), ii.
22.

he wearing it on the present occasion? To be in a position to give an affirmative answer to this question, we need to draw on two kinds of evidence. Recall, in the first place, that according to Locke 'we are apt to think' that fearing, doubting, and the like are the actions of some substance distinct from matter (*E* 2. 23. 5); in other words, we have acquired the habit of thinking in dualist terms. Of itself, this claim of Locke's shows little; it is consistent with supposing that dualism is a mere habit or convention which we could perhaps discard in favour of materialism, but it does not entail it. Even if we have unreflectingly acquired the habit of thinking and speaking in dualist terms, it is still possible that our habit reflects an objective metaphysical truth.

To support the deflationary approach thus requires evidence of a different kind, and it is here that his analysis of our idea of a substratum (substance in general) proves suggestive. For Locke, our idea of a mind, like our ideas of particular sorts of bodies, includes, as an essential component, the idea of a substratum of properties. But, as we have seen, this idea is wholly empty of content; it is the idea of a 'bare particular' whose only property is the relational one of supporting 'accidents'. At the level of our ideas, then, it is difficult to see how there could be a fact of the matter about the mind–body problem; given the emptiness of our concept of substance in general, there is no reason to say that dualism is truer than materialism. We can of course say—and, according to Locke, it is how we think—that thinking inheres in a substratum which is different from the one which supports physical properties. But we could just as easily say that one and the same substratum supports mental and physical properties; since it is so empty, there is nothing in the concept of a substratum which makes it logically resistant to such a combination. It may be said that there is one strand in Locke's account which has been overlooked; in order for properties to be attributable to the same substratum, they must 'go constantly together', that is, they must cluster in the way that the purring, miaowing, and furriness of a cat do. But this condition is satisfied in the present case; in this life at least, pain and the stimulation of C-fibres, for example, go constantly together.

The case for attributing full-blooded Cartesian dualism to Locke has thus been undermined, but it may seem that a heavy price has been paid for this result. For, as we have hinted, Locke's dominant position on the mind–body problem seems to be one of strict agnosticism, and this position is inconsistent with the deflationary approach. An agnostic stance, after all, implies that there is a meta-physical fact of the matter to be discovered; the problem is that we just do not know it. But fortunately, there is a way of salvaging the coherence of Locke's overall position by drawing on features of his doctrine of substance. Recall, from the previous chapter, that Locke does not just say that our idea of substance in general is empty; he also says that it is obscure. Implicitly, then, our idea of substance is to be contrasted with the perfect concept which would be available to an omniscient being such as God. This contrast proves service-able here. At the level of our ideas the issue which divides dualists and materialists can be deflated; the truth of dualism is a matter of convention or custom only. But at the level of the ideas available to an omniscient being, there is more to be known; that is, such a being with perfect cognitive vision can see whether mental and physical properties can be instantiated by the same thing. The deflationary and the agnostic approaches to the mind–body problem can thus be combined, since they concern different epistemological levels—the level of our imperfect ideas and the level of the perfect ideas which are available to an omniscient being.

The Thinking-Matter Hypothesis

The (implicit) contrast between our imperfect ideas and those of an omniscient being resurfaces in that part of Locke's teaching about the mind–body problem which most disturbed his contem-poraries; this is the hypothesis that, in some sense, matter might think. Once again context is important; in a chapter entitled 'Of the Extent of Human Knowledge' (4. 3) Locke seeks to argue that there are certain philosophical problems which we may never be able to solve. Although, as we shall see, the imperfections of our ideas are relevant here, Locke introduces the thinking-matter hypothesis by saying that 'the extent of our knowledge' comes short not only of the reality of things, but even of the extent of our own ideas:

We have the *ideas* of *matter* and *thinking*, but possibly shall never be able to know, whether any mere material being thinks, or no; it being impossible for us, by the contemplation of our own *ideas*, without revelation, to discover, whether omnipotency has not given to some systems of matter fitly disposed, a power to perceive and think, or else joined and fixed to matter so disposed, a thinking immaterial substance: it being, in respect of our notions, not much more remote from our comprehension to conceive, that God can, if he pleases, superadd to matter a faculty of thinking, than that he should superadd to it another substance, with a faculty of thinking; since we know not wherein thinking consists, nor to what sort of substances the Almighty has been pleased to give that power, which cannot be in any created being, but merely by the good pleasure and bounty of the Creator. For I see no contradiction in it, that the first eternal thinking being should, if he pleased, give to certain systems of created senseless matter, put together as he thinks fit, some degrees of sense, perception, and thought. (*E* 4. 3. 6)

Obviously this notorious passage is inconsistent with a dogmatic commitment to substantial dualism of the kind we find in Descartes; by the use of natural reason alone we cannot be certain that mind and body are two really distinct substances. But though Locke's hypothesis of thinking matter proved disturbing to his contemporaries, his claims in this passage are not merely in line with his dominant tendency towards agnosticism; they are carefully crafted to give as little offence as possible to his conservative critics; certainly they are far removed from Hobbesian materialism. Once again the key to Locke's meaning is provided by the distinction between our ideas and those of an omniscient being.

Some readers who have felt that Locke's message in this passage is a modest one have supposed that he is not making any claim to the effect that thinking matter is logically possible, even as a result of God's power. On this view Locke's concern is not with logical but with what is called epistemic possibility; that is, according to Locke, it is possible, as far as we know, that God has endowed matter with a faculty of thinking. It may then be added that there can be no valid inference from epistemic possibility to logical possibility. Consider, for example, Goldbach's famous conjecture that every even number is the sum of two primes. There is as yet no mathematical proof or disproof of this conjecture, though no counter-examples have been found. Thus it is epistemically possible—i.e. as far as we know—that the conjecture is true. But on a standard view of mathematics, if it is true, then it is necessarily true, and its negation is logically impossible, and if it is false, then it is necessarily false, and its truth is likewise logically impossible. Thus from the fact that the truth of Goldbach's conjecture is epistemically possible, it does not follow that it is logically possible.

The reasoning here is valid, but the reading of Locke to which it appeals seems mistaken. It is true that claims about what is possible for us to know are indeed very much in evidence in the passage, but it is wrong to suppose that he makes no claims about the logical possibility of thinking matter. We can interpret him in this way only by ignoring the direction of his argument; as is not infrequently the case with Locke, the fact that there is an argument here may be masked not just by his standard informality but by his habit of stating his conclusion before the premisses. Read carefully, however, Locke can be seen to be relying on a premiss to the effect that a certain state of affairs is in his judgement logically possible; he sees no contradiction in the proposition that God has endowed matter with a faculty of thinking. From this premiss Locke argues for the conclusion that we cannot know a priori whether God has in fact endowed matter with such a faculty. Here Locke is trading on the rather plausible assumption that we can know a priori that p is false only if we can see that p involves a contradiction. God of course might choose to inform us by a special revelation whether he has in fact endowed matter with a faculty of thinking, but a revelation of this sort would not be a priori knowledge; indeed, as we shall see in the penultimate chapter, for Locke we could never, strictly speaking, have knowledge by this means, since there would always be room to doubt whether God has in fact revealed a truth to us. To say this is not of course to impugn God's veracity; it is rather to say that we cannot be sure whether what we take to be a divine revelation really is so.

Locke is thus committed to the claim that it is logically possible for matter to think, at least by an act of divine superaddition. But in fact this claim commits him to less than it might appear to do; for it is clear from his discussion that it is only at the level of our ideas that there is no contradiction in the supposition of matter thinking. It is consistent with everything that Locke says that at the level of the perfect ideas available to an omniscient being there might be such a contradiction; endowed with such ideas, God may be able to see that thinking and material properties cannot coexist in the same subject. This is a coherent position for Locke to adopt, even if he holds that God's ideas and our own pick out the same things. The point can be illustrated by means of a familiar example. The terms 'wingless biped' and 'rational animal' may be extensionally equivalent, but whereas it is consistent to say that some wingless bipeds are irrational, it is a contradiction to say that some rational animals are irrational. Thus once the role of Locke's distinction between the two levels of ideas is appreciated, we can see that his hypothesis of thinking matter is not only consistent with his agnosticism; it is also a strikingly minimal one. To this extent at least, those who believe that his claims are epistemic throughout the passage are not so far off the mark.

There are two further ways in which Locke seeks to draw the sting out of the hypothesis of thinking matter. In the first place, although he is an agnostic about the truth of Cartesian substance dualism, he never seriously questions the truth of what is called property dualism; that is, he never seriously entertains the thought that mental properties such as willing and fearing are not fundamentally different in kind from physical properties such as shape and solidity. The suggestion which is often heard today that pain is simply the stimulation of C-fibres, picked out under a different description, is alien to Locke's approach to the mind–body problem. Thus even if we set aside his agnosticism, there is no danger that his hypothesis will collapse into the reductive materialism of a Hobbes who identifies mental states with states of the brain. It is true that in one place Locke says that we do not know wherein thinking consists, and this concession may seem to leave the door open to a thoroughgoing reductive materialism. But in the absence of further evidence in support of this suggestion, it is natural to suppose that all Locke means is that we do not know enough about thought to pronounce on whether it can inhere in the same subject as physical properties.

A second way in which Locke seeks to mitigate the harshness of the hypothesis is by the conspicuous and seemingly indispensable role that it accords to God. Today perhaps it is tempting to suppose that the theological framework of the discussion is simply a sop to Locke's conservative critics; but that would be a rash judgement. Certainly, before we adopt it we must take account of a distinction which Locke emphasizes on more than one occasion. Although (in some sense) it is possible for matter to think by a divine act of superaddition, Locke is careful to observe that matter cannot produce thought; as we shall see, this last thesis is crucial to his proof of the existence of an immaterial God. Impressed by the fact that Locke is not entertaining reductive materialism, some readers may find in his talk of superaddition an anticipation of the modern view that thought might be an emergent property of matter; in other words, consciousness might be caused by material systems, but in such a way that its presence could not be inferred by one who knew the laws of nature. But this reading would be a mistake. The role of God in Locke's account cannot be brushed aside so easily.

Before I conclude this section, it is worth noting that Locke's appeal to God's power may be more than an attempt to silence the conservatives; it may be designed as part of an *ad hominem* argument against Descartes. Consider, first of all, one way in which Locke may seem vulnerable to a Cartesian critique. Locke starts, as we have seen, from the premiss that there is no contradiction in supposing that God has endowed matter with a faculty of thinking; from this he argues to the conclusion that we can have no a priori knowledge of whether matter thinks. It is natural to suppose that Descartes might respond by simply rejecting the premiss of Locke's argument: it is logically impossible for matter to think, even by an act of divine superaddition. But Locke is in a position to show that the rejection of this premiss is of little help to Descartes in his defence of dogmatic dualism. Here we come up against Descartes's remarkable claims concerning divine omnipotence. In correspondence, in particular, Descartes is fond of warning his readers that it is a mistake to infer from the fact that p is inconceivable to us to the conclusion that God cannot bring it about that p.[3] And in these contexts Descartes is not employing the term 'inconceivable' in a weak Lockean sense; he does not just mean that we have no understanding of the means or mechanism by which a certain state of affairs might be realized; on the contrary, he means 'inconceivable' in the strong sense of involving a contradiction. Thus even if thinking matter is inconceivable in this strong sense, on Descartes's principles it does not follow that God cannot bring it about. And then Locke can challenge Descartes on how he can be certain that God

[3] Descartes to Arnauld, 29 July 1648, in *Philosophical Writings of Descartes*, iii. 358–9.

has not in fact made matter think. If Descartes seeks to meet the challenge by invoking his doctrine of innate knowledge, we know how Locke will respond.

Does the Mind always Think?

It has sometimes been said that one of Locke's virtues as a philosopher is that he is aware of all the difficulties; his stance towards the mind–body problem bears out the truth of such a judgement. Locke emphasizes again and again that substantial dualism and non-reductive materialism, the two leading candidates for a solution, both involve something 'dark and intricate' (E 4. 3. 6); such are the difficulties that they involve that there are no conclusive grounds for deciding in favour of either of them. The two main discussions in the Essay which bear on the mind–body problem are largely consistent with this stance of principled agnosticism, though, as we have seen, we must recognize a conventionalist strand in Locke's approach at least at the level of our ideas. It is true that on occasions Locke protests that the dualist hypothesis is 'the more probable opinion' (E 2. 27. 25), but he provides no real justification for this claim. Indeed, the important point is rather the implication that the hypothesis stops short of certainty.

When we turn to Locke's specific anti-Cartesian polemics we seem to find a rather different situation; there he seems, implicitly at least, to lean more in the direction of materialism. The most prominent case of this tendency is Locke's famous polemic against Descartes's thesis that the mind always thinks, that is, is always conscious. For Descartes, this thesis occupies a place at the heart of his philosophy of mind; as he tells a correspondent, it is a straightforward deduction from the thesis that the mind is a substance whose whole essence is constituted by thought.[4]

In book 2 chapter 1 of the Essay Locke adopts two significantly distinct strategies for attacking this thesis. The first is a modest epistemological one; the thesis is simply unproven dogma. Locke confronts the Cartesian with a dilemma of the sort that was later to be favoured by Hume. Descartes must advance his thesis either as an

[4] Descartes to Hyperaspistes, Aug. 1641, in Philosophical Writings of Descartes, iii. 189.

a priori truth or as a matter of empirical fact. If the thesis is supposed to be the former, then the question is simply begged:

'Tis doubted whether I thought all last night, or no; the question being about a matter of fact, 'tis begging it, to bring, as a proof for it, an hypothesis, which is the very thing in dispute: by which way one may prove any thing, and 'tis but supposing that all watches, whilst the balance beats, think, and 'tis sufficiently proved, and past doubt, that my watch thought all last night. (E 2. 1. 10)

If, by contrast, the thesis is supposed to be an empirical one, then it is not established by the available evidence; on the face of it there appear to be gaps in consciousness as in dreamless sleep. Locke is aware, however, of the difficulty of arguing that the thesis is actually falsified by the empirical evidence; to the objection that I slept dreamlessly all last night, Descartes can reply that my memory is playing me false.

But, as in the case of his opposition to Descartes's nativism, Locke does not confine himself to the claim that the thesis is unproven; he argues that it is actually false. Locke seeks to establish this stronger thesis by means of a *reductio* argument: the Cartesian thesis leads to the absurdity that two distinct persons could share one and the same soul (E 2. 1. 15). Here Locke anticipates his official discussion of personal identity (added in the second edition) by resorting to the kind of science fiction thought-experiment which has proved so strikingly influential in modern philosophy. Suppose, says Locke, as seems possible on Descartes's principles, that one and the same soul systematically alternates between the bodies of two men, Castor and Pollux, who sleep and wake by turns. While Castor is dreamlessly asleep, the soul thinks in Pollux's body, and vice versa. In that case, if there is no continuity of consciousness between the soul's thoughts in the two men, we are forced to say that there are two distinct persons: 'I ask, then, whether *Castor* and *Pollux*, thus, with only one soul between them, which thinks and perceives in one, what the other is never conscious of, nor is concerned for, are not two as distinct persons, as *Castor* and *Hercules*; or, as *Socrates* and *Plato* were?' (E 2. 1. 12). It should be noted that the argument is not a *reductio ad absurdum* in the strict sense, for its conclusion is not a contradiction; it is rather a thesis which, in Locke's eyes, is so counter-intuitive as to serve as a disproof of its dogmatic metaphysical premiss.

For Locke, then, the dogma that the soul always thinks is simply false, and from this he validly infers the further anti-Cartesian conclusion that thought or consciousness is not the essence of the mind. Instead, Locke suggests, it is one of its operations, as motion is of the body. This may seem a relatively uncontroversial claim, but a little reflection leads one to wonder whether it can be coherently combined with the thesis that the mind is an immaterial substance. Traditionally, since Aristotle, a substance is not just a bearer of properties; it is that which persists uninterruptedly through change; in other words, it is a temporal continuant. But it is not clear that Locke's denial of the Cartesian dogmas entitles him to say that the mind is a substance in this sense. Ironically, it is those very commitments he shares with Descartes which cause trouble for the conception of the mind as an immaterial substance. Locke cannot say, as Leibniz could, that during the intervals in consciousness the mind has unconscious perceptual states (*petites perceptions*),[5] for he subscribes to the Cartesian view that all mental states are necessarily conscious (perhaps even self-conscious): 'It is altogether as intelligible to say, that a body is extended without parts, as that anything *thinks without being conscious of it*, or perceiving, that it does so' (*E* 2. 1. 19). It thus seems difficult to see what sense can be attached to the claim that the mind is an immaterial substance which persists across intervals in consciousness.

To defend the intelligibility of this thesis Locke would need to embrace at least one of two options, neither of which seems philosophically attractive. In the first place, he could agree that a substance is, by definition, an entity which persists through time, and say that though there are times when the mind lacks conscious states, it satisfies this condition for substantiality by virtue of the fact that its powers or faculties persist. In other words, during intervals in consciousness, the mind is in a state of pure potentiality. Such a concession seems hard to reconcile with the conviction, which Locke in general seems to share, that unexercised powers cannot be free-floating; such powers, whether they are mental or physical, need to be grounded in something actual. In the case of an immaterial substance, however, there seems to be no obvious candidate for the role of ground. Alternatively, or in addition, Locke could

---

[5] *Leibniz: New Essays on Human Understanding*, trans. P. Remnant and J. Bennett (Cambridge, 1981), preface, 54–8.

drop the continuant requirement for substantiality, and admit the possibility of temporally gappy substances. As we shall see, Locke is prepared to concede the possibility of temporally gappy persons, but he shows no signs of wishing to concede such a possibility with regard to substances.

It is difficult to escape the view that Locke's denial that the mind always thinks seems more favourable to a materialist account, according to which mental states, such as occurrent thoughts and desires, inhere in a physical system such as the brain.[6] On this view the denial that the mind always thinks is free from the conceptual difficulties which are raised by the immaterialist account; Locke agrees of course that materialism itself has its difficulties, but once these are recognized, there is no further puzzle posed by the supposition that body is intermittently the subject of mental states or properties. Locke of course does not explicitly draw this moral, but there are enough hints in the *Essay* to suggest that he wishes his readers to draw the moral for themselves.

Animal Consciousness

No reader of the *Essay* can miss Locke's polemic against the Cartesian thesis that the soul always thinks. By contrast, his attack on Descartes's more notorious thesis that animals are mere machines is singularly muted. Indeed, ostensibly Locke's chief purpose in discussing animals in the *Essay* is to emphasize how they lack some of the mental faculties with which human minds are endowed; in contrast to us, for example, the animals have no capacity for framing abstract or complex ideas. None the less, though it hardly amounts to a polemic, Locke's dissent from the Cartesian thesis is real:

For if they have any *ideas* at all, and are not bare machines (as some would have them) we cannot deny them to have some reason. It seems as evident to me, that they do some of them in certain instances reason, as that they have sense; but it is only in particular *ideas*, just as they received them from their senses. (*E* 2. 11. 11)

---

[6] Cf. J. Bennett, 'Locke's Philosophy of Mind', in Chappell (ed.), *Cambridge Companion to Locke*, 114.

It is tempting for us today to suppose that Locke's defence of animal consciousness is simply a vindication of common sense against a Cartesian dogma; he may appear to be writing in the spirit of his compatriot Henry More, who expressed honest outrage at Descartes's view.[7] But to read Locke in this way would be a mistake. As he is well aware, the status of animals bears on the larger issue of the prospects of a materialist theory of mind; Locke's own treatment of animals may well seem to contribute to the case for materialism.

Locke's discussion of animals in the *Essay* may be muted, but in controversy with Stillingfleet he is more forthcoming; he sketches an argument from animal sensation for the thesis that some matter thinks (by divine superaddition):

But here I take liberty to observe, that if your lordship [i.e. Stillingfleet] allows brutes to have sensation, it will follow, either that God can and doth give to some parcels of matter a power of perception and thinking; or that all animals have immaterial and consequently, according to your lordship, immortal souls, as well as men: and to say that fleas and mites, etc. have immortal souls as well as men will possibly be looked on as going a great way to serve a hypothesis. (*LW* iv. 466)

The full argument, then, has the following form:

(1) Animals have sensations.
(2) If animals have sensations, then either matter thinks in animals (by divine superaddition), or they have immaterial souls.
(3) Therefore, either matter thinks in animals (by divine superaddition), or they have immaterial souls.
(4) If animals have immaterial souls, they have immortal souls.
(5) But animals do not have immortal souls.
(6) Therefore, animals do not have immaterial souls.
(7) Therefore, matter thinks in animals (by divine superaddition).

It is not entirely clear how far Locke himself wishes to endorse this argument. As he himself indicates, (4) is a principle which his opponent accepts, but to say this is not of course to say that Locke also

<hr>

[7] More to Descartes, 11 Dec. 1648, in P. Adam and P. Tannery (eds.), *Œuvres de Descartes*, 12 vols. (Paris, 1897–13), v. 276–7.

accepts it.[8] Perhaps Locke is arguing in an *ad hominem* fashion for a conclusion which he might wish to support on other grounds. But whether or not he accepts it, at least the argument shows him to be well aware of how the fact of animal consciousness could be exploited in the interests of thinking matter.

Even if Locke accepts the argument, its conclusion is still a relatively modest one; it has no immediate implications for the status of the human mind. But on the standard view that the existence of an immaterial soul is a necessary condition of immortality, the thesis that matter thinks in animals is still disturbing, for Locke's philosophy as a whole may well seem to contain the resources for extending the materialist account to the case of human beings. In book 2 of the *Essay* Locke may emphasize the difference between animal and human consciousness; compared with us, the minds of animals are 'tied up within . . . narrow bounds' (*E* 2. 11. 11). But the moral that Locke wishes to draw appears to be that these differences are differences of degree only, not of kind. And if that is so, it is plausible to suppose that the consciousness inheres in the same kind of subject in both cases. If matter can think in animals, then to postulate that the subject of consciousness in us is a wholly different kind of entity—an immaterial soul—may seem an unpardonable metaphysical extravagance of which no one committed to Ockham's razor should be guilty.

Thinking Matter and the Proof of God's Existence

It is natural to claim that in his discussion of our knowledge of God's existence (*E* 4. 10) Locke sounds more like a rationalist metaphysician than he does elsewhere in the *Essay*. Elements of rationalism are visible not just in Locke's confidence that it is possible to offer a deductive proof of the existence of a supersensible being; they are visible also in the principles to which he appeals in support of the project. In contrast to Hume and Kant, for example, Locke does not feel the need to question the epistemological credentials

---

[8] Indeed, if 'immortality' is understood in a full-blooded sense as entailing continuity of consciousness, then there is evidence that Locke does not accept this principle. See Ch. 6 n. 1 below.

of the causal principle that 'nothing cannot produce any real being'; he does not question, as Kant did, whether such a principle can be coherently applied beyond the limits of possible experience. For Locke, the causal principle is as intuitively certain as it was for Descartes. But though this chapter to some degree stands apart in spirit from the rest of the *Essay*, there is none the less an important link with the issues which we have already examined. The rationalist spirit of the discussion of God's existence is certainly in some overall tension with the agnosticism of the thinking-matter hypothesis, but to say this is not necessarily to say that there is any outright inconsistency between the two discussions. Locke himself insists that there is no such inconsistency, and with one single exception perhaps his confidence on this score seems justified.

Although its structure is not always clearly marked, Locke's proof of the existence of God comes in three stages. First, Locke argues for the existence of an eternal being; secondly, he argues that this being is a thinking or 'cogitative' entity which is also all-powerful; indeed, it is the source of power in all other things. Finally, he argues that this eternal thinking and all-powerful being must be wholly non-material. It is above all in connection with this last stage of the proof that Locke touches on issues that have already surfaced in the discussion of the thinking-matter hypothesis.

We have seen that, like many other traditional proofs of the existence of God, Locke's proof relies on the supposedly a priori principle that something cannot come from nothing. Locke deploys this principle as early as the first stage of the argument to prove the existence of an eternal being. To this principle he adds a premiss which has a better claim to intuitive certainty; with a clear echo of Descartes's *cogito ergo sum* Locke remarks that he certainly knows the existence of at least one being, namely himself. From these premisses Locke seeks to infer the conclusion that an eternal being exists. For if something such as himself exists, then either it is eternal or it has a beginning in time; if it has a beginning in time, then by the causal principle it owes its existence to something external. The same argument can then be run with respect to this further being, and so on, until we are led to the conclusion that an eternal being exists.

Since Leibniz critics have been quick to complain that this argument involves an egregious instance of the fallacy of equivocation, and unfortunately this criticism appears to be justified. Locke states the conclusion of his argument in the form: 'From eternity there has been something' (E 4. 10. 3), but he appears not to see that this sentence is ambiguous between: (1) There has never been a time when nothing existed; and (2) Some one thing has always existed. Obviously (2) does not follow from (1), but though Locke clearly intends to assert the stronger (2), he is entitled only to the weaker (1). His argument shows at most that there must be a series of finite beings which extends backwards to infinity in time.

Whatever its defects, Locke's 'proof' of the existence of an eternal being thus depends on the traditional premiss that something cannot come from nothing. His proof that this eternal being is cogitative similarly depends on a traditional principle that is supposedly a priori, but in this case it is the nature rather than the (universal) existence of causality which is in question. In this second stage of the overall argument Locke is committed to what we might call an 'heirloom' model of causality[9] which goes back to the Scholastics; according to this model, properties are literally transmitted from the cause to the effect. Thus, for Locke, if x is the causal source of the properties of y, then x contains these properties in itself (or perhaps grander versions thereof). It is this principle that seems to ground the thesis that mere matter could not produce thinking beings external to itself; for since thought is a non-physical 'perfection', if matter produced thinking beings, it would be the causal source of perfections which it did not itself possess.

Claims about the relationship between thought and matter thus surface in the second stage of Locke's argument, where he seeks to prove that the eternal being cannot be merely material but must be 'cogitative'. But it is the third stage of the overall argument which bears most directly on the issues raised by the thinking-matter hypothesis. There Locke seeks to establish that the eternal cogitative being must be immaterial; he is thus forced to confront the objection that matter might be able to produce thought in itself. In other words, why should not some system of matter be organized or structured in such a way that it gives rise to consciousness? Now Locke, as we have seen, never seriously entertains any alternatives to property dualism; it seems, then, that he is not considering the reductionist thesis that mental states, such as pain, might be identical with certain physical states (for example, the stimulation of C-

---

[9] I owe this phrase to J. Cottingham, *Descartes* (Oxford, 1986), 50.

fibres). Rather, what he is attacking is more like the modern hypothesis that thought or consciousness is an emergent property of some material systems. On this view, thought is a property which is caused by structural features of such systems but is not identical with any physical state. Indeed, for emergentists, no knowledge of the structure of the system and the laws which govern it enable us even in principle to conclude that it would have to have consciousness. In one place Locke dismisses this hypothesis out of hand: 'unthinking particles of matter, however put together, can have nothing thereby added to them, but a new relation of position' (E 4. 10. 16).[10] Thus, for Locke, we can know a priori that no organization of matter can be the causal source of consciousness.

At first sight Locke's dismissal of the emergentist view may seem inconsistent with his willingness to entertain the hypothesis of thinking matter in 4. 3. 6. But this impression is mistaken. The hypothesis which Locke dismisses in 4. 10 is the idea that without outside interference a material system might be able to cause thought in itself, and, by extension, have the power to cause thought elsewhere in the universe. But of course the possibility to which he is more receptive in 4. 3. 6 is a very different thesis: what is at issue there is whether a material system might be endowed with a power of thinking by an external being which already has this power in itself. So even if in 4. 3. 6 Locke is prepared to consider the possibility that the faculty of thinking is the causal source of occurrent thoughts, this faculty is in turn the product of something eternal (and external) which thinks. By contrast, in 4. 10. 16 it is the very origin of mentality in general that is at issue, and thus it is not logically possible to appeal to an external source of consciousness.[11]

So far, then, the two discussions are consistent, as Locke proclaims they are. But though it may be difficult to convict him of an outright inconsistency here, there is one loose end which is left dangling. It is part of the hypothesis which Locke entertains in 4. 3. 6 that the systems of matter to which God superadds the faculty of thinking are 'fitly disposed'. If this last phrase is not mere verbiage, the suggestion seems to be that structural features of a material system make a difference to its receptivity to a faculty of thinking:

[10] Locke offers an elaborate argument against this hypothesis at E 4. 10. 17; for a valuable discussion of this argument, see Bennett, 'Locke's Philosophy of Mind', 102–4.
[11] Cf. ibid. 102.

in other words, some structural arrangements of material particles are inherently more suitable than others for receiving mental powers. By contrast, in the argument against the emergentist hypothesis in 4. 10. 16 Locke seems to reject this thesis; *however* material particles are put together, only physical properties such as motion can result. On this view, no disposition of matter could be inherently fitter than any other to receive the power of thinking; God could as easily superadd such a power to a shoe or a turnip as to a human brain. Although it may not amount to a formal inconsistency, there is thus a clear tension between the two accounts; in the light of 4. 10 it is hard to see what business Locke has to add the qualification 'fitly disposed' into his hypothesis of thinking matter. To put the point another way, the earlier discussion seems rather more sympathetic to the emergentist hypothesis than the later discussion. As we have seen, there is an unaccustomed strain of rationalist metaphysics in Locke's proof of the existence of God, and it would be surprising if the presence of this strain were to have no embarrassing repercussions elsewhere in the *Essay*. In this one instance the repercussions do indeed seem to be embarrassing.

6

PERSONAL IDENTITY

IN book 1 of the *Essay* Locke poses some puzzle cases which are designed to convince the reader that our idea of identity is not as clear and distinct as we suppose, and hence is not innate. He then anticipates the objection that these puzzle cases are merely of academic interest with no bearing on our practical concerns:

Nor let anyone think, that the questions, I have here proposed, about the *identity* of man, are bare, empty speculations; which if they were, would be enough to show, that there was in the understandings of men *no innate* idea of identity. He, that shall, with a little attention, reflect on the resurrection, and consider, that divine justice shall bring to judgement, at the last day, the very same persons, to be happy or miserable in the other, who did well or ill in this life, will find it, perhaps, not easy to resolve with himself, what makes the same man, or wherein *identity* consists: and will not be forward to think he, and everyone, even children themselves, have naturally a clear *idea* of it. (E 1. 4. 5)

Here, as elsewhere, Locke hints at the main motivation for his theory of personal identity; the theory is above all designed to address a theological challenge which arises naturally from his rather radical approach to the mind–body problem. As we have seen, Locke's stance on this issue is officially agnostic, while unofficially it leans in the direction of materialism. Readers who believed that the immortality of the person is the immortality of an immaterial soul would find in Locke a threat to traditional teachings concerning the afterlife and divine justice. In response to this challenge Locke does not seek to prove the fact of personal immortality; that is a truth of divine revelation which is to be believed on the authority of the Bible. But he does offer a theory of personal identity which points the moral that the survival of the person beyond death does not depend logically on the truth of substantial dualism; even if there are no finite immaterial substances, we may none the less be resurrected at the Day of Judgement.[1] Locke's whole theory of personal identity is carefully crafted to be consistent with the doctrine of materialism, whose truth he regards as both logically and epistemically possible.

To introduce Locke's theory of personal identity by way of its theological motivation is not of course to deny that the interest of the theory extends well beyond such issues as the nature of divine justice. Locke's theory of personal identity is perhaps the most influential part of his whole philosophy; it is scarcely an exaggeration to say that all modern discussions of the topic go back to Locke. It is Locke who not only first formulates the problem in a recognizably modern form, but also pioneers some of the techniques which have become standard in recent approaches to solving the problem; the contemporary use of science fiction examples to test our intuitions is in a clear line of descent from Locke. But it is necessary to understand the theological motivation of his discussion if we are to appreciate why it has the form it does have; we thereby come to see that certain options are not available to him and that certain objections are misguided. The need to accommodate the demands of personal immortality and of divine justice rules out various modifications of his basic theory which have attracted some modern philosophers.

Locke's theory of identity, and of personal identity in particular,

---

[1] Cf. *E* 4. 3. 6: 'All the great ends of morality and religion, are well enough secured, without philosophical proofs of the soul's immateriality; since it is evident, that he who made us at first begin to subsist here, sensible intelligent beings, and for several years continued us in such a state, can and will restore us to the like state of sensibility in another world, and make us capable there to receive the retribution he has designed to men, according to their doings in this life.' For Locke, however, a proof of the soul's immateriality, if it were available, would not serve to establish personal immortality. Simply by virtue of being a substance, an immaterial soul would, if it existed, be indestructible, but such indestructibility is not sufficient for personal immortality. What personal immortality essentially involves is continuity of consciousness, and this must be something added by divine grace. Locke's views are close to those of the 'mortalists', that is, those who believed that the soul is naturally mortal. See the journal entry for 20 Feb. 1682, in *An Early Draft of Locke's Essay*, ed. R. I. Aaron and J. Gibb (Oxford, 1936), 121–3.

is embedded within the wider context of his programme of explaining the origin of all ideas in experience. For his nativist opponents the idea of identity was supposed to be a paradigm case of an innate idea, and though Locke did not add this chapter until the second edition, we can see why he feels the need to show how the idea could be accommodated within his empiricist framework of idea-acquisition. Yet it is natural to believe that the official context is little more than a pretext for Locke's real concerns; what really interests Locke, we may suppose, is a set of metaphysical issues concerning identity. But we should not be too quick to accuse Locke of departing from what the order of his discussion requires. For one thing, as we have seen, Locke's analysis of the puzzle cases concerning identity is by no means irrelevant to his anti-nativist account of idea-acquisition. On Locke's view the nativist hypothesis entails that our idea of identity is clear and distinct (*E* 1. 4. 4), and this in turn entails that it is easy to analyse; we shall not be confronted with cases where we do not know what judgement to make about identity. In 2. 27 Locke of course dwells on the puzzle cases concerning identity, and though in his judgement these puzzles can be ultimately resolved, to do so requires careful analysis which shows that the idea of identity is not as clear and distinct as the defenders of the nativist hypothesis suppose. Locke's elaborate analysis of the puzzle cases surrounding identity is thus grist to the mill of the empiricist account concerning idea-acquisition.

But even if we allow that Locke's interest in identity is in some degree a metaphysical one, it does not follow that it is metaphysical in a damaging sense; in other words, he does not violate his own self-imposed strictures on the limits of human knowledge. After all, the theory of personal identity in particular is advanced against the backdrop of metaphysical agnosticism; its context, as we have seen, is Locke's conviction that ultimate knowledge of the nature of the mind—knowledge of the kind that God possesses—is not available to human beings. Locke's theory of personal identity is couched in terms of the concepts which we possess; it is our concept of personal identity which is being analysed. If this is metaphysics, it is descriptive metaphysics which runs no danger of trying to cross barriers which he has declared to be impassable. Perhaps the only general feature of Locke's project which might be criticized is his conviction that the concepts which we employ are also those which

God employs to settle questions about moral responsibility at the Day of Judgement.

The Relativity of Identity

As part of his polemic against the nativist hypothesis Locke thus holds that the idea of identity in general is a difficult one which requires careful analysis. This suggestion, already thrown out in book 1 of the *Essay*, is developed at length in chapter 27 of book 2, where, as order requires, he prefaces his theory of personal identity with an account of identity in general. Locke's analysis of this idea is among the subtlest and most important discussions in the *Essay* as a whole.

Although the importance of Locke's analysis of identity is generally agreed, the nature of his theory remains to some extent controversial. What is not in dispute is that he is committed to at least a weak version of the theory that identity is relative. In Locke's words: 'To conceive, and judge of [identity] aright, we must consider what *idea* the word it is applied to stands for: it being one thing to be the same *substance*, another the same *man*, and a third the same *person*, if *person*, *man*, and *substance*, are three names standing for three different *ideas*; for such as is the idea belonging to that name, such must be the *identity*' (E 2. 27. 7). In other words, the identity conditions for individuals are systematically determined by the sortal or specific concepts under which the individual falls.[2] Thus if, as Locke thinks, the concept of a man (human being) is a different concept from the concept of a person, then what it is for A to be the same person as B will not be the same as what it is for A to be the same human being as B. The identity of a human being over time, for instance, according to Locke, requires spatio-temporal continuity; the identity of a person, however, does not. As we shall see, Locke is under theological pressure to advance this last doctrine.

The correct analysis of human and personal identity is of course controversial, as Locke is well aware, and he is careful to introduce

---

[2] Mackie, *Problems from Locke*, 141.

the general principle by way of less contentious examples. Consider, he says, the difference between the identity of a mass of atoms and the identity of an oak tree. A mass of atoms remains the same no matter how the atoms are jumbled, but it ceases to be the same if one atom is added to or subtracted from the collection. By contrast, an oak retains its identity through enormous variations in the particles of matter which constitute it at a time; one and the same oak was a sapling and is now a full-grown tree, even though there may be no atoms (material particles) which remain constant throughout these changes. Locke plainly thinks that we will all share the same intuitions about such cases. The moral to be drawn is that the identity conditions in the two cases are determined by the very different concepts of a mass of atoms and an oak:

We must therefore consider wherein an oak differs from a mass of matter, and that seems to me to be in this; that the one is only the cohesion of particles of matter anyhow united, the other such a disposition of them as constitutes the parts of an oak; and such an organization of those parts, as is fit to receive, and distribute nourishment, so as to continue, and frame the wood, bark, and leaves, *etc.* of an oak, in which consists the vegetable life. (*E* 2. 27. 4)

Locke proceeds to claim that the identity of a human being is like that of an oak; it consists in 'nothing but a participation of the same continued life, by constantly fleeting particles of matter, in succession vitally united to the same organized body' (*E* 2. 27. 6). In neither case is it required for identity over time that any particular particle of matter remain constant. And more controversially, Locke draws the conclusion that the identity of the soul is neither necessary nor sufficient for the identity of the human being.

Whether Locke is correct in his analysis of these cases may be disputed, but of course the answer to this question does not affect the truth of his general thesis concerning the relativity of identity. And this thesis is not merely plausible; it has also proved highly influential in the literature on the topic. But unfortunately the analysis appears inconsistent with Locke's teachings concerning identity elsewhere in the *Essay*. The philosophical moral of the relativity thesis is that questions about the identity of individuals are vacuous until a sortal term is introduced. We cannot meaningfully ask whether A is the same individual as B; our question only becomes meaningful when it takes the form: Is A the same F (e.g. the same man) as B? In the words of Peter Geach, there is no being the same without being the same such-and-such.[3] But this moral seems to be contradicted by Locke's famous thesis that the individual has no essence:

'Tis necessary for me to be as I am; God and nature has made me so: But there is nothing I have, is essential to me. An accident, or disease, may very much alter my colour, or shape; a fever, or fall, may take away my reason, or memory, or both; and an apoplexy leave neither sense, nor understanding, no nor life. Other creatures of my shape, may be made with more, and better, or fewer, and worse faculties than I have: and others may have reason, and sense, in a shape and body very different from mine. None of these are essential to the one, or the other, or to any individual whatsoever, till the mind refers it to some sort or *species* of things; and then presently, according to the abstract *idea* of that sort, something is found *essential*. (E 3. 6. 4)

The implication of Locke's thesis here seems to be that it is possible to pick out and reidentify an individual independently of any general description (such as man). And this conflicts with the moral of the thesis concerning the relativity of identity. If individuals can be picked out only via a general term, then, logically speaking, they must have essential properties; that is, they must have those properties which are entailed by the sortal concepts under which they fall.

The Theory of Personal Identity

The theory of the relativity of identity is a doctrine of very general application; it has consequences for questions not just about diachronic identity (identity over time), but also about synchronic identity (identity at a moment). But like other philosophers, such as Hume, Locke is most interested in issues about the nature of personal identity over time, and his theory of personal identity is specifically addressed to questions of this sort. But whereas Hume thought that the identity of persons over time was in much the same

[3] P. T. Geach, *Mental Acts* (London, 1957), 68–9. Cf. E. Anscombe, 'Aristotle', in E. Anscombe and P. T. Geach, *Three Philosophers* (Oxford, 1961), 8.

case as the identity of plants and animals, Locke takes a wholly different view; for him the criterion of personal identity proves to be
very distinctive. To understand why this is so we must at least keep
in mind that Locke's whole discussion is motivated by a concern
with personal immortality.

To point out that for Locke the criterion of personal identity is
distinctively different from that for plants and animals is not of
course to convict him of any inconsistency. On the contrary, he is
here faithful to his general principles concerning identity; that is, he
is faithful to his earlier insistence on the role of the concept in question—in this case the concept of person—in determining the identity conditions. As he says, 'such as is the idea belonging to that
name, such must be the identity' (E 2. 27. 7). Indeed, in this case
Locke appears to seek to deduce the criterion of identity for persons
from his analysis of the very concept of a person; for Locke, the
concept of a person is the concept of 'a thinking intelligent being
that has reason and reflection and can consider itself as itself, the
same thinking thing in different times and places' (E 2. 27. 9). Locke
seems to hold that his famous account of the identity conditions for
persons follows from this analysis:

For since consciousness always accompanies thinking, and it is that, that
makes everyone to be what he calls *self*; and thereby distinguishes himself
from all other thinking things, in this alone consists *personal identity*, *i.e.*
the sameness of a rational being: And as far as this consciousness can be
extended backwards to any past action or thought, so far reaches the identity of that *person*; it is the same *self* now it was then; and it is by the same
self with this present one that now reflects on it, that that action was done.
(E 2. 27. 9)

According to Locke, then, A is the same person as B if and only if
A can be conscious of the actions and experiences of B (where A is
a person picked out at t and B is a person picked out at an earlier
time $t - 1$). But if this is intended to be a derivation, then it seems
to be fallacious. A person is, for Locke, by definition a self-conscious
being that has some sense of itself as existing at different times and
places, but it is not clear that he is entitled to infer from this that
I cannot be identified with my 10-year-old self unless I can be conscious of his actions and experiences.

We can throw light on Locke's theory of personal identity by
reflecting on how different it is from his account of the identity con-

ditions for human beings and animals. In the case of human beings he holds that spatio-temporal continuity is a necessary condition for identity over time; an infant 'mewling and puking in the nurse's arms' cannot be the same human being as the judge 'in fair round belly' unless there is a continuous history as a human being connecting the two times. In the case of persons, however, Locke drops the requirement of spatio-temporal continuity; he insists that persons picked out at different times can be identical even though there are gaps in their history (E 2. 27. 10). But Locke still wishes to hold that personal identity implies some kind of psychological continuity, and he offers an analysis instead in terms of the continuity at the level of the content of consciousness.[4] Although this analysis does not impose the strict requirement of spatio-temporal continuity, it is none the less in its way quite as stringent as his analysis of the identity conditions for animals and human beings.

Personal identity is thus to be analysed in terms of psychological continuity, in the sense explained, and from this Locke proceeds to draw some corollaries regarding the doctrine of substance. It is logically possible that the continuity of consciousness required for personal identity should be preserved across a change in immaterial substances; hence, personal identity does not entail the identity of a persisting immaterial substance. Conversely, for Locke, the identity of an immaterial substance does not entail the identity of the person; as his earlier discussion showed, we can conceive that two different persons, Castor and Pollux, might take their turns in one and the same immaterial substance (E 2. 1. 12; cf. 2. 1. 15). These corollaries may seem innocent enough, but of course Locke is committed by his analysis to a stronger, more controversial thesis; personal identity does not entail the presence of any immaterial substance whatsoever. Provided the continuity of consciousness condition is satisfied, there can be no grounds for denying that personal identity is preserved even if it should turn out that such personhood was not instantiated in any immaterial substance. Thus Locke's theory of personal identity is clearly consistent with substance materialism. To say this is not of course to say that it entails the doctrine; nor is it even to say that materialism is in any sense meta-

---

[4] This kind of continuity corresponds to what Derek Parfit calls 'psychological connectedness'. See his 'Personal Identity', *Philosophical Review*, 80 (1971), 3–27. I prefer to speak of psychological continuity, since it stays closer to Locke's phrase 'continued consciousness' (E 2. 27. 25).

physically possible. Locke's concern is simply with what is logically or conceptually possible on his analysis of a person. Indeed, he even ventures to say that 'the more probable opinion is, that this consciousness is annexed to, and the affection of one individual immaterial substance' (E 2. 27. 25). But Locke conspicuously fails to provide any supporting evidence for this opinion, and in the next sentence he changes the subject.

Locke's theory of personal identity thus satisfies crucial constraints; it puts him in a position to answer two objections arising from his approach to the mind–body problem, which is at best agnostic. Consider, first, an objection that might be made by defenders of the thesis that persons are essentially immaterial substances. If we do not and cannot know that there are any such finite substances, then we do not know that there are any persons; *a fortiori*, then, we do not know that there are any persons which survive death. Locke would respond to this objection by conceding first of all that, strictly speaking, we have no a priori knowledge of personal immortality; this doctrine is part of revealed religion, and must be believed on the authority of the Bible. But our invincible ignorance with regard to the mind–body problem has no tendency to call into question the existence of persons; for our concept of a person is, as it were, a phenomenal one. Whether there are persons that preserve their identity over time can be established without knowledge of deep metaphysics; all we need to do is to see whether there is the right kind of psychological continuity.

A second objection might begin with the fact that Locke's approach to the mind–body problem does not rule out a materialist account of finite minds; for all we know, according to Locke, consciousness may inhere in a material system. But if such a form of materialism were true, then personal immortality would be (hypothetically) impossible; for personal immortality entails the survival beyond death of an entity such as an immaterial substance. But, according to materialism, there is no plausible candidate for an entity which literally survives, with a continuous history, from this life to the next. On the materialist account, when Jones is cremated that is simply the end of him.

Locke responds to this objection by conceding that on the materialist hypothesis there is nothing which has a continuous history from this life to the next. But to make this concession does not entail that there cannot be persons at the Day of Judgement who are identical with persons in this life; for, as we have seen, spatio-temporal continuity is not a requirement in the case of the identity of persons over time. On the contrary, our concept of a person is the concept of an entity which can remain the same across gaps in its history; it is the concept of an entity which can go out of existence for stretches of time. Even if there is no continuous person-history which connects us with persons at the Day of Judgement, we can still be identical with them if the continuity of consciousness condition is satisfied.

We are now in a position to criticize a famous objection by Thomas Reid. Reid in fact is the source of two celebrated objections to Locke's theory, and in the final section we shall discuss his 'brave officer' paradox, to which Locke's theory is supposed to lead. Here we are concerned rather with Reid's charge that Locke's theory is internally inconsistent. Reid observes that in denying that sameness of person entails sameness of substance Locke implies that persons are not substances, and thereby embroils himself in a contradiction.[5] For Locke also defines a person as 'a thinking thing' and, according to Reid, Locke's basic meaning for 'substance' is simply that of thing.

Reid is clearly right that a person is, by Locke's definition, a thinking thing, but he is wrong in his account of what it is to be a substance for Locke. The reply to be made on Locke's behalf is that when he denies that persons are necessarily substances, what is at issue is a stronger sense of the term 'thing' than when he calls persons things. Such a defence of Locke might take two complementary forms. In the first place, we might come to his rescue by invoking his famous account of the substratum, which is supposed to be an ingredient of our concept of any kind of substance. When Locke denies that personal identity over time entails the identity of a substance, he may be denying that it entails the identity of a substratum (where a substratum is supposed to be unobservable even in principle). By contrast, to say that a person is a thinking thing of some sort is not to say that there is an unobservable substratum or bare particular in which its mental properties inhere. Secondly, and more promisingly perhaps, we can mount a defence of Locke by invoking the traditional definition of substance. From Aristotle onwards, a substance is not just a bearer of properties, or ultimate

---

[5] T. Reid, 'Of Identity', in *Essays on the Intellectual Powers of Man* (1781).

subject of predication; it is that which persists uninterruptedly through changes of qualities. But of course, as we have seen, Locke has dropped the requirement of strict temporal continuity for personal identity over time; persons, for Locke, are beings of the sort which may have gappy histories. Thus if persons are things, it is in a weaker sense than that which is implied by the traditional Aristotelian understanding of what it is to be a substance.

The metaphysical status of personhood on Locke's account can be illuminated by means of an analogy deriving from Jonathan Bennett.[6] It seems accurate to say that a person, for Locke, is less like a substance than it is like an institution. A monarchy, for example, is not intuitively a substance, but it is in some weak sense a thing; the term is at least a substantive, and it is perfectly coherent to say that it is a thing of which people can approve or disapprove. The analogy can be developed further in two significant ways. Just as the same monarchy may be successively realized in different human beings, so, for Locke, it seems, a person can be successively realized in different immaterial substances. And further, we can say that the English monarchy in 1660 was the same institution as the monarchy in 1640 (before the Civil War), despite the fact that it ceased to exist during the Interregnum. In this way too, then, a monarchy is like a Lockean person; its identity conditions do not require strict spatio-temporal continuity.

Personal Identity and Strong Relativity

We saw in an earlier section that Locke is committed to a version of the doctrine that identity is relative; as he says, 'such as is the idea belonging to that name, such must be the identity'. In connection with his theory of personal identity, it is natural to ask whether he is committed to a stronger version of the doctrine. To understand what is at issue, let us suppose that 'two' individuals A and B both fall under different sortal or specific concepts F and G. The thesis of the strong relativity of identity then asserts that A and B may be the same F without being the same G. Defenders of the thesis might

---

[6] Bennett, 'Locke's Philosophy of Mind', in Chappell (ed.), *Cambridge Companion to Locke*, 108.

say that it is convincingly illustrated by Stevenson's famous short novel *Dr Jekyll and Mr Hyde*. In this story the kindly figure of Dr Jekyll is transformed every night into the sinister and diabolical figure of Mr Hyde. Now here, clearly, Jekyll and Hyde are both men and both persons, but it is rather plausible to say that although Jekyll is the same man as Hyde (by virtue of the bodily continuity between the two), he is not the same person (by virtue of the wide difference in character). In order to move from the weak thesis to the strong thesis, we need to insert the premiss that sortal terms F (e.g. 'man') and G (e.g. 'person') may both be applied to A and B, even though F and G have different identity conditions.[7]

Does Locke's theory of personal identity show him to be committed to this stronger thesis? Locke does not of course think that it is continuity of character which constitutes personal identity, but it is none the less tempting at first sight to suppose that, *mutatis mutandis*, he would agree with proponents of the strong-relativity thesis in their analysis of such cases. But it would be a mistake to reach this conclusion too hastily; it is important to be clear about what can and cannot be safely attributed to Locke. As we have seen, he certainly believes that the identity of the person is logically independent of the identity of the substance. And closer to hand, he believes that the identity of the human being does not entail the identity of the person; to this extent he would agree with the proponents of strong relativity. He likewise agrees with them that the identity of the person does not entail the identity of the human being: if, as in Kafka's *Metamorphosis*, I were to wake up one morning with the body of a bug, then I would be the same person as before the transformation (provided I have the appropriate consciousness), but on Locke's analysis I could not possibly be the same human being, for I would have ceased to be a human being at all. To adapt one of Locke's own examples, if the person of Heliogabulus were to enter one of his hogs, no one would say that the hog was the same man as Heliogabulus. But of course the example from Kafka's short story is of a very different nature from Jekyll-and-Hyde cases, where one and the same individual is supposed to satisfy the general descriptions 'human being' and 'person' both before and after the transformation.

The evidence for Locke's subscription to the stronger thesis

---

[7] Cf. Lowe, *Locke on Human Understanding*, ch. V.

concerning identity is, I believe, inconclusive. The issue is complicated by the fact of his principled uncertainty concerning what sort of entity realizes personality. For example, he is not in a position to say that one and the same individual satisfies the general descriptions 'person' and 'human being'. If, as is epistemically possible, personality is realized in immaterial substances, then there is and perhaps can be nothing of which we could say that it is both a person and a human being; immaterial substances would be joined to human beings, but be distinct entities from them. And, on the other hand, if, as is epistemically possible, there are no finite immaterial substances, and persons are realized in physical systems, then there is not and perhaps cannot be any individual of which we could say that it is both a person and an immaterial substance. Perhaps it will be said that Locke believes that one of the two accounts of personality is correct; that is, persons are realized either by immaterial substances or by human beings. Thus either there is an individual which is both a person and a human being or there is an individual which is both a person and an immaterial substance. In this way a commitment to strong relativity of identity might be attributed to Locke. But even this seems to go beyond what Locke says.[8]

The Memory Criterion and Divine Justice

One of Locke's most revealing remarks is that the word 'person' is a forensic term appropriating actions and their merit (E 2. 27. 26). For Locke, to use the language of persons is to speak of bearers of responsibility, both moral and legal; it is persons who are punished and rewarded, and they are punished and rewarded for what they did. As we shall see, he is concerned to show how his theory of personal identity can accommodate our intuitions about human justice, but it is fair to say that he has his eyes more firmly fixed on divine

[8] Some readers may feel that there is other evidence in favour of attributing the strong-relativity thesis to Locke. For example, it might be said that, for Locke, A and B may be the same oak but not the same mass of matter, though A and B are both oaks and masses of matter. But it seems likely that Locke would deny that there is one individual thing which is both an oak and a mass of matter; rather, he would regard these as two distinct objects of different kinds.

justice as meted out at the Resurrection (e.g. *E* 2. 27. 15); in particular, he is interested in the question of how it can be just for God to punish and reward beings in the afterlife for actions performed here on earth. As I suggested at the beginning of this chapter, Locke's concern with divine justice in an eschatological setting helps to throw light on his theory of personal identity in general, and to explain why some friendly amendments to his theory which have been proposed by recent philosophers would not suit his purposes.

Although in explaining his doctrine Locke tends to speak of consciousness, it is generally accepted that his theory offers an analysis of personal identity in terms of memory. It is then said that, in order to be remotely plausible, it must be genuine remembering which is at issue; otherwise his theory will have wildly counter-intuitive consequences. For example, if honest pseudo-memories are allowed to count, it will follow that George IV was indeed the same person as the one who led British troops to victory at Waterloo, for towards the end of his life this monarch honestly suffered from the delusion that he had done just this. But in that case Locke's theory may be in trouble. The worry takes the following form. Philosophers have pointed out that the concept of genuine memory is a causal one; genuine remembering, unlike pseudo-remembering, is causally related to the original experience which is recalled.[9] Now the causal links which are involved in such genuine remembering must run through one and the same body. But then the memory criterion simply collapses into the criterion of bodily continuity. Employing one of his own favourite strategies of argument, we can thus confront Locke with a dilemma: either his theory is wildly counter-intuitive in its consequences or it does not offer an analysis of personal identity which is independent of bodily continuity.

Some philosophers have sought to respond to this objection on Locke's behalf by going through the horns of the dilemma. According to this line of defence, we should agree that his theory needs to be couched in terms of genuine memory and that the concept of genuine memory is indeed a causal one. None the less, there is no need to accept the further thesis that the causal links require sameness of body. It is conceivable at least that there should be transfers of consciousness across different bodies such that the later

---

[9] Cf. Mackie, *Problems from Locke*, 184.

consciousness is caused by an earlier consciousness in a different body.[10] In this way, then, the memory criterion does not simply collapse into the criterion of bodily continuity.

Philosophers who propose this line of defence may be right about the conceivability of such transfers, and they may indeed be able to rescue a memory theory in this way. But it is not clear that Locke is in a position to accept such offers of assistance, however well-meaning; here again the theological motivation of his theory comes into play. For, as we have seen, it is vitally important to Locke to be able to say that persons at the Day of Judgement can be identical with persons here on earth, and justly punished or rewarded for their actions. Now if the identity of persons over time is constituted by genuine memory, then on the proposed analysis there must be causal connections between the memories of people at the Day of Judgement and the original actions on earth which they recall; Jones's memory at the general Resurrection of the dead of fornication must be ultimately caused by the action and experience of fornication itself in this life. And it is not clear that this idea is coherent. It is perhaps intelligible to suppose that my memory of an experience or action may be causally related to actions in another body in the same world. But the scenario which we are invited to imagine here is much more radical than that. To come up with a theory which is adequate to Locke's purposes, we are required to suppose that a memory experience can be causally related to an original action which was performed not only in a different world but in a body which has ceased to exist. And on any ordinary understanding of causality this makes no sense.

In this light we can consider Locke's actual struggle with the problem of the transfer of consciousness from one mind or 'intellectual substance' to another. Locke is concerned with the following kind of case. Suppose that at the Day of Judgement I have a vivid consciousness of having committed the Whitechapel murders, which were in fact committed by Jack the Ripper (where the proper name picks out the human being by whom those heinous crimes were committed). Locke is worried that since consciousness entails personal identity, and personal identity in turn entails accountability, I am responsible for the notorious Whitechapel murders. Locke,

---

[10] Cf. Mackie, *Problems from Locke*, 184.

then, appeals to the goodness of God to guarantee that such cases do not arise:

> that which we call the *same consciousness*, not being the same individual act, why one intellectual substance may not have represented to it, as done by itself, what it never did, and was perhaps done by some other agent, why I say such a representation may not possibly be without reality of matter of fact, as well as several representations in dreams are, which yet, whilst dreaming, we take for true, will be difficult to conclude from the nature of things. And that it never is so, will by us, till we have clearer views of the nature of thinking substances, be best resolved into the goodness of God, who as far as the happiness or misery of any of his sensible creatures is concerned in it, will not by a fatal error of theirs transfer from one to another, that consciousness, which draws reward or punishment with it. (E 2. 27. 13)

A natural modern response to the problem is once again to confront Locke with a dilemma: the consciousness at issue is either genuine memory or it is not. If it is merely pseudo-memory, then he need not worry about such cases; since personal identity is not in question, there is not even a prima-facie problem of accountability to be resolved. But if it is genuine memory, then on Locke's analysis I am indeed morally responsible for the Whitechapel murders, and thus there is no ground for the kind of appeal to God's goodness which Locke envisages. In other words, there is no entity which needs to be protected against injustice in such cases.[11] By assuming that there is, Locke is illicitly departing from his theory that genuine memory and moral accountability entail each other. Thus his response to his own problem either is unnecessary (for there is no problem to be resolved) or it is not one to which he is entitled.

This is a deft analysis, but it is also an unsympathetic one, for it fails to take account of the constraints under which Locke's theory labours. As we have seen, if genuine memory requires a causal analysis, it is not clear that he can formulate his theory in these terms, for it is very obscure how the memory experiences of people at the Day of Judgement can be causally related to original experiences in this life. Since the causal analysis of memory appears to be unavailable to Locke, it is natural for him to state his theory, as he

[11] Ibid.

does, in terms of consciousness; he thereby allows even memory beliefs without causal links to the original experience to enter into the analysis.

To recognize the constraints under which Locke labours is not of course to endorse his actual approach to the problem with its seemingly clumsy appeal to divine benevolence. Indeed, his response to the problem seems doubly vulnerable. In the first place, if personal identity is constituted by consciousness alone (without the causal link), then the objections to the revised theory arise in a new form; if I am conscious of having committed the Whitechapel murders, then even if there is no causal link, I am indeed accountable, and it cannot be the case that my consciousness needs to be protected by divine goodness against a miscarriage of justice. Secondly, since personal identity is constituted by consciousness, the identity of an intellectual substance is no more nor less relevant to questions about accountability than the identity of the human being. Thus if there were a problem about the transference of consciousness from one intellectual substance to another, there would be an analogous problem about the transference of consciousness from one human being to another. Now a case can be made for saying that Locke is in fact committed to recognizing the reality of transferences of this kind. For as a Christian he is required to believe that the general Resurrection of the dead will take a physical form; the persons who will be punished or rewarded at the Day of Judgement will be realized by (or at least joined to) human beings. But Locke surely does not think that there is any human being in this life with whom a given human being at the Day of Judgement can be identical, for the requirement of spatio-temporal continuity would be violated. Thus Locke seems to be in a curious position. On the one hand, he is under theological pressure to recognize the existence of transfers of consciousness, at least across human bodies; on the other hand, he is logically committed to holding that the existence of any such transference would constitute an injustice which the goodness of God can be guaranteed to forestall. As applied to the Day of Judgement, then, Locke's theory seems curiously self-undermining.

Although there is an element of incoherence in Locke's account, it is a mistake to imagine that nothing can be made of his appeal to the goodness of God, whether in this life or the next. We can see this by means of the following scenario. Let us recall our earlier supposition that at the Day of Judgement I have a vivid recollection of having committed the Whitechapel murders; among the details of these recollections are images of a London full of hansom cabs and the kind of pea-souper which we associate with old Sherlock Holmes films. Suppose also that my other memories of London are of a city full of modern cars, tower blocks, and the clean air which has been standard since the passage of legislation after the Second World War. God could play a role in ensuring that my memories do not exhibit this kind of incoherence; he could play this role with respect to my consciousness in either this life or the next. Whether he in fact plays this role in the present life seems put in doubt by counter-examples of the George IV variety. But the objection here is not that Locke's appeal to God is muddled, but that it is belied by the empirical facts. Even if we admit the existence of such counter-examples, however, we have no reason to suppose that God does not play a role in guaranteeing the coherence of memories of persons at the Day of Judgement. If, in the presence of God, I were to remember committing heinous crimes in dark alleys in late Victorian London, I would indeed be guilty, but I can rely on the goodness of God to ensure that I will have no memories which are incoherent with my actual recollections of the clean, car-filled city of today.

Molyneux and the Drunkard

That Locke has his sights fixed on divine justice is evident even in his discussions of issues whose explicit focus is questions of human justice. In a notorious passage which led to a debate with William Molyneux, Locke seeks to bring his theory into line with our moral and legal intuitions about the case of the person who claims to have lost consciousness of crimes committed when drunk:

But is not a man drunk and sober the same person, why else is he punished for the fact he commits when drunk, though he be never afterwards conscious of it? Just as much the same person, as a man that walks, and does other things in his sleep, is the same person, and is answerable for any mischief he shall do in it. Human laws punish both with a justice suitable to their way of knowledge: because in these cases, they cannot distinguish certainly what is real, what counterfeit; and so the ignorance in drunkenness or sleep is not admitted as a plea. For though punishment be annexed to personality, and personality to consciousness, and the drunkard perhaps be not conscious of what he did; yet human judicatures justly punish him; because the fact is proved against him, but want of consciousness cannot be proved for him. But in the great day, wherein the secrets of all hearts shall be laid open, it may be reasonable to think, no one shall be made to answer for what he knows nothing of; but shall receive his doom, his conscience accusing or excusing him. (E 2. 27. 22)

The judgements which human law courts hand down thus do not conflict with the implications of Locke's theory of personal identity, but because of the limitations on our knowledge, they are necessarily provisional compared with divine justice.

Molyneux naturally objected that Locke's theory mischaracterizes the moral and legal basis for punishing the drunkard. Somewhat curiously, he believes that it is just to punish the sleepwalker, and he accepts the Lockean account of why this is so, but otherwise he points to a clear disanalogy between the two kinds of cases. Drunkenness, he observes, is a voluntary act; indeed, it is itself a crime, and human laws are based on the principle that persons are responsible for the consequences of such actions; as he says, no crime shall be alleged in excuse for another crime. Molyneux illustrates the principle through the example of the person who accidentally shoots a human being while he is out poaching; the law holds that the person is culpable for this unintended act of homicide (Molyneux to Locke, 23 December 1693, CL iv. 767).

It has sometimes been suggested that in the course of the exchange Locke comes to capitulate to Molyneux, but this is a mistake;[12] on the contrary, Locke consistently reaffirms and defends the position which he had articulated in the Essay. His statement which concludes the exchange is easy to misunderstand in this respect. Locke tells Molyneux that he agrees with him that 'drunkenness being a voluntary defect, want of consciousness ought not to be presumed in favour of the drunkard' (26 May 1694, CL v. 58). We should not be misled here by Locke's conciliatory tone, which is designed simply to bring the exchange to a close. The point that

---

[12] H. E. Allison, 'Locke's Theory of Personal Identity: A Re-Examination', *Journal of the History of Ideas*, 27 (1966), 47; repr. in Tipton (ed.), *Locke on Human Understanding*, 111.

he is making is not that though the drunkard (that is, the man who was drunk and is now sober) is indeed unconscious of his criminal act, his want of consciousness ought not to be allowed to count in his favour; it is rather that he should not be presumed to lack the consciousness which he says he does. In other words, the courts should not accept as genuine his possibly self-serving plea about his mental state. Locke's point concerns fact, not right.[13]

Locke's exchange with Molyneux about the drunkard raises some interesting methodological issues. In places Locke implicitly concedes that the laws concerning drunkenness may have in fact been motivated by the principle which Molyneux adduces; a voluntary criminal act cannot be alleged in excuse of another crime. None the less, Locke argues that this is irrelevant to the assessment of his theory. On the methodological issue Locke seems right; it is not a constraint on the adequacy of his theory that it should capture the actual reasoning of the lawyers or parliamentarians who framed the law. Consider, by way of analogy, the debate between J. S. Mill and William Whewell over the moral basis of sanitary legislation.[14] Whewell argued that the justification for such laws is paternalistic; their goal is to force people to be clean for their own good. On the contrary, replied Mill, such laws are not paternalistic at all; they are justified on the ground that they prevent harm to others by inhibiting the spread of disease. Now Whewell may be perfectly right about the actual motives of those who introduced the sanitary laws; they may indeed have been activated by the spirit of paternalism. But that is no objection to Mill; it is enough for his purposes that these laws can be justified on non-paternalistic grounds. Similarly, it is enough for Locke's purposes if the punishment of the drunkard who claims to have lost consciousness of his crime can be justified in a way that is consistent with his overall theory of personal identity.

Locke, then, is entirely justified in setting aside the legal principles which Molyneux adduces. But it must be admitted that in order to reconcile his theory of personal identity and responsibility with legal practice and our intuitions about who should be punished, he is driven to adopt slightly desperate measures; he is forced to invoke

---

[13] This was originally pointed out by P. Helm, 'Did Locke Capitulate to Molyneux?', *Journal of the History of Ideas*, 42 (1981), 669–71.
[14] For an account of this debate, see A. Ryan, *J. S. Mill* (London, 1974), 147.

epistemic considerations about our necessary ignorance of other people's mental states; the courts do not and cannot know whether the drunkard's plea of lost consciousness is made in good faith. In this respect Locke's defence of his theory is less elegant than, say, Mill's defence of his anti-paternalism in response to Whewell. Locke's resort to such considerations also underlines how far apart are he and Molyneux, even though Locke closes the exchange by pretending they agree. Molyneux is committed to the counterfactual conditional thesis that it would still be just to punish the drunkard even if we did know that his plea of loss of consciousness was genuine; Locke of course is committed to denying this thesis, for he is committed to denying that the now-sober man is the same person as the criminal drunkard. Locke and Molyneux are as far apart as ever.

Reid and the 'Brave Officer'

Locke may believe that he can reconcile his theory with all our intuitions about who is deserving of punishment, but in this he seems mistaken. Most of us would be inclined to side with Molyneux about the counterfactual situation in which we have certain knowledge regarding the drunkard's sincerity. In the grip of his theory Locke is prepared to override some of our intuitions. To admit this is not necessarily to say that his procedure is indefensible; it may be good philosophical practice to do this if our intuitions are either weak or demonstrably confused. What is perhaps most interesting about Locke's intransigence in response to Molyneux is that it suggests how he might respond to an even more famous objection proposed after his death.

Thomas Reid sought to show, by means of an anecdote, that Locke's theory of personal identity leads to paradox. Suppose, he says, that a brave officer, who was flogged as a boy for robbing an orchard, captures a standard from the enemy, and in later life becomes a famous general. The officer can remember being flogged as a boy, and the elderly general can remember capturing the standard, but the general cannot remember the flogging. On Locke's theory the general is the same person as the officer, and the officer is the same person as the boy; but the general is not the same person as the boy. But this is paradoxical, for identity is a transitive relation.[15] In other words, if A is the same person as B, and B is the same person as C, then A is the same person as C.

How might Locke have responded to such an objection? The usual defence which is presented on his behalf accepts the transitivity of identity as a principle which cannot be sensibly challenged. The strategy then is to weaken the analysis of personal identity to the point where no violation of transitivity occurs. In response to Reid, then, we might say that though as a matter of fact the general cannot remember the flogging, he could remember it in principle, and that it is this weak construal of the 'could remember' relation which the theory needs. In this manner Locke's account can be reconciled with the transitivity of identity. But such a defence steers the theory away from Scylla only to drive it in the direction of a new Charybdis. For the only justification that can be offered for the thesis that the general can in principle remember the flogging is that he is the same person. Thus the defence of the theory looks circular.[16]

The failure of this defence prompts us to look around in a different direction, and here Locke's policy of 'no surrender' in response to Molyneux provides us with a clue; it is tempting to speculate that Locke might again bite the bullet, and in this case deny that personal identity over time is indeed a transitive relation. Some readers may feel that this is a desperate move of last resort, and it is certainly true that we should not gratuitously saddle Locke with defences of his theory which involve untenable commitments. But perhaps this move is not as desperate as it seems. It can at least be pointed out that diachronic identity has some distinctive logical features of its own; Leibniz's law, for instance, states that if A is identical with B then they have all their properties in common, but though this principle holds with respect to judgements of synchronic identity, it does not hold for judgements of identity over time. In view of this precedent, it is not obviously foolish to question whether the transitivity relation holds for identity over time. But of course this is only a speculation as to how Locke would have answered Reid.

Earlier in this chapter I suggested that, for Locke, the concept of

[15] Reid, 'Of Identity'.
[16] Cf. Mackie, *Problems from Locke*, 179.

a person is a phenomenal one, and in one way this is indeed the case. Certainly Locke seeks to show that, despite our metaphysical agnosticism, the self is accessible to us in consciousness; it is not hidden away in a mysterious immaterial substance or substratum below the level of consciousness. But in another way it would be misleading to stress the phenomenal nature of the Lockean self, for though it is available from a first-person perspective, as his handling of the drunkard case shows, from a third-person point of view it is as difficult of access as a substratum would be; this being so, the judgements of the law courts can only be at best provisional. Thus it is a striking characteristic of Locke's theory of personal identity that it is by no means tailored to the requirements of human justice. Locke does not start from the assumption that it is possible in principle for human tribunals to reach definitive judgements about responsibility, and then ask what sort of an entity a person must be in order for this to be the case. It would be more accurate to say that Locke's theory is tailored to the requirements of divine justice. Indeed, the requirements of divine justice supply Locke with a kind of unofficial argument for his theory of personal identity; it is an argument based on the premiss that unless personality were constituted by continuity of consciousness at the level of content, divine justice could neither be done nor be seen to be done. It is perhaps Locke's confidence in the truth of this conditional which allows him, in the name of his theory, to ride roughshod over some of our intuitions.

7

FREEDOM AND VOLITION

L IKE his famous theory of personal identity, Locke's discussion of freedom and volition is above all a contribution to the metaphysics of morals; once again he is enquiring into the necessary conditions of being a bearer of moral responsibility and hence subject to reward and punishment. Punishment, according to Locke, is annexed to personality, and personality to consciousness; in other words, people can be justly punished only for what they can be conscious of having done. In the present chapter we shall see how punishment is likewise annexed to a certain kind of human freedom.

But the parallels between the two discussions are even closer than this. At the end of the previous chapter I suggested that divine justice supplies Locke with at least an unofficial argument for his theory of personal identity. At a later stage in the *Essay* he explicitly sketches a similar argument from theological premises for human freedom. In opposition to the Scholastic insistence on syllogistic methods of argument he outlines a more informal and, as he believes, more perspicuous kind of inference which proceeds by a series of conceptual entailments; he then offers the following illuminating example:

To infer is nothing but by virtue of one proposition laid down as true, to draw in another as true, *i.e.* to see or suppose such a connexion of the two *ideas* of the inferred proposition. *V.g.*, Let this proposition be laid down, *Men shall be punished in another world*, and from thence be inferred this other, *then men can determine themselves* . . . In the instance above-mentioned, what is it that shows the force of the inference, and consequently the reasonableness of it, but a view of the connexion of all the intermediate *ideas* that draw in the conclusion, or proposition inferred? *V.g. Man shall be punished,—God the punisher,—just punishment,—the punished guilty—could have done otherwise—freedom—self-determination,* by which chain of *ideas* thus visibly linked together in train, *i.e.* each intermediate *idea* agreeing on each side with those two it is immediately placed between, the *ideas* of men and self-determination appear to be connected . . . (*E* 4. 17. 4)

Although he thus believes that divine punishment (i.e. in an after-life) implies human freedom, we must remember that for Locke we cannot strictly be certain of the proposition that we shall be punished or rewarded in an afterlife;[1] thus the argument stops short of a full demonstration (despite the certainty of its conditional premisses). Moreover, it would be quite wrong to suggest that Locke's case for human freedom is dominated by theological concerns; in 2. 21, as in 2. 27, Locke is often engaged in a close analysis of secular concepts. But Locke's underlying interest in formulating the necessary conditions of divine justice is one that we ignore at the cost of distorting his aims and purposes.

Locke is clear, then, that divine justice requires human freedom, but what is the nature of the freedom that is thus required? In spite of Locke's explicit insistence that it is the ability to do otherwise, with respect to 2. 21 of the *Essay* readers have traditionally found difficulty in making out Locke's position on the issue of free will. Some critics, such as O'Connor, have accordingly pronounced the whole chapter a failure;[2] others, by contrast, have rendered a more favourable verdict. Even the normally hostile Leibniz privately told a correspondent that Locke's discussion of freedom was among the most subtle in the *Essay*.[3] The existence of such divergent verdicts is not as puzzling as it may appear at first; Locke might easily be criticized for the unclarity of his overall position, while being praised for the many incidental insights into issues concerning human freedom. But in this chapter I shall argue that the central tendency of Locke's position is clear, even though there are some passages which are hard to reconcile with it. In general, Locke

---

[1] *The Reasonableness of Christianity, LW* vii. 122.

[2] O'Connor, *John Locke*, 113; cf. 116–17.

[3] Leibniz to Jaquelot, 28 Apr. 1704, in *Die philosophischen Schriften von G. W. Leibniz,* ed. C. I. Gerhardt, 7 vols. (Berlin, 1875–90), iii. 473.

argues for a compatibilist approach to the problem; in other words, the freedom that is required for moral responsibility is consistent with determinism. We shall then look at some problematic passages and see how far they are really at odds with what appears to be his central thesis. If there are certain tensions in Locke's account, they may be traced to his attempt to reconcile a strongly anti-Scholastic position with his intuition that moral responsibility and divine justice require a robust concept of human freedom.

The Critique of Faculty Psychology

In Locke's philosophy as a whole a dominant tendency towards agnosticism is accompanied by what I have called a deflationary tendency; in Chapter 5 we have seen how both these tendencies are at work in his approach to the mind–body problem. There is no doubt about which of these two tendencies is in the ascendant in his discussion of freedom and volition, particularly perhaps in the early sections. Locke's approach is characterized by a strongly deflationary, anti-Scholastic stance which is strikingly reminiscent of Hobbes. In company with Hobbes Locke argues that the whole issue of free will has been shrouded in unnecessary mystification by his Scholastic predecessors. Philosophers have got off to a bad start by formulating the central questions in terms that are strictly nonsensical and, led astray by this initial error, they have constructed so many metaphysical cobwebs which can be destroyed by the first touch of critical scrutiny. Locke is particularly hard on attempts to construct an elaborate psychology of mental faculties. His intention, however, is not really to deny that there is a metaphysical issue about human freedom to be resolved; indeed, in some sense he offers a positive theory of his own. But Locke is clear that the problems can be resolved without postulating dubious theoretical entities; all the metaphysical facts lie open to our view.

In the early stages of 2. 21 Locke mounts a swift and challenging argument for the thesis that the question whether the will is free is unintelligible. The crucial point, for Locke, is to see that will and freedom are alike powers or faculties, not agents. Freedom is, roughly, the power to do what we will, and will in turn is the power to choose one course of action over another from the alternatives which are physically possible for us (we cannot will to fly). Thus if freedom is predicated of the will, then one power is predicated of another power, but this is incoherent; powers can be predicated, not of powers, but only of agents:

> It is plain then, that the *will* is nothing but one power or ability, and *freedom* another power or ability: so that to ask, whether the *will* has *freedom*, is to ask, whether one power has another power, one ability another ability; a question at first sight too grossly absurd to make a dispute, or need an answer. For who is it that sees not, that *powers* belong only to *agents, and are attributes only of substances, and not of powers* themselves? (E 2. 21. 16)

From these premisses Locke's conclusion straightforwardly follows.

The argument is certainly valid, but one may wonder whether it is sound. Locke regards it as uncontroversial that one power cannot coherently be predicated of other powers, and at first sight the thesis seems plausible; however, reflection suggests that there may be counter-examples. Consider the following admittedly somewhat strained scenario: I buy a set of a dozen wineglasses and discover that they are more fragile than I realized; within weeks of my purchase the set is significantly reduced in number through constant breakages. Here we might say that the fragility of the glasses is irksome to me (meaning thereby that it has the power to irk or irritate me). But fragility is of course a classic case of a dispositional property, and hence a power. So it seems that, contrary to Locke, one power can be coherently predicated of another power. Of course it may be pointed out that fragility is simply a placeholder for a manifest property, namely, the actual physical structure of the glass; dispositional properties, such as fragility, will not figure in a mature scientific explanation of breakages. But we must still beware of confusing a dispositional property with its ground, and it is surely the fragility, not some physical microstructure, which is irksome or irritating to me.

The premiss that one power cannot be coherently predicated of another power perhaps needs more defence than it receives. Locke in fact shows much more concern to defend the premiss that will is merely a power or faculty of the mind. In his view, philosophers have, as it were, sought to disguise from themselves the absurdity of predicating freedom of another power by treating the will as if it were something more; they have converted it and other mental faculties, such as the intellect, into so many little agents within the mind. It is of course the Scholastic philosophers whom Locke is attacking, but though his critique of faculty psychology has been highly influential, it is arguable that its lesson has not always been learned. Freudians who say that a person's id or superego caused him or her to act in a certain way are as much guilty as any Scholastic of the mistake which Locke diagnoses.

Locke's main criticism of the tendency to treat mental faculties as agents is that it violates Ockham's razor: entities are not to be multiplied unnecessarily. In Locke's view the violation of this principle in general is a leading characteristic of the Scholastic style of physical explanation which he and his contemporaries, such as Boyle, were seeking to overthrow: Scholastics characteristically disguised the emptiness or circularity of *vis dormitiva* explanations by reifying faculties or powers into agents. Locke makes the point with characteristic irony: 'For it being asked, what it was that digested the meat in our stomachs? it was a ready, and very satisfactory answer, to say, that it was the *digestive faculty*. What was it that made anything come out of the body? The *expulsive faculty*. What moved? The *motive faculty*' (E 2. 21. 20). This error of reifying powers into agents had been amply exploded in the physical sciences, but, in Locke's view, it was proving surprisingly tenacious in the philosophy of mind. People who would not make the mistake of supposing that the digestive faculty is anything more than a power to digest were still inclined to suppose that the will is something more than a mere power to choose in a certain way. But Locke is insistent that there is a strict parity between the two kinds of cases; will and intellect must not be gratuitously privileged at the expense of the physical faculties.

Locke's critique of a debased kind of faculty psychology is largely persuasive, but it may be asked how far he remains faithful to his original insights. When discussing the nature of motivation in particular, he seems to slip back into the kind of linguistic habits which he had earlier excoriated. Locke criticizes those who speak as if the will operates on the understanding on the ground that one power cannot coherently be said to operate on another (E 2. 21. 18). Yet he himself is led to treat the question what determines the will as a perfectly coherent one; he is even capable of saying such things as that the will is a power to direct the operative faculties (E 2. 21. 71). Perhaps Locke would insist that this is simply a manner of speaking which can be harmlessly cashed out in a way that does not involve any metaphysical error (see *E* 2. 21. 20). But Locke at least excites the suspicion that he has forgotten one of his own earlier lessons.

A Compatibilist Approach

For Locke, then, the question whether the will is free is strictly unintelligible; the sensible question to be asked in this area is rather whether the man, or human being, is free. It is tempting to agree with Locke's strictures, and yet insist that the original question need not be as foolish as it seems; it can be reformulated, more defensibly, as a question about human freedom.[4] Locke himself anticipates this objection when he says that 'the next thing demanded is, *whether a man be at liberty to will which of the two he pleases, motion or rest*' (*E* 2. 21. 25). However, Locke shows himself no more sympathetic to the question in this new form; he thinks it manifest that the answer is 'no'. Although this is supposed to be obvious, he in fact offers an infinite-regress argument to this conclusion. Here he relies on two related premises: free actions are necessarily voluntary, and the voluntariness of such actions is to be understood in terms of their being preceded by acts of volition. However, to generate the infinite regress which he wants, Locke needs the further assumption that the second, earlier act of volition was itself free, and so on down the line.[5]

The moral which Locke draws, then, is that 'liberty concerns not the will' (*E* 2. 21. 25); it pertains rather to overt acts of behaviour. In developing this insight he sketches a compatibilist approach to the problem of human freedom which was anticipated by Hobbes in *Leviathan* and elsewhere. The freedom that matters in connection with moral responsibility is consistent or compatible with determinism; it does not require a contracausal power of willing, that is, a power of willing in a causally undetermined fashion. This is clear from Locke's explicit definition of freedom: '*Liberty* . . . is the power

---

[4] See *Leibniz: New Essays on Human Understanding*, trans. P. Remnant and J. Bennett (Cambridge, 1981), 2. 21, p. 182.

[5] This point is made by Vere Chappell, 'Locke on the Freedom of the Will', in Rogers (ed.), *Locke's Philosophy*, 109.

a man has to do or to forbear doing any particular action, according as its doing or forbearance has the actual preference in the mind, which is the same thing as to say, according as he himself *wills* it' (E 2. 21. 15). Other clarifications point the same moral:

. . . *as far as this power reaches, of acting, or not acting, by the determination of his own thought preferring either, so far is a man free. (E 2. 21. 21)*

. . . *freedom consists in the dependence of the existence, or not-existence of any action, upon our volition of it, and not in the dependence of any action or its contrary, on our preference. (E 2. 21. 27)*

Thus, for Locke, A is free with respect to doing x just in case if he wants to do x he is able to do x and if he wants not to do x he is able not to do x.[6]

Locke's account of human freedom is not identical to Hobbes's, but one difference between them is more verbal than real.[7] Hobbes famously expresses his central compatibilist thesis by saying, with his usual terseness, that liberty and necessity are consistent;[8] in other words, a free action may be part of a causal nexus. Now Locke may appear to contradict this thesis in places, for he seems to oppose freedom to necessity: 'So a man striking himself or his friend by a convulsive motion of his arm, which is not in his power by volition or the direction of his mind to stop or forbear, nobody thinks he has in this liberty; everyone pities him as acting by necessity and constraint' (E 2. 21. 9). But the appearance of contradiction with Hobbes's compatibilism is only an appearance. Indeed, the point that Locke is making in this passage is one that Hobbes would endorse, though he would express it in different terms: what prevents convulsive motions of the arm from counting as free actions is that they are involuntary. Doctor Strangelove does not want his arm to rise in a Nazi salute. Hobbes and Locke are agreed that, in the case of human agency at least, voluntariness is a necessary

[6] That this is Locke's analysis is clearest perhaps in a statement made in correspondence with Limborch during the course of an extended discussion of free will: 'Liberty for me is the power of a man to act or not to act, according to his will: that is to say, if a man is able to do this if he wills to do it, and on the other hand to abstain from doing this when he wills to abstain from doing it.' Locke to Limborch, 12 Aug. 1701, *CL* vii. 406; De Beer's trans. from Locke's original Latin.

[7] Cf. Chappell, 'Locke on the Freedom of the Will', 104.

[8] Hobbes, *Leviathan*, 2. 21.

condition of freedom. Of course it may be pointed out correctly that convulsive motions are causally determined, but Locke is clear that it is not causal determination *per se* which is at issue here, but that kind of causal determination which bypasses the will, as it were. Unlike Hobbes Locke is capable of using the term 'necessary' as a synonym for 'unfree', but we should not be misled by this linguistic usage into seeing a substantive conflict where none exists.

In one way, however, Locke's understanding of the freedom that matters for moral responsibility does differ from Hobbesian doctrine. Consider Locke's illuminating and remarkable discussion of a man transported into the company of his friend:

> Again, suppose a man be carried, whilst fast asleep, into a room, where is a person he longs to see and speak with; and be there locked fast in, beyond his power to get out: he awakes, and is glad to find himself in so desirable company, which he stays willingly in; *i.e.* prefers his stay to going away. I ask, is not this stay voluntary? I think, nobody will doubt it: and yet being locked fast in, it is evident he is not at liberty not to stay, he has not freedom to be gone. (*E* 2. 21. 10)

The general moral which Locke wishes us to draw from this example is that an action may be voluntary and yet constrained, hence unfree; voluntariness is a necessary condition for free agency, but it is not a sufficient one. Hobbes would agree, but Locke reaches the conclusion via a subtly un-Hobbesian route. For Locke, the reason why the person is not a free agent in this case is that one of the conjuncts in his definition of freedom is not satisfied; it is not the case that if he wanted not to stay in the room he would be physically able to do so. Thus the Lockean definition of freedom imposes the requirement that a person be physically able to satisfy non-actual preferences. Hobbes's definition of free agency, by contrast, imposes no such requirement; for him, 'a free man is he that in those things, which by his strength and wit he is able to do, is not hindered to do what he has a will to'.[9] On the basis of this definition Hobbes would have to conclude that the man was indeed a free agent in the case, for he is not hindered in doing what he wills to do, namely, stay and talk with his friend.

---

[9] Hobbes, *Leviathan*, 2. 21.

The Problem of Consistency

In Locke, then, we find one of the classic statements of the compatibilist thesis that the freedom that matters in ethics is consistent with causal determinism: freedom is to be analysed in terms of the ability to act according to actual and hypothetical volitions. But later in the chapter he introduces a new definition of freedom which is clearly not equivalent to the first. Locke tells us that in order to prevent us from acting too hastily: 'we have a power to *suspend* the prosecution of this or that desire, as everyone daily may experiment in himself. This seems to me the source of all liberty; in this seems to consist that, which is (as I think improperly) called *free will*' (E 2. 21. 47). Locke may still hold that, strictly speaking, 'free will' is a nonsensical expression, but he seems to retreat here from his earlier insistence that freedom 'concerns not the will' but rather overt acts of behaviour.

To address the charge of inconsistency we need to distinguish two issues. In the first place, we can ask whether Locke is departing from the compatibilist position which seems to dominate the first half of the chapter; in other words, the question is whether he is introducing a definition of the freedom that matters in ethics which requires a contracausal power of willing, that is, a power to make causally undetermined choices. Secondly, we can ask whether Locke is now committing himself to a libertarian position; in other words, the question is whether he asserts that we actually possess such freedom. Incompatibilism and libertarianism are positions that naturally tend to go together in the writings of philosophers, but it is important to recognize that they are logically independent of one another. It would be perfectly possible to maintain the truth of determinism while holding that the freedom that matters in ethics is inconsistent with the truth of this doctrine; indeed, such a position is known as 'hard determinism'. Thus incompatibilism does not entail libertarianism. In the other direction, libertarianism does not logically oblige one to accept incompatibilism. It is perfectly possible to maintain that we are in possession of contracausal freedom while holding that even if determinism were true, we could still be free in the way that matters in ethics; in other words, the libertarian can concede that the freedom which is required by moral responsibility is simply the absence of coercion. This last combination of views is indeed rare, and it is difficult to see what philosophical motives one could have for subscribing to it. Typically, one of the main reasons for adopting libertarianism is the intuition that unless agents are in possession of contracausal freedom, they are not morally accountable for their actions; thus it would be odd to assert the existence of such freedom while denying that it played any role in ethics. But to say that a combination of views would be philosophically unmotivated is not to say that there is no logical space for it.

In terms of this distinction how should we assess Locke's position in the later sections of 2. 21? On the face of it, Locke appears to be at least a libertarian, for he seems to invite us to picture the antecedents of action in terms of a causal chain which has significant gaps in it. Desires are aroused in a person's mind by a causal process, but it is causally possible for a person to yield or not to yield to a desire (or complex of desires perhaps); the state of desire does not causally necessitate its successor state. Rather, a person exercises a power to yield or not to yield to the desire in a causally undetermined way.

For our purposes, however, the crucial question is not so much whether Locke is a libertarian in these later sections as whether he is an incompatibilist; it is compatibilism rather than determinism for which he is chiefly concerned to argue in the earlier part of the chapter. Thus Locke cannot be convicted of inconsistency simply by pointing to passages which have a libertarian flavour. (As we have seen, it is possible to be both a libertarian and a compatibilist.) But it may appear, unfortunately, that in those passages which seem libertarian in tendency Locke is also simultaneously retreating from the dominant compatibilist position of the early sections of 2. 21. For not merely does he seem to say that we are in possession of a contracausal power of willing; but he also states that it is in precisely this power that freedom consists. Locke adds that the expression 'free will' is improper, but he none the less seems to recognize that freedom in this apparently contracausal sense is a necessary condition of moral responsibility.[10]

---

[10] Chappell believes that in an addition made for the fifth edition (at *E* 2. 21. 56) Locke came to see an inconsistency between his doctrine of suspension and

The principle of charity requires that we should avoid such a reading if we can, and further reflection suggests some doubts about its accuracy. In the first place, it is possible that Locke's remarks about our ability to suspend the prosecution of our desires are not intended as a challenge to the truth of determinism in general. Locke's target may rather be a crude deterministic account of human motivation according to which human beings are simply at the mercy of irrational motives such as greed and envy. As against this Locke may wish to point out that among the causal antecedents of human action may be processes of reasoning and deliberating; we can deliberate not just about how to satisfy our desires, but whether to satisfy them at all. On this reading Locke is not a libertarian, for he does not recognize a contracausal power of willing. And he has not suddenly become an incompatibilist either. There is a freedom relevant to moral responsibility that involves the ability to suspend the prosecution of our desires, and this freedom is obviously different from the freedom to which Locke appeals in his classic compatibilist statements. But even the second kind of freedom is consistent with the truth of determinism.

The issue of Locke's stance on the freedom of the will is complicated by his remarks about indifference. Traditionally, liberty of indifference has been taken to mean contracausal freedom or the absence of causes.[11] When Hume dismisses such liberty as a chimera, he is rejecting the thesis that in a situation where, for example, I choose a doughnut over a chocolate éclair, I could have chosen the éclair without any change in my antecedent motivational state; in other words, I am supposed to be indifferent between the two choices in the sense that either is causally possible for me. Now Locke, on the whole, is not very complimentary in his remarks about indifference; he says that a perfect indifference in the mind would not be 'an advantage and excellency of any intellectual nature' (E 2. 21. 48), but rather an imperfection. Superficially such claims may seem to support the compatibilist reading, but the evidence is inconclusive. For what is at issue in such passages is not indifference with regard to causes, but indifference with regard to

his 'volitional determinism'. See Chappell, 'Locke on the Freedom of the Will', 118.

[11] Hume, A Treatise of Human Nature, 2. 3. 2. Locke uses the phrase in this sense at E 2. 21. 71.

reasons. That which would constitute a great imperfection in our mind is indifference with respect to reasons on matters of importance to us.

We may illustrate Locke's meaning by considering two bridge players, of whom one is an expert, the other a hapless beginner. At some stage in the game the beginner is confronted with a choice between playing the ace of spades and playing the king of diamonds; he is indifferent with regard to this choice in the sense that he can see no reason for preferring to play one card rather than the other. By contrast, in the same situation the expert bridge player experiences no such indifference; he sees that there is overwhelming reason to play the ace of spades. Now Locke's entirely valid point is that the expert's state of mind is more perfect in this case than that of the beginner; the kind of indifference which the latter enjoys is not something which any reasonable person would desire. That this is Locke's point is confirmed by his further recognition that there are cases in which such indifference is not an imperfection in our nature. Playing a game of bridge is a matter of some consequence in which it is desirable to be guided by reason; by contrast, it is no imperfection in me if I am indifferent with regard to which foot I put forward in entering a room. If I am asked my reasons for playing a particular card and cannot answer, I shall be embarrassed; I shall not be embarrassed if I cannot cite any reason for putting my left foot forward rather than my right on crossing a threshold.

Locke's remarks about indifference in 2. 21. 48 seem entirely defensible, but it is important to see that they have no bearing on the debate between libertarians and determinists. The fact that the beginner is indifferent with respect to reasons has no tendency to show that his choice of cards is not causally determined; his choice may be determined by non-rational, perhaps even unconscious, motives. He may play the king of diamonds, for example, because of an unconscious association between the picture on the card and a friend's face. And on the other side, lack of indifference with respect to reasons does not imply determinism. There is no inconsistency in holding that it is causally possible for a person not to do what he or she has overwhelming reason to do (in the sense that the course of action in question is the necessary means to achieving some desired goal). The libertarian may concede that the expert is guided by reason to play the ace of spades, yet add that, in the very same situation, he could have played the king of diamonds on a whim.

Locke's discussion of freedom of indifference is thus neutral with respect to his stance on human freedom. A further problem for a consistent compatibilist reading of Locke comes from a different quarter. We began this chapter by noting that, for Locke in 4. 14. 4, human freedom is a necessary condition of divine justice. Now in setting out his chain of entailments Locke indicates that divine punishment implies that the person punished 'could have done otherwise'. Prima facie at least this admission is something of an embarrassment, for this is an entailment which compatibilists typically deny. According to a standard compatibilist position, in order for me to be morally responsible for an action it is sufficient that I act freely in the sense of being uncoerced and that I am in possession of my rational faculties at the time of acting. (Even this second condition might be waived by some philosophers.) On this view, it is certainly not a necessary condition of moral responsibility that I could have done otherwise. We might try to come to Locke's rescue by invoking features of his initial definition of freedom; according to Locke, freedom is the ability to satisfy non-actual as well as actual preferences. To say, then, that an agent could have done x rather than y is to say that if the agent had willed to do x, he or she would have been physically able to do so. But to many readers such an analysis will appear unsatisfactory; intuitively it fails to do justice to our conception of what is involved in the ability to do otherwise. When it is said that I could have kept a promise which I in fact broke, what is being asserted is something about my will; I could have willed or chosen to keep the promise. It may be true to say that if I had chosen to keep the promise I would have been physically able to do so, but this fact is not sufficient to establish that I could have done otherwise.

Whatever problems are posed by his later remarks, in the chapter on power Locke seems to present a reasonably consistent position. Here as elsewhere (for example, in his discussion of the existence of the external world) it is helpful to imagine Locke as engaged in a kind of debate with an imaginary adversary; if we see the discussion as shaped in these terms, the puzzling sense that he somehow changes direction in midstream can be largely dispelled. Locke begins by taking up a bold deflationary stance; the question to be asked is not whether the will is free but whether the human being is free; in this spirit he advances what is clearly a compatibilist definition of freedom. An imaginary adversary then objects: the issue of free will is not simply a nonsensical question and there is a freedom that is relevant to ethics which is not captured by Locke's initial compatibilist definition. Locke then makes a concession; he introduces his second definition of freedom in terms of the ability to suspend the prosecution of our desires. The opponent is tempted, as it were, to imagine that this is a victory for incompatibilism and also libertarianism inasmuch as we possess this kind of freedom. But Locke would take a different view: to say that we are in possession of the second kind of freedom is simply to recognize our capacity for rational deliberation, and in no way implies a commitment to contracausal freedom.

The Theory of Motivation

An overall compatibilist reading of Locke draws support from the fact that in 2. 21 the discussion of human freedom is followed by— or, more accurately, run in tandem with—a theory of human motivation. On the compatibilist interpretation the two discussions fit together rather snugly. Locke advances a theory of how the will is causally determined that suggests an affirmative answer to the question whether the will is causally determined. It is a slightly complicating fact that, as we have seen, Locke shows little interest in arguing for determinism itself, but both his compatibilism and his theory of motivation would be idling unless he accepted the truth of this doctrine.

The theory of motivation, or of the causal antecedents of human action, is one of those few topics on which Locke underwent a serious change of heart between successive editions of the *Essay*. We might say that he moves from a cognitive account of motivation in the first edition to a conative one. Let us allow Locke himself to describe his change of heart in his own words:

It seems so established and settled a maxim by the general consent of all mankind, that good, the greater good, determines the will, that I do not at all wonder, that when I first published my thoughts on this subject, I took it for granted . . . But yet, upon a stricter inquiry, I am forced to con-

clude that *good*, the *greater good*, though apprehended and acknowledged
to be so, does not determine the *will*, until our desire, raised proportion-
ably to it, makes us *uneasy* in the want of it. (*E* 2. 21. 35)

Locke does not just draw the reader's attention here to his candour;
he wishes him to notice that he is breaking with tradition and developing an original theory. Some philosophers have thought that the
theory which Locke offers in the second edition is indeed close to
what has come to be a modern orthodoxy; but how far this is so
remains to be seen.

Why did Locke become dissatisfied with the theory of the first
edition? He himself suggests that his first thoughts on the topic were
vulnerable to objections to which his second theory is immune.
Curiously, however, one of the objections which he states seems
easily answered. Locke says that he is concerned by what we might
call the problem of 'action at a distance'. The greater good in
prospect, being future or merely possible, is not present to the mind,
'and it is against the nature of things, that what is absent should
operate, where it is not' (*E* 2. 21. 37). Yet in the next breath he goes
on to indicate how this objection can be met. Although the greater
good is not directly present to the mind, it can be present by way
of representation; Locke calls this representation an idea, but it
might be more plausible to think of it as a belief, namely a mental
item with propositional content. Thus it is open to the Locke of the
first edition to say that what determines me to study long hours at
nights is the belief that by doing so I shall become a rich and successful lawyer.

The obvious way of blocking this first argument immediately
leads Locke into a more promising objection to the theory of the
first edition. Although some future or possible good may be present
to the mind by way of representation, such a representation is not
the sort of thing that by itself is sufficient to propel a person to
action. Locke suggests that his cognitive theory of the first edition
is vulnerable to counter-examples: 'Convince a man never so much,
that plenty has its advantages over poverty; make him see and
own, that the handsome conveniences of life are better than nasty
penury: yet as long as he is content with the latter, and finds no
uneasiness in it, he moves not; his *will* never is determined to any
action, that shall bring him out of it' (*E* 2. 21. 35). A similar point
has been made by modern philosophers who tend to see themselves

as following the lead of Hume rather than Locke: my belief that by doing x I can obtain y will never cause me to act unless I have some desire for y. Locke himself would say that unless I am uneasy (dissatisfied) with my present state, I will not act, and the relationship between uneasiness and desire in his account is somewhat obscure.[12] But there is little doubt that Locke is close to the Humean view that desire is a causally necessary condition of voluntary action.

A final reason why Locke shows himself to be dissatisfied with the theory of the first edition is that it cannot accommodate the phenomenon known as weakness of the will. It is important to see that this objection to his earlier theory is logically distinct from the previous one. To say that judgement about the greater good is causally insufficient of itself to motivate action does not entail recognition of weakness of will. A philosopher might admit the causal insufficiency of such judgement and hold that it needs to be supplemented by desire—for example, a desire to pursue the greater good. But it would be absurd to say that a person who was motivated by such a combination of judgement and desire was *ipso facto* weak of will. For Locke, the weak-willed person is not just someone who is not moved to action by a judgement about the greater good alone; he is someone who acts against what he judges to be the greater good. In other words, Locke is committed to the thesis that such a judgement is not even a necessary condition of voluntary action. That this is his view of weakness of will is confirmed by the case of the drunkard and by the tag from Ovid which he cites with approval:

Let a drunkard see, that his health decays, his estate wastes; discredit and diseases, and the want of all things, even of his beloved drink, attends him in the course he follows: yet the returns of *uneasiness* to miss his companions; the habitual thirst after his cups, at the usual time, drives him to the tavern, though he has in view the loss of health and plenty, and perhaps the joys of another life: the least of which is no inconsiderable good, but such as he confesses, is far greater, than the tickling of his palate with a glass of wine, or the idle chat of a soaking club. It is not for want of viewing the greater good: for he sees, and acknowledges it, and in the intervals of his drinking hours, will take resolutions to pursue the greater good;

[12] Bennett, 'Locke's Philosophy of Mind', in Chappell (ed.), *Cambridge Companion to Locke*, 96–7.

but when the *uneasiness* to miss his accustomed delight returns, the greater acknowledged good loses its hold, and the present *uneasiness* determines the *will* to the accustomed action . . . And thus he is, from time to time, in the state of that unhappy complainer, *Video meliora proboque, deteriora sequor;* which sentence, allowed for true, and made good by constant experience, may this, and possibly no other, way be easily made intelligible. (E 2. 21. 35)

Locke is thus as explicit as one could wish that the theory of his first edition is inconsistent with weakness of will.

The desire to accommodate the phenomenon of weakness of will, as Locke understands it, helps us to understand the relationship between his first and second thoughts on the subject of motivation. It has recently been suggested that the theory of the second edition is intended not so much as a replacement for, but rather as a supplement to, the theory of the first edition;[13] in other words, Locke comes to hold that there is both a cognitive and a conative component in motivation. Behind this interpretative suggestion presumably lies a concern to bring him close to the standard modern view according to which belief and desire in combination explain action; my desire for y and my belief that x is the means to achieve y are individually necessary and jointly sufficient for my doing x. Now it may be right to say that the theory of the second edition allows some role for belief, or some other kind of mental representation. But it surely cannot be right to say that Locke's second thoughts are intended to supplement his first. For the theory of the first edition does not say simply that action is to be explained in terms of belief; it says that action is to be explained in terms of a very specific belief, namely a judgement about the greater good. And this theory, whether by itself or supplemented by the doctrine of uneasiness, is clearly inconsistent with the phenomenon of weakness of will on Locke's understanding; as we have seen, he comes to hold that a judgement about the greater good is not even a necessary condition of voluntary action.

One objection to Locke's theory of uneasiness goes back to Leibniz, and has been revived in recent times. Locke's theory, it is said, states that voluntary action is always an attempt to cure some dissatisfaction with a present state of affairs, and this implies the falsehood that the peak of satisfactoriness would involve perfect

[13] Ibid. 96.

inactivity.[14] In the words of one contemporary writer, everyone knows that inactivity is a source of misery. But this objection is misguided, for it misdescribes Locke's thesis. What Locke is saying is that voluntary *changes of state* are always attempts to cure an uneasiness: 'The motive for continuing in the same state or action is only the present satisfaction in it; the motive to change is always some uneasiness; nothing setting us upon the change of state, or upon any new action, but some uneasiness' (E 2. 21. 29). Here a state need not be something passive; it can be an activity such as an early-morning jog. Locke is formulating a psychological version of the the law of inertia. He is thus committed to saying that I will not change my state (for example, stop jogging) unless I experience some dissatisfaction with it, and that claim seems rather plausible. Whatever the shortcomings of Locke's theory of motivation, it is not committed to the counter-intuitive consequences with which some philosophers have charged it.

The Absence of Agnosticism

Near the beginning of this chapter I observed that there is a strongly deflationary strand in Locke's approach to the issue of free will. Now though the deflationary strand in Locke's philosophy is a significant one, it is not the most pervasive or conspicuous; more prominent, as we have seen, is the tendency towards agnosticism. And this reflection serves to draw our attention to the fact that in Locke's discussion of free will agnosticism plays no part; where freedom of the will is at issue he conveys no sense that there are metaphysical facts which are hidden from our mental view. The disappearance of agnosticism from his discussion of this issue is not to be explained by saying that the nature of the topic does not allow it. On the contrary, it is rather easy to see how agnosticism might shape a discussion of free will. For example, a philosopher might say that it does indeed appear to us that we are endowed with a liberty of indifference, in respect of at least many of our choices; none the less, it is epistemically possible that at a deeper level such

---

[14] Bennett, 'Locke's Philosophy of Mind', in Chappell (ed.), 95. Cf. *Leibniz: New Essays on Human Understanding*, 2. 21, pp. 188–9.

choices are causally determined by motives of which we are not aware. Alternatively, a philosopher might say that as beings who are part of nature we must be subject to the thoroughgoing determinism which governs the whole realm of spatio-temporal phenomena; hence, as events in time, all our choices are causally determined. None the less, it is epistemically possible that at a deeper 'noumenal' level we are endowed with the contracausal freedom required for moral responsibility. Such positions employ ways of contrasting appearance and reality which are reminiscent of Leibniz and Kant respectively, although it would not be correct to describe either philosopher as an agnostic on the issue of free will.

Perhaps the explanation is to be found in the centrality of human freedom to Locke's metaphysics of morals. As we have seen, one of the principal themes of the *Essay* is the thesis that a science of morality is possible; we can have demonstrative knowledge of what our moral duties are. Now Locke may well believe that it would be incoherent to combine this thesis with an agnostic stance on human freedom. If we could not know whether we have the freedom required for moral responsibility, it would seem to make little sense to go on to assert that we can know what our moral duties are; on the plausible assumption that 'ought' implies 'can' the whole question whether we have any moral duties at all would seem to be moot if agnosticism about our freedom were justified. Thus the metaphysical transparency of human freedom is required by Locke's commitment to a demonstrative science of morality. To say this is not of course to provide a philosophical justification for his anti-agnostic stance on free will; Locke would surely would not wish to appeal to the possibility of a demonstrative science of ethics as a premiss in the argument for the transparency of human freedom, for the possibility of such a science is a controversial thesis which is not established until later in the *Essay*. But it does help us to understand the motivation for this account and its coherence with Locke's project of a metaphysics for morals.

I should like to conclude this chapter on a more speculative note; the idea is that Locke's commitment to a demonstrative science of ethics may throw light on the tensions in his account of human freedom. On the one hand, if he is to defend the possibility of such a science he needs to show that our freedom (in the morally relevant sense) is beyond serious doubt; here the compatibilist definition of freedom serves Locke well, for, as Hume was to observe, freedom in this sense is available to everyone who is not in chains.[15] On the other hand, Locke hankers in places, it seems, for freedom in a more robust sense; there are passages which might be read as suggesting that it is liberty of indifference or contracausal freedom which is required for moral responsibility and divine justice. It is true that the 'could have done otherwise' requirement may not be inconsistent with compatibilism, but Locke does not explain how the reconciliation is to be brought off.

Locke may thus have been drawn to the compatibilist account in part because it puts our freedom beyond doubt. By contrast, liberty of indifference or contracausal freedom for which he sometimes seems to hanker may seem vulnerable to sceptical challenge; it is open to a critic, such as Leibniz, to say that what appear to us to be free choices in the contracausal sense (such as putting one's left foot forward rather than one's right in entering a room) are really determined by motives and desires of which the agent is not aware. Now Locke may appear to have the resources to defeat such an objection; for he holds a version of the Cartesian doctrine of the transparency of the mental. At least for occurrent mental states, he holds that there is nothing in the mind of which we are not conscious. But Locke's general tendency towards agnosticism about the nature of the mind might seem to make it difficult for him to offer a defence of this thesis. Whether or not he felt that liberty of indifference could be defended against sceptical assault, it seems likely that the certainty of freedom on the compatibilist account was one of the recommendations of this theory; yet Locke could not entirely dispel the suspicion that morality requires a stronger concept of freedom. Ironically, the epistemic and the moral dimensions of the science of morality may have pulled Locke in different directions.

[15] Hume, *An Enquiry Concerning Human Understanding*, 8. 1.

8

CLASSIFICATION AND LANGUAGE

IN book 3 of the *Essay* Locke sets himself at least two important goals. In the first place, he seeks to lay the philosophical foundations for the main theme of the last book; this is the thesis that knowledge in a strong sense is possible in mathematics and ethics but not on the whole in metaphysics and the natural sciences. Secondly, Locke seeks to advance a radically anti-Aristotelian theory of classification which is inspired by the corpuscularian hypothesis; according to Locke, it is a mistake to think that species are already marked out for us by nature. Once again we encounter an interesting tension in his thought which none the less stops short of an outright contradiction. In pursuit of the first goal Locke is led to insist sharply on the distinction between essences of substances and essences of modes or non-substances. In pursuit of the second anti-Aristotelian goal, by contrast, Locke is led to minimize this distinction, at least in an important respect; for he holds that substances, no less than modes, are classified according to essences which are what he calls the 'workmanship of the understanding'.

One of the main themes of book 3 is thus the mind's inevitable role in constructing the ideas by which we interpret the natural and the moral world. Here Locke is not just presenting an anti-Aristotelian argument concerning the nature of classification; he is also developing his characteristically anti-Cartesian thesis that the ideas which are not given in sensation and reflection are human constructions. But it would be a mistake to suppose that the constructionist thesis elbows out the other strands in Locke's thought in book 3; on the contrary, one of the fascinations of this book lies in seeing how the various tendencies in his thought come together. In the previous chapter we saw how, when free will was at issue, the deflationary side was in the ascendant and the agnostic side tended to disappear from view. In book 3 the deflationary strand is evident in Locke's characteristic tendency to approach questions of classification as if there were no fact of the matter to be discovered; such questions are to be settled rather by an appeal to convention. And the agnostic tendency reappears in Locke's insistence that the inner constitutions of bodies are unknown to us, and thus cannot constitute the basis for classification. However, we shall see that even if we did know the inner constitutions of bodies, such knowledge could not straightforwardly settle questions about classification.

Book 3 is officially entitled 'Of Words', and it is certainly true that in this book Locke advances a number of philosophically important and debatable theses concerning language. His theory of the signification of 'natural kind terms' is particularly striking, and in recent years it has often been invoked among contemporary analytic philosophers. Important as they are, Locke's linguistic theories are not perhaps as central to his purposes in book 3 as they may appear to be; much of this book is occupied with metaphysical and epistemological issues concerning classification which can be treated independently of the role of language. Accordingly, I shall postpone discussion of Locke's linguistic theories until the last section of this chapter.

The Corpuscularian Hypothesis and the 'Workmanship of the Understanding'

It is impossible to understand the thrust of Locke's anti-Aristotelian theory of classification without some reference to the revolution introduced by the corpuscularian hypothesis; it is this revolution which is in the background of his theory, even when it is not expressly articulated. According to the Aristotelian picture which the corpuscularian hypothesis displaces, the physical world is divided up into a number of mind-independent natural kinds such as gold, lead, and human beings. Locke himself famously characterizes the traditional view as holding that there are 'a certain number of forms or moulds, wherein all natural things that exist, are cast and do equally partake' (E 3. 3. 17); on this view, the task which faces human beings in classifying is simply to sort things out according to the moulds from which nature has produced them. The point might be expressed through a famous metaphor by saying that we must carve nature up at her deep joints. But on the corpuscularian hypothesis the thesis that nature has any such deep joints has become problematic at least. In the first place, our commonsensical division of the world into natural kinds such as gold and lead can no longer claim to be metaphysically basic; what underlies such divisions into putative kinds is a realm of corpuscles which are not observable by the naked eye. Secondly, these corpuscles at ground level are all supposed to share the same fundamental nature; the phenomenal, qualitative differences which we observe between gold and silver are anchored in merely quantitative differences of size, shape, and motion of the insensible particles.

Following the lead given by his friend Boyle (who made a number of suggestive remarks in this area), Locke sees that on the corpuscularian hypothesis the whole nature of classification needs to be rethought.[1] Although he decisively rejects the Aristotelian theory, he does not make a total break with the past; like many of his contemporaries he seeks to reinterpret some of the traditional claims within the new framework. As we shall see, Locke is concerned to tackle a number of different questions concerning classification which he does not always clearly distinguish. The first and fundamental issue is whether there are mind-independent natural kinds. To this question Locke replies with a resounding 'no'; it is the human mind, not nature, which classifies: species are the workmanship of the human understanding.

Although the corpuscularian hypothesis is in the background, it is a mistake to suppose that it straightforwardly entails Locke's positive thesis. Locke indeed offers at least three arguments for his thesis, only one of which makes any use of corpuscularian assumptions against the Aristotelians; this is the argument from the existence of borderline cases. According to Locke, if all things in nature

---

[1] '. . . it [is] very much by a kind of tacit agreement that men had distinguished the species of bodies, and . . . those distinctions [are] more arbitrary than we are wont to be aware of'. *Origin of Forms and Qualities*, in *Selected Philosophical Papers of Robert Boyle*, ed. M. A. Stewart (Manchester, 1979), 72.

were produced from a certain number of forms or moulds, as the
Aristotelians suppose, there would be no room for such cases; all
species would be hard-edged, as it were. But 'the frequent produc-
tions of monsters, in all the species of animals' testifies to the fact
that there are plenty of borderline cases (*E* 3. 3. 17). Strictly speaking, of course, as Locke realizes, this argument establishes only that
not all things in nature belong to hard-edged natural kinds; it does
not establish that nothing does. But if Locke generalizes the claim
about the existence of borderline cases to all natural things, then he
is entitled to draw the stronger conclusion; in other words, there are
no mind-independent natural kinds.

At first sight Locke seems to be mounting an *ad hominem* argument against the Aristotelians, since they are supposed to accept its
conditional premiss. But as some commentators have observed, it is
not clear that the Aristotelians need to accept this premiss; even the
'forms and moulds' metaphor does not seem to commit them to
the existence of hard-edged boundaries to species. For it is a familiar fact of everyday life that two things which are produced from
the same mould may turn out very differently; one cake or jelly may
have a perfect shape, another may be such a poor approximation of
the first that it will be discarded. But Locke seems to evade this
objection by appealing to his rationalist model of scientific explanation: the phenomenal, macroscopic properties are supposed to
flow from the internal constitution or real essence as the properties
of a circle flow from its essence; on this model, if things were produced from 'moulds', there would be no room for the variations
which this metaphor seems to allow.[2] Here of course Locke would
be going against what the Aristotelians would accept; for they are
obviously not committed to the view that the macroscopic properties of substances flow from internal constitutions with geometrical rigour. But Locke could reply that within the corpuscularian
framework the Aristotelian theory of moulds and forms calls for
reinterpretation if it is to make any sense at all, and that on this rein-

---

[2] It has recently been argued that Locke uses the term 'property' in a stronger
sense than is current today; writing in the tradition of Porphyry's doctrine of
predicables, Locke is supposed to mean by 'property' a quality which is entailed by
the essence. See Ayers, *Locke*, ii. 20–1. However, it is worth pointing out that
sometimes Locke seems to use the terms 'property' and 'quality' interchangeably
(e.g. *E* 3. 3. 17). Here I use the term 'property' in the standard, broad modern
sense.

terpretation it is inconsistent with the existence of the anomalies in nature to which he draws our attention.

Even so Locke's reply is not entirely convincing; for it seems to push the problem one stage further back. It may still be possible to defend the thesis that there are mind-independent natural kinds against his objections. Suppose the defender of this thesis concedes that phenomenal properties flow from internal constitutions with geometrical rigour; thus if two individuals share qualitatively the same internal constitution, they will indeed not differ in terms of their phenomenal properties. He may then further concede to Locke that the 'form or mould' is to be interpreted in corpuscularian terms, but he could still insist that to say that two individuals come from the same mould does not entail the absence of significant variations between them; here he would point to the moral of the cakes and jellies case. But the best way of defending this thesis against Locke would involve an appeal to teleology; nature seeks to endow a class of individuals with the same inner constitution, but sometimes fails to do so. Unfortunately, the appeal to teleology is unlikely to impress Locke.

A further problem with Locke's argument was pointed out by Leibniz.[3] Locke seems to assume that if there are hard-edged species, they must have many members. But this assumption may appear gratuitous; far from ranking as a borderline case or defective approximation to another species, the putative 'monster' may constitute a separate species in its own right. Thus, on this view, the facts of nature may be consistent with the existence of hard-edged natural kinds. Perhaps Locke would respond that he is arguing here from the principles of his Aristotelian opponents, and that on these principles there is no room for species with single members.

A second argument that Locke deploys for his workmanship of the understanding thesis comes from an entirely different quarter; it turns, not on the existence of borderline cases, but rather on considerations concerning language and the nature of abstract ideas:

That then which general words signify, is a sort of things; and each of them does that, by being a sign of an abstract *idea* in the mind, to which *idea*, as

---

[3] Leibniz: *New Essays on Human Understanding*, trans. P. Remnant and J. Bennett (Cambridge, 1981), 3. 3, p. 292.

things existing are found to agree, so they come to be ranked under that name; or, which is all one, be of that sort. Whereby it is evident, that the *essences* of the *sorts, or* (if the Latin word pleases better) *species* of things, are nothing else but these abstract *ideas*. For the having the essence of any species, being that which makes any thing to be of that species, and the conformity to the *idea*, to which the name is annexed, being that which gives a right to that name, the having the essence, and the having that conformity, must needs be the same thing: since to be of any species, and to have a right to the name of that species, is all one. (*E* 3. 3. 12)

In other words, general terms such as 'man' signify abstract general ideas, and, as we saw in Chapter 3, such ideas are human construc- tions; they are framed by eliminating from a number of particular ideas everything except that which is common to all. But to say that *x* has, or instantiates, the essence of the species 'man' is just to say that it conforms to the abstract idea of man; thus the essence of the species is identical with the abstract idea. Since abstract ideas are man-made, it follows that the essences of species are also man- made. This conclusion is intended to yield not just the positive thesis that human minds classify, but the further negative thesis that nature does not. Classification into species is nothing but the workmanship of the understanding.

This argument crucially depends on the premiss that the concepts signified by general terms are human, mental constructions, and this premiss is of course controversial. A Platonist, for example, might concede to Locke that to have, or instantiate, an essence is to conform to or fall under a concept; none the less, he would take issue with the claim that to fall under a concept is to fall under a construction of the human mind. On the contrary, according to the Platonist, concepts are not mental entities of any sort, whether these are supposed to be constructed (as Locke thinks) or innate (as Descartes thinks); rather, they are abstract entities which do not exist in space and time. But Locke of course would hardly regard this objection as devastating. Quite apart from the difficulty of making sense of anything like a Platonic theory of forms or ideas, he would say that his own theory is to be preferred on grounds of ontological economy.

One might also seek to challenge Locke's argument in a more Leibnizian spirit. Suppose we ask: by virtue of *what* do individual things conform to abstract general ideas? For Leibniz, the natural as

well as the correct answer is that they do so by virtue of the existence of objective resemblances which are out there in the world.[4]
Our classifications, then, are founded in something which is indeed
mind-independent; thus, according to Leibniz, Locke's thesis that
classification is the workmanship of the understanding is simply
false.

But Locke of course has not overlooked the existence of such
resemblances; in the paragraph which follows his statement of the
argument from abstract ideas, he assures the reader: 'I would not
here be thought to forget, much less to deny, that nature in the
production of things, makes several of them alike: there is nothing
more obvious, especially in the races of animals, and all things prop-
agated by seed' (E 3. 3. 13). Why, then, does Locke not believe that
his thesis is thereby refuted? The answer to this question brings us
to what is probably Locke's best argument for his thesis—one which
does not turn on the existence of borderline cases or the untidiness
of nature. The crucial point, for Locke, is not that nature fails to
present us with resemblances; it is rather that she offers us so many.
From the plethora of resemblances with which nature does confront us, we must inevitably select those which we deem important
enough to constitute species. Nature cannot perform this task for
us; only we are capable of doing so. Locke makes the point best in
connection with artefacts (watches), but it holds for natural substances as well. In a passage which has attracted some attention
recently, Locke writes:

For what is sufficient in the inward contrivance, to make a new *species*?
There are some *watches* that are made with four wheels, others with five:
is this a specific difference to the workman? Some have strings and physies,
and others none; some have the balance loose, and others regulated by a
spiral spring, and others by hog's bristles; are any, or all of these enough
to make a specific difference to the workman, that knows each of these,
and several other different contrivances in the internal constitutions of
watches? It is certain, each of these hath a real difference from the rest: but
whether it be an essential, a specific difference or no, relates only to the
complex *idea*, to which the name *watch* is given: as long as they all agree
in the *idea* which that name stands for, and that name does not as a generical name comprehend different *species* under it, they are not essentially nor
specifically different. But if anyone will make minuter divisions from

---

[4] *Leibniz: New Essays on Human Understanding*, 3. 6, p. 311.

differences, that he knows in the internal frame of watches; and to such precise complex *ideas* give names, that shall prevail, they will then be new *species* to them, who have those *ideas* with names to them; and can, by those differences, distinguish watches into these several sorts, and then *watch* will be a generical name . . . (*E* 3. 6. 39)

As Guyer has observed, this is a powerful argument, whose force Leibniz did not appreciate.[5]

Nominal Essences and the Basis of Classification

For Locke, then, classification of things into sorts is necessarily the workmanship, not of nature, but of the human understanding. He then proceeds to take up the logically posterior question how does the human mind classify. On the face of it Locke appears to offer two different answers to this question which agree in their negative component but not in their positive thesis:

(1) We classify substances according to their nominal essences, not according to their real essences.

(1) is illustrated by the following passage:

The next thing to be considered is, by which of these essences it is, that *substances are determined into* sorts, or species; and that, 'tis evident, is *by the nominal essence*. (*E* 3. 6. 7)

(2) We classify substances according to their observable properties, not according to their real essences.

(2) is illustrated by the following passage:

Nor indeed *can we* rank, and *sort things,* and consequently (which is the end of sorting) denominate them *by their real essences,* because we know them not. Our faculties carry us no farther towards the knowledge and distinction of substances, than a collection of those sensible *ideas,* which we observe in them; which however made with the greatest diligence and exactness, we are capable of, yet is more remote from the true inter-

---

[5] P. Guyer, 'Locke's Philosophy of Language', in Chappell (ed.), *Cambridge Companion to Locke,* 137–8.

nal constitution, from which those qualities flow, than . . . a countryman's *idea* is from the inward contrivance of that famous clock at *Strasburg*. (*E* 3. 6. 9)

These two answers—(1) and (2)—are clearly non-equivalent, for observable properties are features of the substances themselves, whereas nominal essences are said to be abstract ideas, and hence are constructions of the human mind. It is true that in 3. 6. 9 Locke initially speaks of 'sensible ideas' (i. e. mental items), but he goes on to correct this mistake when he later refers back to 'qualities' ; from this it appears that he was talking all along of mind-independent features of bodies. In any case, even if we allow that the sensible ideas are mental items, they are clearly not constructions of the human mind; rather, they are the data of sensory experience. Hence, on no possible reading does (2) simply collapse into (1).

Fortunately, the suspicion that Locke offers two non-equivalent answers to the same question concerning classification can be easily dispelled. A little reflection suggests that (1) and (2) are not addressed to the same issue. In the first place, Locke seeks to answer a strictly philosophical question: what logically determines membership in a species? He answers this question by an appeal to (1): in other words, x is gold if and only if x instantiates all the properties contained in my nominal essence or abstract idea of gold. Now since, according to Locke, nominal essences are abstract ideas, and hence human constructions, the answer to this logical question naturally gives rise to a psychological or genetic question: how does the abstract idea come to be formed? Locke's response is that we frame such abstract ideas by observing properties (e.g. yellowness and malleability) which are regularly coinstantiated and by making decisions about which such regularities are important enough to enter into the nominal essence.

Although (1) and (2) are answers to different types of question, we can see that Locke is also telling a single story about the stages of cognitive development. The first stage described by Locke is that at which we acquire a given abstract idea or nominal essence. Once we have reached this stage (and only then), we are in a position to pass to the second stage and answer questions about species membership: we determine whether a particular individual is a human being by consulting the nominal essence which we have framed for ourselves. At neither stage, however, are we guided by the real essence or internal constitution of substances. Our nominal essence is not framed by reference to the real essence because we do not know what this is. And once we have framed the nominal essence it is this alone which logically determines whether an individual belongs to a given species.

Locke is insistent, then, that the nominal essence is formed on the basis of observable sensible ideas or, strictly, properties. But though he does not stress the point, it would seem that this is not a necessary truth about nominal essences; it depends on contingent limitations of our ability to know. If our cognitive faculties allowed us to achieve detailed knowledge of the facts about internal constitutions, then there is no reason in principle why such facts should not be incorporated into our nominal essences. But even if nominal essences did include reference to the internal constitutions, they would not thereby simply collapse into real essences; for the nominal essence is, by its nature, an abstract idea, and hence the work of the human mind, whereas real essences are out there in the world of substances. And whatever the content of our nominal essences, the classification of substances is inevitably the work of the human mind; it cannot be transferred from our shoulders on to those of nature.

It is in the course of developing his theory of nominal essences that Locke displays most clearly the deflationary and conventionalist side of his thought concerning classification. When we are confronted with a taxonomic anomaly we tend to think that there is some fact of the matter to be discovered which will settle the question; we wish to know whether a given individual is really a man or whether a discoloured lump of metal is really gold. In Locke's view, such an approach is muddle-headed. All that is at issue in such cases is whether x conforms to or instantiates a certain nominal essence. Moreover, he further holds that nominal essences may vary from person to person, and that there is no standard for arbitrating between different nominal essences, at least in respect of how many properties are included. Locke recognizes, for instance, that people will differ over whether to include fusibility in the nominal essence of gold:

Wherein no one can show a reason, why some of the inseparable qualities, that are always united in nature, should be put into the nominal essence, and others left out: or why the word *gold*, signifying that sort of body the ring on his finger is made of, should determine that sort, rather by its colour, weight, and fusibility; than by its colour, weight and solubility in *aqua regia*. (*E* 3. 9. 17)

Thus the only sense in which there is a fact of the matter concerns the question whether a given individual instantiates a nominal essence; relative to a given standard there is an objective answer. But there is no further standard for adjudicating between nominal essences that are constituted by properties that tend to occur regularly together.

The deflationary side of Locke's thought is not without its own difficulties. For one thing, it tends to sit rather uneasily with what we may call the accommodationist strand in Locke's thought. Like other seventeenth-century philosophers he seeks to do justice, where possible, to traditional philosophical claims concerning essences; in this spirit he examines the credentials of the doctrine that essences are ingenerable and incorruptible, and suggests that its truth appears in connection with nominal, not real, essences:

That such *abstract* ideas, with *names to them . . . are essences*, may further appear by what we are told concerning *essences*, viz. that they are all ingenerable, and incorruptible. Which cannot be true of the real constitutions of things, which begin and perish with them. All things, that exist, besides their author, are all liable to change; especially those things we are acquainted with, and have ranked into bands, under distinct names or ensigns. Thus that, which was grass today, is tomorrow the flesh of a sheep; and within few days after, becomes part of a man: in all which and the like changes, 'tis evident, their real *essence*, *i.e.* that constitution, whereon the properties of these several things depended, is destroyed, and perishes with them. But *essences* being taken for *ideas*, established in the mind, with names annexed to them, they are supposed to remain steadily the same, whatever mutations the particular substances are liable to. (*E* 3. 3. 19)

But the negative thesis here is more convincing than the positive. For one thing, the claim that nominal essences are ingenerable does not readily accord with Locke's overall theory that, as abstract ideas, they are all constructed by the human mind; it would be easier to reconcile with a Platonic view of essences as abstract entities which are outside space and time. Further, and more importantly, it is not clear how the incorruptibility thesis is to be made consistent with Locke's view that nominal essences may vary from person to person, and that there is no criterion for deciding between them. If we take seriously the normative connotations of the term, the nominal essences would be incorruptible only in the trivial sense that the issue of corruption does not arise; for we can say that x has fallen away from a standard only where there is a standard to fall away from. But if the term 'incorruptible' simply means 'immutable', then nominal essences are not incorruptible in this sense, for they can be added to; for example, I may come to include the property of fusibility in my nominal essence of gold. Perhaps it will be said that in such a case my nominal essence has not changed by the addition of the new property; rather, it has given way to a wholly new nominal essence. But such a defence of Locke's thesis again threatens to make it trivial.

One may also wonder how consistently Locke adheres to his deflationary and conventionalist account of classification. In one place Locke speaks of our uncertainty about the boundaries of species: 'So uncertain are the boundaries of *species* of animals to us, who have no other measures, than the complex *ideas* of our own collecting: and so far are we from certainly knowing what a *man* is; though, perhaps, it will be judged great ignorance to make any doubt about it' (E 3. 6. 27). A reader may be forgiven for supposing that Locke is advancing here the very thesis he is meant to be attacking. For if we are uncertain of the boundaries of species, it seems that there is a mind-independent fact of the matter which it is the task of our classification to capture; in other words, our taxonomies are to be judged adequate only to the extent that they succeed in tracking objective natural boundaries. Yet this is perhaps an uncharitable reading. There is a legitimate sense in which Locke can allow that we do not know what a man is: we are ignorant of the real essence presumed to underlie the phenomenal resemblances among the individuals we call men. But that is not to concede that, if we knew the real essence, we should discover any objective natural boundaries as postulated by the Aristotelians; all the old problems of classification would simply reappear in a new form.

Essences of Modes

We saw at the beginning of this chapter that an important task of book 3 is to lay the foundations for Locke's central epistemological distinction between mathematics and ethics on the one hand and natural science and metaphysics on the other. The key to the epistemological superiority of the former two disciplines is that, unlike the latter, they are concerned not with substances but with modes— that is, 'such complex *ideas*, which however compounded, contain not in them the supposition of subsisting by themselves, but are considered as dependencies on, or affections of substances; such are the *ideas* signified by the words *triangle, gratitude, murder etc.*' (E 2. 12. 4).[6] Since general knowledge is knowledge of essences, Locke thus needs to find a way of distinguishing the essences of modes from the essences of substances. But this project is not as easy to execute as it seems, for through his general anti-Aristotelian theory of classification he has tied his hands in one crucial respect; he cannot say that what is distinctive about modes is that their classification is the workmanship of the understanding, for, as we have seen, he is committed to just this thesis with regard to the taxonomy of substances; their nominal essences, no less than the nominal essences of modes, are abstract ideas which are constructed by the mind.

Locke has indeed limited his options, but he has not wholly painted himself into a corner; his philosophy still has the resources to formulate a distinction which can bear epistemological fruit. His considered solution to the problem invokes the distinction between real and nominal essences: the nominal essences of modes (like those of simple ideas) have the remarkable characteristic of being always identical with their real essences:

Essences being thus distinguished into *nominal and real*, we may further observe, that *in the species of simple* ideas *and modes*, they *are always the same*, but *in substances, always quite different*. Thus a figure including a space

---

[6] This definition suggests some confusion of ideas of modes with modes themselves. We have complex ideas of modes but modes (as opposed to their essences) are not themselves complex ideas.

between three lines, is the real as well as nominal *essence* of a triangle; it being not only the abstract *idea* to which the general name is annexed; but the very *essentia*, or being, of the thing itself, that foundation from which all its properties flow, and to which they are all inseparably annexed. But it is far otherwise concerning that parcel of matter, which makes the ring on my finger, wherein these two *essences* are apparently different. For it is the real constitution of its insensible parts, on which depend all those properties of colour, weight, fusibility, fixedness *etc.* which are to be found in it. . . . But yet it is its colour, weight, fusibility, and fixedness, *etc.* which makes it to be *gold*, or gives it a right to that name, which is therefore its nominal *essence*. Since nothing can be called *gold*, but what has a conformity of qualities to that abstract complex *idea*, to which the name is annexed. (*E* 3. 3. 18)

As an objection to Locke, it will not do to say that the sense in which properties flow from, or depend on, the real essence of gold is quite different from the sense in which properties flow from, or depend on, the definition of a triangle; we cannot accuse him of simply muddling causal and logical relations. As we have seen (in Chapter 4 above), Locke holds, as a matter of theory, that what is involved in both cases is a relation of logical or geometrical necessity. Locke may of course be wrong about the kind of necessity which is possessed by bridge laws connecting micro- and macroscopic properties, but his error would need to be established by argument; we must beware of simply begging the question against him.

Locke's claim that there is a disanalogy in this respect between modes and substances is none the less open to challenge. Leibniz, for one, turned to geometry in order to refute Locke's thesis that the nominal essences of modes are always identical with their real essences. Mathematicians prove non-trivial theorems concerning triangles, for example, and thus discover properties which might be said to flow from the real essence, but when they do so they are not merely explicating the nominal essence; in other words, they are not merely unpacking the definition of the term 'triangle'.[7] But this objection is perhaps unfair, for Locke does not say that there is nothing more to modes than is explicitly contained in their nominal essence; he says rather that the nominal essence, by virtue of its identity with the real essence, is 'that foundation from which all its

---

[7] *Leibniz: New Essays*, 3. 3, pp. 294–5.

properties flow, and to which they are all inseparably annexed' (*E* 3. 3. 18).[8] But Leibniz may be right to this extent: the logical foundation for the properties which are established in a geometrical theorem is not just a definition but a set of axioms as well; hence it is the package of axioms and definitions which constitutes the real essence, and thus this real essence is not strictly identical with the nominal essence. The issue of assessing the force of this objection is complicated by the fact that Locke has definite views of his own on the status of axioms; he regards them in general as empty of content, and thus as theoretically dispensable in the search for knowledge. But even if he is wrong on this score, it seems fair to say that Leibniz's objection is not seriously damaging; it shows at most that Locke's thesis needs qualification, but not that it needs to be abandoned altogether.

Leibniz's objection concerns geometry, which is occupied with what Locke calls simple modes. A more serious objection perhaps arises in connection with those social and moral properties which Locke groups under the heading of mixed modes. John Mackie has observed that it is not only natural scientists who seek to discover real essences; sociologists, for example, seek to discover the real essences of social phenomena such as suicide, and this search is not simply an enquiry into the meaning of a term or its logical consequences.[9] The aim of a sociological investigation is rather to formulate a unitary theory of how and why suicides occur; in this respect the enquiry is on all fours with research in the natural sciences. Thus Locke is simply mistaken to believe that in the case of mixed modes the real essence coincides with the nominal.

It is tempting to try to meet this objection by challenging the assumptions about social phenomena on which it rests. Surely, we might say, it is implausible to suppose that there is some underlying causal basis which is common to all cases of adultery and suicide. It is true, for example, that people who commit suicide are often severely depressed, and depression is a candidate for an internal physiological state, but many of those who kill themselves are not depressed at all. In some cultures suicide in certain circumstances is dictated by a code of honour: the officer who is left alone in a room

---

[8] Editors' Introduction, in *G. W. Leibniz: New Essays on Human Understanding*, trans. P. Remnant and J. Bennett, abridged edn. (Cambridge, 1982), p. xxxi.

[9] Mackie, *Problems from Locke*, 90–1.

with a revolver on the table may feel a sense of relief, perhaps even exaltation, that now at last he has a chance to salvage his reputation. Neither suicide nor adultery can be regarded as a natural kind. Hence in the case of such phenomena it is simply misguided to search for a common real essence which is distinct from the nominal and explains those readily observable properties in terms of which the phenomenon is identified. But despite its attractions, this approach is not one that is available to Locke, for it would seem to involve him in inconsistency with his other commitments concerning classification; it makes assumptions about real essences to which he is not entitled. For, as we have seen, there is nothing in Locke's account of what it is to be gold which logically guarantees that all its instances share an internal constitution or real essence; at most, it is a reasonable presumption that they do. It may indeed be a necessary truth, for Locke, that any lump of gold will possess a real essence which explains its nominally essential properties, but of course to say this is not to say that the same internal constitution must be common to all instances of gold. The fact that this is not a logical truth is the import of his thesis that it is the nominal essence, not the real, that ranks substances into sorts.

Some of Locke's remarks about mixed modes suggest a different way of meeting Mackie's objection. As their name suggests, mixed modes are by their nature in some sense hybrid properties, and it is this feature of them which might be exploited for the purposes of defending Locke's thesis that their nominal essence is necessarily identical with their real essence. In particular, a number of Locke's own hand-picked examples appear clearly to be hybrids of natural and normative properties. Adultery and incest, for instance, are not just complex human activities describable in natural terms; they are activities which essentially involve the violation of a norm of sexual behaviour. Even jealousy—to take another of Locke's examples—is not just suspicion, but suspicion of unfaithful conduct; here too there is an implicit reference to a norm of conduct as having been violated. We might try to argue, then, that in the case of mixed modes it is this combination of natural and normative properties which, for Locke, makes it misguided to hunt for a real essence distinct from the nominal. In this respect adultery and incest are in a quite different category from gold or swans.

This is a suggestive line of defence, and it is perhaps the most promising which is available; but as it stands, it needs to be supplemented. It is not plausible to maintain that all mixed modes are hybrids of just this kind. But it does seem possible to claim that all Locke's remaining examples of mixed modes are hybrids of a relevantly similar type; that is, they are all hybrids of natural and non-natural properties. In the other cases that Locke considers, the non-natural properties are not so much normative as institutional. Take the case of a Roman triumph which Locke discusses at some length: we cannot understand what a triumph is without reference to such institutional concepts as those of an army, a victory, and an official celebration. Unfortunately, however, as Mackie points out, this line of defence suffers from one drawback: it fails to drive a wedge between mixed modes and certain artefact substances whose nature similarly cannot be understood without reference to institutional concepts.[10] We cannot explain to someone what a cricket bat is by simply saying that it is a physical object of a certain characteristic size and shape which is traditionally made of willow; we must specify the role that it plays in a highly complex institutional practice. Certainly we may wish to say that there is no underlying real essence of cricket bats which causally explains their nominally essential properties. But it is not clear that Locke would be happy with this result.

Even apart from this difficulty, it may still be wondered whether this defence is of sufficiently general application. It is true that all Locke's examples of mixed modes appear to be hybrids of natural and non-natural properties, whether normative or institutional. But it is not clear that there is anything in Locke's definition of mixed modes that logically guarantees this happy result; when he introduces the term he says that they are composed of simple ideas (properties) of various kinds (E 2. 12. 5), and he seems to have in mind simply the point that they are composed of primary and secondary qualities (for example, figure and colour). But if this is so, then the door is open to admitting purely natural states or processes, such as diseases, into the category of mixed modes; once these are admitted, it will be hard to defend the thesis that the real essences of mixed modes are always identical with the nominal. In the case of tuberculosis, for example, it is extremely plausible to

[10] Mackie, 99.

claim that there is a distinct real essence (a bacillary infection) which causally explains the nominally essential properties in terms of which we pick out the disease. Perhaps Locke may be able to find grounds for denying that diseases are mixed modes, but this will bring him only cold comfort, for he can hardly deny that diseases are modes of some kind; they are clearly not substances, but rather, in Locke's terms, 'dependencies on, or affections of substances' (E 2. 12. 4).

For all its difficulties, Locke's thesis about the identity of the nominal and the real essence remains his most considered and intriguing way of distinguishing modes from substances in terms of their essences. Certainly his other ways of making the distinction seem most unpromising. In particular, Locke says a number of things about the distinctive features of essences of mixed modes which do not seem to stand up to critical scrutiny. In places, for example, he emphasizes the arbitrary character of such essences (E 3. 5. 6). But if nominal essences are in question, arbitrariness does not supply Locke with a criterion for distinguishing mixed modes from substances; for, as he himself recognizes, there is an arbitrary element in the constitution of the nominal essence of gold, for example; that is, it is simply up to human beings to decide how many properties to include in the nominal essence. Again, Locke says that there is a pragmatic element in the framing of the essences of mixed modes; the mind puts together such ideas 'as may best serve its purposes' (E 3. 5. 6); but our decision about where to draw the line around the nominal essences of substances may similarly be made on pragmatic grounds. Of course, it may be said on Locke's behalf that our nominal essences of substances are constrained by nature in a way that the nominal essences of mixed modes are not; it is not up to us to decide that yellowness, malleability, and fusibility are regularly co-occurring properties. This is true, but the contrast will not be helpfully captured by saying that the nominal essences of mixed modes are arbitrary, whereas those of substances are not. At most we can say that there is a difference in the degree of arbitrariness in the two kinds of case.

The idea that nominal essences of substances are responsive to nature in a way that nominal essences of modes are not is one that intrigues Locke, but which he has difficulty formulating in a defensible manner. Sometimes he says that the nominal essences of mixed modes, unlike those of substances, are not always copied from patterns in nature. But, as Leibniz saw, there is a respect in which the two kinds of nominal essence may be on a par here.[11] It is true that nominal essences of substances are typically framed by observing regularly co-occurring properties, but there is no logical necessity for them to be framed in this way. Consider Locke's anecdote about how Adam frames the nominal essence of jealousy. He observes Lamech to be troubled and supposes that his trouble arises from the fact that his wife is too familiar with another man; in time Adam discovers his mistake: Lamech's troubled state of mind proceeded from another cause (E 3. 6. 44). None the less, Adam has framed a new nominal essence and attached a name to it. Similarly there is no reason in principle why the nominal essence of gold might not be framed by someone who had never observed the relevant co-occurrence of properties in nature; I might, for example, dream of a substance which is yellow, malleable, and soluble in aqua regia, and subsequently find a hunk of metal that satisfies this description. Thus there is no philosophically interesting distinction here between the two kinds of nominal essence in respect of how they are framed.

A second difficulty attends Locke's claim that in framing ideas of mixed modes 'for the most part' the mind 'searches not its patterns in nature' (E 3. 5. 6). This suggests that sometimes nature does supply the mind with patterns for essences of mixed modes; certainly it commits Locke to the claim that it is logically possible for nature to supply the mind with such patterns. But in that case he seems vulnerable to an objection in the form of a dilemma. If nature can supply the mind with such patterns, this can only be in cases of purely physical states and processes such as diseases; but then Locke will not be able to defend his thesis that the nominal and the real essences of modes always coincide. If, however, he is to defend this latter thesis, he must recognize that mixed modes are necessarily hybrids of natural and non-natural properties; but in that case nature could not possibly supply the mind with patterns for such modes.[12]

---

[11] Leibniz: New Essays, 3. 6, p. 321.

[12] Locke says of substances not merely that their nominal essences are always framed from patterns in nature, but also that their constituent properties are united in nature, that is, they tend to cluster; by contrast, mixed modes do not, or at least do not always, satisfy either criterion. But if Locke supposes that these criteria are equivalent, he is mistaken. The fact that my nominal essence consists of

Language and Signification

Many of Locke's major theses concerning the metaphysics and epistemology of classification can be understood independently of his
teachings about language. But it is not for nothing that book 3 of
the *Essay* is entitled 'Of Words' , for in this book he advances a
theory of what he calls signification in general, as well as a more
particular theory of the meaning of 'natural-kind terms' (a con-
venient phrase which is none the less something of a misnomer in
connection with Locke). Not surprisingly in view of his interest in
developing an anti-Aristotelian theory of classification, Locke tends
to focus his attention on general terms. But he has more than
merely polemical reasons for doing this; he correctly sees that it is
of the very nature of language that most of its names will be general
terms, not proper ones. Indeed, unless this were the case, language
could not fulfil its chief function, which is that of communication,
for proper names 'could not be significant, or intelligible to another,
who was not acquainted with all those very particular things, which
had fallen under my notice' (*E* 3. 3. 3). Moreover, even if it were possible to impose proper names on every individual, such an achievement would be of little use for the advancement of knowledge
which is essentially general in nature; knowledge, though founded
in particular things, enlarges itself by general views (*E* 3. 3. 4). Once
again, we see how even in book 3 Locke seeks to lay the foundations for the culminating theory of knowledge in book 4. He rarely
loses an opportunity to remind the reader that it is general,
systematic knowledge (*scientia*) which he is above all concerned
to analyse and whose prospects in the various disciplines he is
concerned to assess.

Locke's general theory of 'signification' might be said to be constituted by the following three theses:

(1) Words immediately signify ideas in the mind of him who uses
them. ('*Words in their primary or immediate signification, stand*

properties which are united in nature does not entail that it is framed from a natural
pattern. For example, in the above case my nominal essence of gold was framed
in a dream, in advance of seeing any instances of gold, but it is none the less true
that its constituent properties are united in nature.

for nothing, but the ideas *in the mind of him that uses them.'*
E 3. 2. 2)

(2) Ideas are private to individual minds. ('It was necessary, that man should find out some external sensible signs, whereby those *invisible* ideas, which his thoughts are made up of, might be made known to others.' E 3. 2. 1; emphasis added)

(3) Successful communication requires that the speaker's words excite the same ideas in the hearer as in the speaker. ('Unless a man's words excite the same *ideas* in the hearer, which he makes them stand for in speaking, he does not speak intelligibly.' E 3. 2. 8)

Philosophers have tended to be puzzled not merely by individual theses here, but by the implications of the package as a whole. In the first place, Locke's claim that words stand for nothing but ideas in the mind has suggested to many readers that he is muddled about the distinction between sense and reference. The difference can be brought out by means of a classic illustration: the terms 'the morning star' and 'the evening star' have different senses or meanings, but the same reference, for they pick out one and the same object in the world. Locke is charged either with ignoring this key distinction altogether or with implausibly holding that words never refer to things in the world but only to our ideas. But this criticism is unfair. In his most careful formulations at least, Locke is explicit that it is in their primary or immediate significations that words stand for our ideas; this qualification obviously leaves open the possibility that in their mediate or derivative significations they stand for things in the world. It is true that he sometimes says that people are misguided if they suppose that words stand also for the reality of things (E 3. 2. 4). But, as we shall see, Locke can be understood here as making the point that we cannot refer to things except by the mediation of the ideas which we associate with our words. And such a point may well be in large measure defensible, for, as we shall see, it anticipates modern criticisms of theories of direct reference.

A criticism which is no less often heard is that Locke's theory makes communication impossible, or at best problematic. The conjunction of theses (1) and (2) appears to imply that the meanings of words are mental entities which are private to the speaker; they are ideas which are 'invisible' to others. By contrast, philosophers in the tradition of Frege have insisted that the senses or meanings of words must be public entities if communication is to be possible. For example, two speakers cannot disagree about a proposition unless it is the same proposition which they have in mind, and this condition in turn cannot be satisfied unless the meanings are public rather than private entities. It is true, on this view, that different individuals may associate a train of mental imagery with their words, but such mental images are not to be mistaken for senses or meanings.

One might try to come to the defence of Locke here by invoking the distinction between idea-types and idea-tokens. The general distinction between types and tokens can be readily illustrated by means of its application to language. In the horror film *The Shining* the Jack Nicholson character covers sheets of paper with the words: 'All work and no play makes Jack a dull boy.' If we ask: 'How many sentences has he written?', the question is susceptible of two interpretations, depending on whether it is sentence-types or sentence-tokens which are in question. If sentence-types are at issue, the answer is 'one'; if, on the contrary, it is sentence-tokens which are at issue, the answer is (say) 'a thousand'. Applying this distinction to the case of ideas we could say that the ideas which are said to be invisible are idea-tokens; they are indeed private to the speaker. But it does not follow from this that the idea-type (the pattern common to the idea-tokens in different minds) is a private mental object; this could be an object in the public domain. Whether Locke would be happy with such a defence of his theory is not entirely clear, for it seems to introduce a public dimension into his account of meaning only if idea-types are construed in a Platonic way as abstract entities over and above mental particulars, and it may be objected that Locke's ontology leaves no room for such entities. But at least his philosophy has some of the resources for meeting the Fregean objection on its own ground.

Less controversially, the type–token distinction can be invoked to defend Locke's commitment to (3). On the face of it, this thesis appears to impose an impossible requirement on successful communication; the speaker's words must excite the same ideas in the hearer as those in his mind, but it will be naturally objected that ideas, being private mental objects, are not things of the sort that can migrate from one mind to another. But Locke is not committed to this absurd requirement. Successful communication indeed requires that the speaker's words excite the same idea-types in the mind of his hearer, but it obviously does not require that his words excite immediately the same idea-tokens.

Locke's theory of communication can thus to some extent be defended against familiar objections by means of the type–token distinction. But the theory may still seem to leave us with a sceptical epistemological problem on our hands. How do I know that when I utter the word 'gold', the idea-token aroused in your mind is of the same idea-type as the idea-token in mine? My idea of gold is of a substance that is yellow, heavy, shining, and malleable, but, for all I know, you attach a quite different idea to the word. But (as Guyer says), the fact that Locke's theory has sceptical consequences hardly amounts to a refutation of the theory; indeed, he wants to make us aware of a problem about successful communication.[13] Locke sketches a theory of the conditions for successful communication, but that does not commit him to saying that these conditions can be known to be satisfied.

Locke's theory of signification in general thus differs from Fregean orthodoxy concerning the nature of meaning. But when we turn to Locke's views on the signification of natural-kind terms so-called, we find that in one important respect he and the Fregeans are on the same side; in contrast to some recent philosophers they agree in holding that the reference of such terms is fixed by what they more immediately signify. For Frege, it is the sense of natural-kind terms which determines their reference; for Locke, it is the nominal essence or abstract idea. Thus, for Locke, if the nominal essence which I associate with the word 'gold' is the idea of a substance which is heavy, yellow, and metal, then all and only those items in the world which answer this description fall within the extension of the term 'gold'. The Lockean theory has a consequence which has appeared counter-intuitive to some people: if two substances differed in respect of their real essence or inner constitution, they would both be gold provided they instantiated the nominal essence. Conversely, however, if two substances had the same internal constitution, they would not both be gold if one of them failed to instantiate the nominal essence of gold.

Although the thesis may seem to us a purely semantic one, it is importantly motivated by epistemological considerations.

---

[13] Guyer, 'Locke's Philosophy of Language', 121.

According to Locke, the intelligible use of language requires that our words function as signs of entities with which we are acquainted, and in context this further implies that it must be the nominal essence which fixes the extension of our natural-kind terms. The only alternative is to allow the extension of these terms to be fixed by means of the real essence or internal constitution, but to do this would be to violate the requirement for intelligibility, for real essences are unknown to us. Locke sees that some people seek to do just this, but he believes that they are thereby guilty of an abuse of language:

Another abuse of words, is the setting them in the place of things, which they do or can by no means signify. We may observe, that in the general names of substances, whereof the nominal essences are only known to us, when we put them into propositions, and affirm or deny anything about them, we do most commonly tacitly suppose, or intend, they should stand for the real essence of a certain sort of substances. For when a man says *Gold is malleable*, he means and would insinuate something more than this, that *what I call gold is malleable*, (though truly it amounts to no more) but would have this understood, viz. that *gold*; i.e. *what has the real essence of gold is malleable*, which amounts to thus much, that *malleableness depends on, and is inseparable from the real essence of gold*. But a man, not knowing wherein that real essence consists, the connection in his mind of malleableness, is not truly with an essence he knows not, but only with the sound gold he puts for it. (*E* 3. 10. 17)

Although Locke does not say so explicitly here, the target of his attack on this abuse of language is presumably the Aristotelians.

In recent years the Lockean view (or more strictly its Fregean descendant) has been disputed. Unwittingly following a trail which was blazed by Leibniz, philosophers such as Kripke and Putnam have argued for a theory of direct reference which rather resembles the account of the signification of natural-kind terms which Locke attacks as an abuse of language. On their view, when we introduce a term such as 'gold', we intend it to refer to all and only those things which have the same internal constitution as the stuff we baptize as 'gold'.[14] According to this theory, then, it is not the nominal essence

[14] S. Kripke, 'Naming and Necessity', in D. Davidson and G. Harman (eds.), *Semantics of Natural Language* (Dordrecht, 1972); H. Putnam, 'Meaning and Reference', *Journal of Philosophy*, 70 (1973), 699–711. Cf. Mackie, *Problems from Locke*, 93–100. Mackie misleadingly claims that Locke anticipates the views of Kripke.

which fixes the extension of the term 'gold', for if we found a metal which had all the properties contained in our nominal essence, it would not be gold if it had a different internal constitution from the initial sample. In modern terms no stuff is gold which fails to have atomic number 79. Locke's worry that on such an account our words thereby become signs of something we do not know is met by an appeal to the division of linguistic labour.[15] Just as there are people whose 'job' it is to wear gold wedding-rings, so there are others whose 'job' it is to tell whether a given ring is really gold; such experts are of course presumed to have the kind of knowledge of internal constitutions which Locke believes to be beyond our cognitive grasp.

But is the Lockean account of natural-kind terms thereby refuted? Some philosophers have drawn attention to a difficulty in the theory of direct reference which suggests how the Lockean account might be rehabilitated: the difficulty is sometimes known as the *qua* problem. According to the Kripke–Putnam account, the term 'gold' is supposed to apply to all and only those substances which have the same underlying nature as our initial samples. But this raises the question which underlying nature is the relevant one. The samples share a number; they share, for example, the nature of metal. Those who press the *qua* problem observe that the nature relevant to fixing the reference of the term 'gold' is established by a particular description under which a person thinks of the samples.[16] In other words, then, Locke is right after all to insist that it is inescapably the nominal essence which logically determines whether something is or is not gold.

It is only fair to conclude this chapter on a note of caution. Although there are some intriguing parallels between Locke's views and contemporary positions in debates in the philosophy of language, it is controversial how deep the similarities go; some philosophers have sought to play down these similarities quite radically. At a minimum estimate Locke's approach to language is driven by concerns which play little or no part in contemporary debates. His attack on the abuses of language is a contribution to a larger

---

[15] The idea of the division of linguistic labour is found in Putnam, 'Meaning and Reference', 704.

[16] M. Devitt and K. Sterelny, *Language and Reality* (Cambridge, Mass., 1987), 73. I am indebted here to an unpublished paper by Kyle Stanford, 'Reference and Natural Kind Terms: The Real Essence of Locke's View'.

polemic against the Aristotelians and their teachings concerning classification. And even Locke's theory of natural-kind terms is informed by epistemological preoccupations that dominate the *Essay* as a whole: unless such terms signify items of which we have some knowledge, our discourse will fail to be intelligible. More broadly, Locke's whole concern with the linguistic and conceptual dimensions of generality cannot be understood apart from an epistemological commitment: with the exception of existential knowledge, any knowledge that is really worth having is by its nature general, though it may begin in particulars. The discussion of language and generality in book 3 is not free-standing; it is essentially a propaedeutic to book 4.

9

KNOWLEDGE AND FAITH

IT is sometimes said that in book 4 of the *Essay* Locke appears most like a rationalist. There is more than a grain of truth in this claim. Although he is in some sense a concept-empiricist, he is not a knowledge-empiricist; that is, although he holds that all our ideas are either given in experience or constructed from the data which experience supplies, he does not hold that all our claims to knowledge can be justified by experience. It is also true that, like the rationalists, Locke operates with a strong conception of knowledge such that its paradigm examples are a priori truths. But in terms of this strong conception of knowledge he develops a theory which, in its pessimistic side, sets him apart from his rationalist predecessors such as Descartes and Spinoza; knowledge is possible in mathematics and morality but not (with rare exceptions) in metaphysics and the natural sciences.

Making good on this commitment is perhaps Locke's main goal in book 4, but the last book of the *Essay* is also remarkable for a subsidiary theme; he develops an often brilliant analysis of the role of reason in relation to religious faith. Here it is helpful to place Locke's aims in a historical setting; he seeks to defend the claims of reason against two groups of contemporary opponents. On the one hand, the role of reason must be vindicated against those such as the Catholics who supposedly require submission to authority; on the other hand, it must also be vindicated against those such as the Puritan fanatics and enthusiasts, who claim to possess 'a light from heaven' which is superior to natural reason. Rather like Hobbes in *Leviathan*, then, Locke is fighting a war on two fronts. Brilliant as it often is, Locke's account of faith and reason in the *Essay* does not constitute his whole philosophy of religion; it is in the *Letter on Toleration* rather than the *Essay*, for instance, that he deploys a powerful argument for toleration from the involuntary nature of belief. But even in the *Essay* no one can miss Locke's commitment to freedom of conscience in religion or his critique of authoritarianism.

The Nature of Knowledge in General

'*Knowledge* then seems to me nothing but *the perception of the connection and agreement, or disagreement and repugnancy of any of our ideas*' (*E* 4. 1. 2). Ever since Leibniz readers have tended to be surprised by Locke's austere, uncompromising definition; the definition may be satisfied by conceptual truths, such as 'All squares have four sides', but it appears to disqualify much that we would normally call knowledge. We would be inclined to say, for example, that I know that there is a table in front of me and that the Prime Minister of Britain is Tony Blair; however, it is difficult to see how either of these epistemic commonplaces satisfies Locke's definition.

Perhaps the best way of approaching Locke's account of knowledge in general is from the direction of the Aristotelian tradition. Locke is engaged in a task of creative reinterpretation; he seeks to appropriate the Aristotelian doctrine of *scientia* in a way that excludes those unappealing aspects of the doctrine which he associates above all with Scholasticism.[1] According to the doctrine of *scientia*, which derives from the *Posterior Analytics*, knowledge is essentially of universal, necessary truths; such truths are either themselves first principles or they are derived from first principles by means of syllogistic reasoning. As we shall see, Locke seeks to find room for a category of existential knowledge—we can have knowledge of the existence of the self, the world, and God—and this category does not easily satisfy the requirements for *scientia* or Locke's definition of knowledge, but he shares the traditional

---

[1] On the relationship between Locke's theory of knowledge and the Aristotelian tradition of *scientia*, see R. S. Woolhouse, *Locke* (Brighton, 1983). Cf. P. Phemister, 'Locke, Sergeant, and Scientific Method', in T. Sorell (ed.), *The Rise of Modern Philosophy* (Oxford, 1993), 231–49.

assumption that knowledge is paradigmatically of universal necessary truths. However, Locke rejects other elements of the traditional Aristotelian theory or else at least reinterprets them in the
light of commitments which he shares with Descartes.

We have seen that one such commitment is to a kind of epistemological individualism. For Locke, it is a conceptual truth that
knowing is knowing for oneself. As he says, 'I think, we may as rationally hope to see with other men's eyes, as to know by other men's
understandings' (E 1. 4. 23). This claim should be understood to
imply more than the apparent truism that if I know that p, then it
is I who am in the state of believing that p; it further implies something about the nature of my justification for believing that p. (We
should note, however, that strictly speaking for Locke knowledge
excludes believing.) Locke's epistemological individualism is
expressed in his emphasis on *perceiving* the agreements and dis-
agreements among ideas; in order to know the truth of the
Pythagorean theorem, we must perceive that the square on the
hypotenuse must be equal to the sum of the squares on the other
two sides. According to Locke, then, someone who believes a
theorem which is true on the authority of Newton does not strictly
speaking know the truth of the theorem. It is also a consequence
of Locke's position that he would reject the orthodox modern
definition of knowledge as justified true belief; in the above example
the person's mental state satisfies the orthodox definition of knowledge but not the Lockean one; for he does not perceive the agreements or conceptual connections of the constituent ideas.

Locke's commitment to epistemological individualism in this
sense is something he shares with Descartes, but in one way he goes
beyond his great predecessor. Or to put the point another way,
he seeks to be more faithful to this commitment than Descartes
himself. For Locke, as we have seen, epistemological individualism
requires the rejection of innate ideas. Locke's complaint against
Descartes on this score is easy to understand. Descartes holds that
knowledge paradigmatically consists in having clear and distinct perceptions, but he none the less allows room for innate knowledge of
propositions (for example, in mathematics and metaphysics). In
Locke's view, he is thus prepared to ascribe propositional knowledge
to infants who cannot see why the propositions in question are true;
indeed, they cannot even believe the propositions. In this way he
runs foul of the commitment to epistemological individualism.

It is fair to question the consistency of Locke's own commitment to individualism since he recognizes a category of habitual knowledge:

A man is said to know any proposition, which having been once laid before his thoughts, he evidently perceived the agreement, or disagreement of the *ideas* whereof it consists; and so lodged it in his memory, that whenever that proposition comes again to be reflected on, he, without doubt or hesitation, embraces the right side, assents to, and is certain of the truth of it. This, I think, one may call *habitual knowledge.* (*E* 4. 1. 8)

Locke is even prepared to ascribe habitual knowledge to people who can no longer perceive the connections or logical relations among their ideas. It is significant that he himself admits to having second thoughts on this issue, and only reluctantly comes to the conclusion that such habitual knowledge 'comes not short of perfect certainty, and is in effect true knowledge' (*E* 4. 1. 9). In defence of Locke's second thoughts it can at least be said that such people are in a different epistemological situation from someone who believes that *p* on the authority of Newton, for the former have had insight into the grounds for the truth of *p*.

A second element in Locke's reinterpretation of *scientia* is its opposition to the formalism which he associates with the Aristotelian tradition. According to this tradition, *scientia* essentially depends on form or structure; that is, it depends on laying out a proof in a series of syllogisms, where syllogisms are governed by strict rules of logical form. On this view, then, claims to know a theorem are to be justified by reference to the formal structure of the proof and to the status of the premisses as first principles or necessary truths. Formalism of this kind was to be revived and defended in Locke's own time by Leibniz.

Anti-formalism is a characteristic which is common to the theories of knowledge of both Descartes and Locke, and it is instructive to compare the positions of the two philosophers. Descartes's anti-formalism is perhaps most evident in the distinction which he draws between intuition and deduction in his early work the *Rules for the Direction of the Mind*. Descartes there explains that intuition is a 'conception of a clear and attentive mind, which is so easy and distinct that there can be no room for doubt about what we are understanding';[2] we can intuit, for example, that we think or that we exist. Deduction, by contrast, is defined as 'the inference of something as following necessarily from other propositions which are known with certainty'.[3] It is natural to suppose that it is axioms or first principles which are the province of intuition, and all and only formal inferences are the province of deduction, but this is belied by Descartes's further insistence that even inferences may be intuited. Indeed, it has been plausibly suggested that the distinction, for Descartes, is a psychological, not a logical, one; it is psychological in the sense that it is relative to an enquirer's level of epistemological sophistication.[4] Simple truths such as '2 + 2 = 4' can be intuited by almost everyone, but with regard to the knowledge of more complex truths the situation is different: one person may need to rely on deduction, whereas another may be able to intuit. Descartes seems to envisage that as rational enquirers we should aim, as far as possible, to replace deduction by intuition. What makes this goal a rationally desirable one is the fact that we would thereby dispense with reliance on the fallible faculty of memory, which detracts from the complete certainty of deduction. Descartes's worry here seems to turn on the fact that deduction involves a temporal succession of steps. At a later stage of the deduction I no longer directly intuit the earlier steps but must rely on my memory to assure me that I did.

Locke makes a seemingly analogous distinction between intuitive and demonstrative knowledge; he even follows Descartes to the extent of saying that demonstrative knowledge is a lesser degree of certainty than intuition by virtue of its dependence on memory (E 4. 2. 7). But in one way Locke seems to diverge from Descartes, at least as he has been presented above. In Locke there is no suggestion that the distinction between intuition and demonstration is relative to an enquirer's level of epistemological sophistication; there is also no suggestion that with practice we may be able to

---

[2] *Rules for the Direction of the Mind*, Rule III, in *The Philosophical Writings of Descartes*, trans. J. Cottingham, R. Stoothoff, and D. Murdoch, 3 vols. (Cambridge, 1985), i. 14.

[3] Ibid. 15.

[4] See I. Hacking, 'Leibniz and Descartes: Proof and Eternal Truths', in A. Kenny (ed.), *Rationalism, Idealism, and Empiricism* (Oxford, 1983), 47–60. On Locke's antiformalism, cf. M. Wilson, 'Leibniz and Locke on "First Truths"', *Journal of the History of Ideas*, 28 (1967), 347–66.

replace deduction with intuition. On the contrary, there are truths which by their nature cannot be intuited, and must be demonstrated because the relevant ideas cannot be directly compared with one another; the intervention of further ideas is required in order to make us perceive the agreement, or disagreement, which knowledge entails. Locke's example is characteristically drawn from geometry. In order to perceive the truth of the proposition that the internal angles of a triangle are equal to two right ones, we must introduce ideas of other angles (E 4. 2. 2). We can do this by drawing through the apex of a triangle a straight line which is parallel to its base; new angles are thereby created which are visibly equal to the two opposite internal angles.[5]

Locke's insistence that the distinction between intuition and demonstration is not relative to an enquirer's level of intellectual vision strikes a more pessimistic note than Descartes's seemingly contrary view; for Locke, we are condemned to rely on demonstration, which depends on memory and thus stops short of the certainty of intuitive knowledge. But it would be a mistake to suppose that he is hereby returning to the kind of formalism which Descartes had rejected in the Aristotelian tradition. For Locke, as for Descartes, formal proof, as understood by the Aristotelians, is neither necessary nor sufficient for demonstrative knowledge. It is not necessary, for syllogistic reasoning has no privileged status; as we saw in connection with the issue of free will in Chapter 7, demonstration may assume the character of informal reasoning set out in a series of conceptual entailments. And it is not sufficient either; merely checking a proof for formal validity, and knowing the truth of the premisses, will not yield demonstrative knowledge. For Locke, as for Descartes, one must see the conceptual connections, or at least have seen them in the past.

It is natural to suppose that Locke's epistemological individualism and his anti-formalism are somehow linked, but the issue of the logical relationship between the two doctrines needs to be treated with some care. Whether the first of these doctrines entails the second seems to depend on how strong a thesis we take formalism to be. Consider the question of the circumstances under which someone might be said to have knowledge of the truth of a

---

[5] Here I follow the account given by Woolhouse, 'Locke's Theory of Knowledge', in Chappell (ed.), *Cambridge Companion to Locke*, 153.

theorem-hypothetical—that is, a conditional proposition of the form: if the premisses are true, then the theorem to be proved is true. It is possible to conceive of a strong version of formalism which is committed to the following. Suppose that a computer which is known to function correctly is programmed to check the formal validity of proofs: then the operator of the machine knows the truth of the theorem-hypothetical even though he may have no understanding of the logical processes involved and cannot check for himself to see whether the machine has made a mistake. But claiming that the conditions for knowledge are satisfied in this case would clearly be inconsistent with epistemological individualism, for this states that in order to have knowledge of the theorem-hypothetical, the person must be able to perceive for himself that the conclusion follows from the premisses. Such perceptions need not be occurrent; it is sufficient that a person have a disposition to have them which is based on past occurrent perceptions.

Yet it is also possible to imagine a more moderate version of formalism which would stand in a different relationship to epistemological individualism. According to this version of the doctrine, formal structure still plays some role in justification; in justifying his claim to know the truth of the theorem-hypothetical, the operator cites the fact that the proof has the appropriate logical structure. But on this version it is further required, for knowledge, that the operator be able to see for himself that the proof is valid; if he has doubts about whether the computer is functioning properly, he can use his own logical competence to check the results it produces. Such a position is clearly consistent with epistemological individualism (as we have understood it), for not merely does the operator believe the theorem-hypothetical p, but he believes it on the basis of his own logical insight, actual or potential; he sees, or at least can see, that the proof has the right logical form.

A third element in Locke's theory of knowledge might be called its psychologism. The term is a slippery one which needs clarification. 'Psychologism' is often used to mean the view that logic is the study of the way in which people actually think and reason; in other words, on this view logic is part of the science of psychology. Psychologism in this sense seems clearly mistaken, and indeed is widely regarded as a wholly discredited doctrine; it is urged in opposition that logic is a normative discipline, not a descriptive science which studies actual mental processes. Here I shall use the term in a more neutral sense; by 'psychologism' I shall mean the view that not merely is propositional knowledge a psychological state but the objects of such knowledge are themselves psychological entities. On this interpretation, then, psychologism stands in opposition to the Platonic thesis that knowledge involves access to a realm of logical concepts and truths which are not reducible to psychological items.

We may bring out the hold that the Platonic thesis which Locke opposes tends to have on our intuitions by means of a quotation. Locke is here concerned to defend his claim that habitual knowledge is genuine knowledge:

> The immutability of the same relations between the same immutable things, is now the *idea* that shows him that, if the three angles of a triangle were once equal to two right ones, they will always be equal to two right ones. And hence he comes to be certain, that what was once true in the case is always true; what *ideas* once agreed will always agree; and consequently what he once knew to be true he will always know to be true, as long as he can remember that he once knew it. Upon this ground it is, that particular demonstrations in mathematics afford general knowledge. (*E* 4. 1. 9)

It is natural to react to this passage by saying that it is concepts and propositions which remain unchangeably the same, and that concepts and propositions are not psychological entities but logical ones; as we might say, they are 'third realm' entities. But Locke's opposition to any form of Platonism is clear in his account of the eternal truths; according to Locke, they have no existence until people come to construct abstract ideas:

> Many of these [general certain propositions] are called *aeternae veritates*, and all of them indeed are so; not from being written all or any of them in the minds of all men, or that they were any of them propositions in anyone's mind, till he, having got the abstract *ideas*, joined or separated them by affirmation or negation. (*E* 4. 11. 14)

From a polemical standpoint, this is a rich and challenging passage, for Locke has two targets in his sights. Not merely is he setting himself against the Platonic (and in Locke's time Malebranchean) account of the eternal truths; he is also picking a quarrel within the ranks of his fellow anti-Platonists. Locke clearly rejects the Cartesian thesis that while 'the eternal truths have no existence outside our thought',[6] they have been inscribed on our minds by a benevolent God in the form of innate propositional knowledge.

For Locke, then, knowledge of the eternal truths of mathematics is not conversant about a Platonic realm of abstract objects; it is conversant rather about eternal relations between ideas, and ideas are psychological items which can be acquired in the course of time. Now Locke surely does not mean to say that it is my mental states which 'eternally have the same relations', for mental states are essentially transitory; moreover, *qua* mental states, they are not entities of the sort that can enter into logical relations. It is true of course that if I thought of a triangle yesterday and think of it again today, then my mental states will be similar, and in that sense might be said to agree. Moreover, there is a trivial sense in which the relation of similarity is eternal; it has always been true and will remain true for the rest of time that such a relation of similarity holds between my mental states at *t*. But as an account of our knowledge of the eternal truths such a strategy is wholly unpromising; for it provides no way of distinguishing between my perception of eternal truths on the one hand and my experience of qualitatively similar pain sensations on the other.

The natural move to make at this point is to appeal to Locke's official definition of the term 'idea': ideas are said to be, not mental states, but objects of the understanding when a man thinks. Understood in this sense, ideas are things of the sort that can enter into eternal logical relationships. The fact that mental states cannot do so is thus strictly irrelevant. It is true that the ontological status of ideas is still psychological, but to say this is simply to deny the Platonic thesis that there is a realm of abstract entities about which knowledge is conversant. It may be objected that Locke does not consistently adhere to this definition; sometimes he seems to regard ideas as occurrent mental events (perceptions). But this difficulty is perhaps not as serious as it seems, for we can come to Locke's rescue with the aid of Cartesian resources. Even if ideas are mental events, they essentially have representational content, and it is when they are considered in terms of their representational content that they are capable of entering into logical relationships.

The issue of how ideas enter into logical relationships is complicated by the assumption that Locke is an imagist. As we have seen,

---

[6] *Principles of Philosophy*, 1. 48, in *Philosophical Writings of Descartes*, i. 208.

the extent of his commitment to imagism is highly controversial, and the difficulty of making sense of logical relationships on this assumption may appear to some readers to be strong evidence against this reading. But we may conclude this section by noticing one way in which the imagist reading is confirmed by Locke's account of knowledge in general; it has the potential to throw light on a widely recognized problem of interpretation. Philosophers have often complained that there is an ambiguity in Locke's notion of the disagreement of ideas. Sometimes Locke seems to mean that two ideas (i.e. mental contents) are logically distinct. At other times he appears to have a stronger criterion of disagreement in mind; ideas which disagree are those which fail to entail one another or even logically exclude one another (that is, are 'repugnant'). On a standard non-imagist reading of Locke such ambiguities are simply gratuitous; it is hard to make sense of what is going on here. But on an imagist interpretation this is far from being the case. It would be natural for an imagist to take the notion of distinctness as basic, and then to seek to provide a reductive analysis of other logical relations (such as non-entailment and exclusion) in terms of this basic concept. To say this is not of course to say that Locke executes his programme successfully, or even that he avoids the mistakes of which he is accused; but it does throw light on what he is doing here. Once again, it is more instructive to see difficulties in Locke as arising from an overambitious programme than from a series of gratuitous muddles and mistakes.

Mathematical and Moral Knowledge

In terms of the general theory outlined above Locke seeks to show how we can have knowledge of mathematics and morality that is both certain and universal. More ambitiously he builds on the results of book 3 to show how such knowledge in these disciplines can also be real. The argument takes the following form. According to Locke, knowledge is real if and only if our ideas conform to their archetypes (E 4. 4. 5, 8); and this in turn is equivalent to saying that our nominal essences coincide with the real essences. Locke, then, is in a position to show how the conditions for real knowledge can be satisfied in the case of the two disciplines. For the province of mathematics is simple modes (geometry and most of arithmetic) and at least one simple idea (namely, unity); the province of morality is mixed modes. And, as we have seen, in the case of simple ideas and modes in general the nominal and the real essences are supposed to coincide. In perceiving, then, how the Pythagorean property follows from the nominal essence of a right-angled triangle, I do not merely perceive an agreement between ideas; I have insight into the real essence of such triangles. My knowledge is thus not merely certain and universal; it is also real.

This is a very important argument for Locke, but it needs clarification and defence. In the first place, it may seem that he offers two criteria for real knowledge which are not equivalent. The argument above turns on the criterion that our knowledge is real to the extent that our ideas conform to their archetypes. But Locke also prominently states that our knowledge is real only so far as there is a conformity between our ideas and the reality of things (*E* 4. 4. 3); indeed, this seems to be his primary criterion for real knowledge. At first sight, it may seem that moral and mathematical knowledge satisfies the first criterion for real knowledge but not this second one (*E* 4. 4. 3). For the real essences or archetypes in mathematics and morality are ideal entities; they are standards of 'the mind's own making'. By this criterion, then, it appears that real knowledge involves no reference to the reality of things.

But this objection is misguided. For Locke aims quite clearly to show how, properly understood, the two criteria turn out to be equivalent; by satisfying the first criterion, then, mathematical and moral knowledge also satisfies the second. One argument for this equivalence is a significant contribution to philosophy. Focusing on the case of geometry, Locke argues that the propositions of this discipline are not existential; they do not assert that such-and-such figures exist. Nor do geometrical propositions have what is called existential import; that is, they do not imply or presuppose the existence of such figures. Rather, what is characteristic of mathematical propositions in general is their hypothetical nature; if anything falls under the concept of a triangle, for example, then its internal angles add up to 180 degrees:

The mathematician considers the truth and properties belonging to a rectangle, or circle, only as they are in *idea* in his own mind. For it is possible he never found either of them existing mathematically, *i.e.* precisely true, in his life. But yet the knowledge he has of any truths or properties belonging to a circle, or any other mathematical figure, are nevertheless true and certain, even of real things existing: because real things are no farther concerned, nor intended to be meant by any such propositions, than as things really agree to those *archetypes* in his mind. Is it true of the *idea* of a *triangle*, that its three angles are equal to two right ones? It is true also of a triangle, wherever it really exists. (*E* 4. 4. 6)

Thus we can be sure that any existing figure which answers to the description of a triangle has this further property by virtue of the relations of entailment among ideas. Locke can show, then, that mathematical knowledge has this kind of indirect reference to the reality of things.

Locke has thus given some thought to showing how his criteria of real knowledge are equivalent. But his conception of real knowledge raises a further problem of a rather similar nature. Consider his well-known distinction between knowledge that is instructive and knowledge that is merely verbal or 'trifling'. Locke explains the difference as follows:

We can know then the truth of two sorts of propositions, with perfect *certainty*: the one is, of those trifling propositions which have a certainty in them, but it is but a *verbal certainty*, but not instructive. And, secondly, we can know the truth, and so may be *certain* in propositions, which affirm some thing of another, which is a necessary consequence of its precise complex *idea*, but not contained in it: As that *the external angle of all triangles, is bigger than either of the opposite internal angles.* (*E* 4. 8. 8)

One might lazily assume that all and only real knowledge would be instructive; at the very least, one might suppose that all real knowledge would also be instructive. But this passage suggests that these assumptions are mistaken, for by the criterion which Locke states, it does not follow from the fact that a proposition counts as an item of real knowledge that it is thereby instructive. For, as we have seen, in mathematics and morality whatever true propositions are trivially deduced from the nominal essence are cases of real knowledge, since in these areas the nominal essence coincides with the real essence. Thus, for example, I have real knowledge when I perceive the truth of an analytic entailment such as 'All triangles have three sides'. But analytic entailments of this kind obviously fail to satisfy Locke's criterion for instructive knowledge; for the property of having three sides is contained in the complex idea of a triangle. Locke, then, is committed to the thesis that there can be real knowledge which is not instructive, and it is not clear that he would be happy with this result.

One might try to allow Locke to escape this surprising result. It might be objected that from the fact that the nominal essence trivially entails p, it does not follow that the real essence also trivially entails p, even though the putatively two essences are identical. Thus, by analogy, from the fact that it is trivially true that the morning star is visible in the morning, it does not follow that it is trivially true that the evening star is visible in the morning, even though the morning star is identical with the evening star. But this attempted defence is unsuccessful, for the parallel is not exact. In the astronomical case what is at issue is one thing under two descriptions which are co-referring but logically non-equivalent. In the cases of essences what is at issue is rather the same concept under different labels.

Locke's distinction between trifling and instructive knowledge is relevant to assessing his claims for moral knowledge. He famously and repeatedly claims that a demonstrative science of morality is possible, and it is clear that this thesis is of great importance in the overall scheme of the *Essay*. But it has often been objected that Locke's confidence in this project is entirely misplaced. A demonstrative science of ethics, as he envisages it, is clearly supposed to justify substantive moral truths, and it is natural to observe that it cannot deliver these goods. Locke's own specimens of demonstrated moral truths are not encouraging: propositions such as 'No government allows absolute liberty' and 'Where there is no property there is no injustice' (E 4. 3. 18) are simply 'trifling' by his own criterion, for their certainty depends on their being analytic entailments; they are true by virtue of the meanings of the terms. By contrast, any attempt to come up with a science of substantive moral truths would seek to proceed from uncontroversial factual premisses and definitions to normative conclusions about conduct such as 'Human beings ought to keep their promises'. And since Hume we supposedly know that it is impossible to deduce 'ought' statements from 'is' statements.[7]

This line of criticism prompts two responses, one minor, one

---

[7] Hume, *Treatise of Human Nature*, 3. 1. 1.

major. The minor response is that in this case Locke may be able to exploit the non-equivalence of real and instructive knowledge to his advantage; even if he concedes that a demonstrative science of ethics cannot justify instructive, substantive moral truths, he is not thereby committed to admitting that it falls short of real knowledge. The major response is that the force of the objection depends on a traditional but controversial conception of ethics; it assumes that moral imperatives are essentially categorical. Other philosophers, by contrast, have held, implicitly or explicitly, that moral prescriptions are hypothetical imperatives of a special kind; they prescribe the necessary means to an end which human beings seek or desire. On this conception of ethics, the supposed logical gap between 'is' and 'ought' statements does not exist; there is no fallacy, for example, in inferring from 'You desire self-preservation' and 'If you desire self-preservation, you ought to seek peace' to the conclusion: 'You ought to seek peace'. If Locke were prepared to regard morality as a system of hypothetical imperatives, he would be in a strong position to defend his project of a demonstrative science of ethics. But whether he would be willing to pay this price is open to dispute, for he might be uneasily conscious that the two most prominent exponents of such an approach to ethics in his own time were Hobbes and Spinoza, 'those justly decried names' (*LW* iv. 477).

Whatever his success in coping with the Humean objection to his project, Locke has at least sought to protect it from criticism from one quarter. As we have seen, he devotes considerable space in the *Essay* to outlining and defending a metaphysics of morals; that is, he has sought to show that the metaphysically necessary conditions for moral agency and responsibility can be known to be satisfied. We can know that we are persons and we can know that we are free in the sense relevant to ethics. Thus, as Locke sees it, he is not vulnerable to an objector who says that we do not know that doing *x* is morally obligatory because we do not know that we have the power to do *x*.

Prospects for Scientific Knowledge

Locke not merely lived in an age of unparalleled scientific achievement; he was also the champion of Newton and of the work of the

Royal Society. Readers who are familiar with this side of Locke might expect him to offer an optimistic appraisal of the prospects for knowledge in the natural sciences; but if they do, they are in for a disappointment. In striking and deliberate contrast to his optimism about mathematics and morality, he argues that the prospects for systematic knowledge or *scientia* of the natural world are decidedly poor; as he famously puts it, 'how far so ever human industry may advance useful and *experimental* philosophy *in physical things, scientifical* will still be out of our reach' (*E* 4. 3. 26). Locke has a principled case for this negative thesis; once again he deploys the results of book 3 in order to establish his position. Real knowledge is knowledge of real essences and the properties which derive from them. But in the case of substances the real and nominal essences fail to coincide, and since we do not and cannot know essences of the former sort, our knowledge cannot be real.

For the most part our knowledge of the natural world is not instructive either. Locke thinks that we have instructive knowledge of substances to the extent that we perceive relations of necessary coexistence or connection between the nominal essence and other properties; in other words, to be more than trifling our knowledge must be of qualities of bodies that are consequences of the nominal essence, but not contained in it. And he further thinks that there are very few cases where we perceive such necessary connections. Indeed, if there is a criticism to be made here, it is not that he is too pessimistic, but rather that he is too sanguine.

Our ignorance of real essences, for Locke, is crucially relevant for explaining our lack of real scientific knowledge, but it may be doubted whether he offers a consistent account of the relevance. Indeed, he seems to alternate between two accounts which may represent different stages in his thought. According to what seems the more primitive account, our ignorance of real essences implies that we are unable to carve nature up at her deep joints; that is, we cannot track nature's own classifications, and hence our knowledge of the world is not real. Locke here presupposes that nature does have deep joints at which she could in principle be carved up. Such an account is suggested in the following places:

So uncertain are the boundaries of *species* of animals to us, who have no other measures, than the complex *ideas* of our own collecting. (*E* 3. 6. 27)

But in substances, wherein a real essence, distinct from the nominal, is supposed to constitute, determine, and bound the species, the extent of the
general word is very uncertain: because not knowing this real essence, we
cannot know what is, or is not of that *species*; and consequently what may,
or may not with certainty be affirmed of it. (*E* 4. 6. 4)

The primitive view seems specially striking in this second passage,
though it is true that in what follows Locke appears to go back on
himself. But in any case, whether or not he means to embrace it, he
should not adopt this account, for it is plainly inconsistent with his
mature anti-Aristotelian theory that classification is the workmanship of the understanding.

The second account poses no such problem of consistency, for
it does not presuppose that the role of real essences is to bound
species. On this view, the reason why, lacking insight into real
essences, we fail to have real knowledge is not that we do not know
how things are naturally classified; it is rather that we do not know
why they have the properties which we observe in them; in other
words, it is impossible for us to deduce such properties from an
internal constitution which we do not know. Thus on this account
it is explanation, rather than classification, which is beyond our cognitive grasp. It might be thought that this separation of the real
essence from the role of classification leads to incoherence, but this
would be a mistake. On this view it is indeed (logically and epistemically) possible that qualitatively identical observable properties
are grounded in quite dissimilar internal constitutions, each of
which is sufficient for the properties in question; thus the qualities
we observe in water may be equally founded in H_2O or some other
chemical structure. Such a claim may be hard to reconcile with
Locke's thesis that even the real essence relates to a sort, but it is
not philosophically incoherent in its own right.

The stage is now set for a theme in Locke's philosophy which is
remarkably fruitful; it pioneers the inductive scepticism generally
associated with Hume. Locke is led in this direction by drawing out
the consequences of his thesis that real essences are beyond our cognitive grasp. On this basis Locke argues that universal scientific
knowledge is condemned to be either trivially certain or impossible
for us to attain. For a proposition such as 'All gold is fixed' either
explicates the nominal essence, and is hence merely verbal, or
(leaving aside the few cases of perceived necessary coexistence) it

makes a claim that goes beyond what is justified in terms of perceived agreements of ideas. Locke thus states a thesis which was
to be emphasized by Hume: if the certainty of a universal proposition is not guaranteed by relations of ideas, then we cannot strictly
know it to be true. It must be admitted that Hume wants to go
much further than Locke in this sceptical direction; he famously
argues that our experience of a 'constant conjunction' between Fs
and Gs gives us no reason at all to believe that 'All Fs are Gs' (where
G is a property not contained in the concept or 'nominal essence'
of F). Locke, by contrast, makes no such sweeping statement about
what it is rational for us to believe; he stops at the thesis that such
universal propositions do not satisfy the criteria for strict knowledge. None the less, his insight is a significant step on the road
to Hume.

Locke deserves full credit for this insight, but it must be admitted that his handling of the point is not impeccable. In successive
books of the *Essay* Locke offers two inconsistent treatments of our
knowledge of the universal proposition 'All gold is fixed'. At 3. 6. 50
he writes that either the word 'gold' signifies the nominal essence,
in which case the proposition is said to be trivially true, since
fixedness is part of the definition, or it signifies a real essence
marked out by nature, in which case it is uncertain. Later, at 4. 6. 8,
however, he again states the second disjunct, but now the other
possibility he recognizes is that the word 'gold' signifies a nominal
essence, in which case it is uncertain (i.e. fixedness is not contained
in the nominal essence of 'gold'). On each occasion Locke overlooks
a possibility regarding the nominal essence. What he should say
concerning the nominal-essence disjunct is that it is either trivially
true or uncertain (if fixedness is not contained in the nominal
essence).

Sensitive Knowledge

Locke's overwhelming epistemological interest lies in analysing
the nature of universal knowledge. But we should expect Locke to
show some interest in existential knowledge, and this expectation
is indeed satisfied; as we have already seen, he offers a supposedly
demonstrative proof of the existence of God. Even here, however,

the topic of universal knowledge is not far away, for God's existence is clearly relevant to the project of the science of morality. Locke follows up his proof of God's existence with a chapter on what he calls sensitive knowledge, or knowledge of the existence of bodies. The juxtaposition of the chapters may be significant. Descartes had notoriously deployed the existence of a non-deceiving God as a premiss in his proof of the existence of physical objects; by putting the two discussions side by side Locke may be seeking to draw the reader's attention to the fact that he is not following Descartes down that road.

Locke may refuse to adopt Descartes's theological strategy, but it has usually been thought that on this topic he shares some key assumptions with his predecessor. Locke and Descartes are traditionally held to agree that there is a logical gap between the data of experience and the existence of an external world; hence some kind of rational inference is required in order to bridge the gap. Locke is supposed to offer a number of flawed proofs of his own, or at best to regard the existence of bodies as a hypothesis which is strongly confirmed by its success in predicting the course of our experience. More recently, the assumption that for Locke the existence of bodies requires any sort of proof has come in for strong criticism. It has been argued by Michael Ayers that Locke follows the precedents set by Epicurus and Gassendi in holding that we have non-inferential knowledge of bodies through sensation.[8]

I believe that this whole debate may be misguided. Locke's discussion of the issue in 4. 11 is best regarded as a kind of dialogue in which he responds to progressively more rigorous sceptical challenges. The dialogue comes in three stages. First, he begins by asserting the commonsensical view that we know the existence of bodies through sensation, not reason. Next, Locke imagines, as it were, a critic who is not satisfied with this appeal to sensation, but demands a rational justification for believing in the existence of bodies. Locke accordingly obliges by offering what he calls 'concurrent reasons'; significantly, he does not speak of arguments or proofs, and with good grounds, for judged strictly as proofs the concurrent reasons clearly fail; they appear either question-begging or inconclusive. Thus when Locke says that 'it is plain, those perceptions are produced in us by exterior causes affecting our senses:

[8] Ayers, *Locke*, i. 155–65.

because *those that want organs of any sense, never can have the* ideas *belonging to that sense* produced in their minds' (*E* 4. 11. 4), he is vulnerable to the charge that he is assuming the existence of sensory organs which are part of the very external world whose existence is in question. And when he adds that we sometimes find that we cannot avoid having sensory ideas produced in the mind (*E* 4. 11. 5), he is vulnerable to such counter-examples as Macbeth's dagger: Macbeth's ideas of a dagger came to him willy-nilly, but they were not caused by the presence of a real physical object. Finally, in response to an extreme sceptic who might point out that these 'concurrent reasons' fall short of proof, Locke concedes that demonstration in this quarter is impossible; none the less, we have all the assurance that we need and are capable of having for the purposes of life.

An approach of this kind suggests that Locke's discussion of sensitive knowledge is more carefully thought out than is often supposed. But it is still fair to ask whether sensitive knowledge qualifies as knowledge at all, by his definition. It is tempting to say that Locke is guilty of a conflation here. Locke famously claims that '*the notice we have by our senses of the existing of things without us*, though it be not altogether so certain, as our intuitive knowledge, or the deductions of our reason, employed about the clear abstract *ideas* of our own minds; yet it is an assurance that *deserves the name of knowledge*' (*E* 4. 11. 3), and we might react to this by saying that it runs together the question of the degrees of certainty with the question whether such assurance satisfies Locke's definition of knowledge. But this reaction is perhaps premature. In his initial account of the divisions of knowledge Locke allows room for existential knowledge; the fourth and last sort is of 'actual real existence' agreeing with any ideas (*E* 4. 1. 7). And with this passage in mind we can see how mistaken it is to suppose that he defines knowledge in general in terms of the agreement or disagreement *between* ideas. Thus Locke is not in the uncomfortable position of having to claim that in cases of sensitive knowledge we perceive that our sensory ideas agree with the idea of existence. But this observation is a source of only modest comfort. Although Locke avoids falling into a verbal trap, it is still the case that his notion of 'agreement' seems tailored to conceptual relations among ideas, and that we are given no real account of what it is for ideas to agree with 'actual real existence' (*E* 4. 1. 7).

Faith and Reason

....

A major theme of book 4 is thus the very limited nature of our knowledge in the strict sense; in many areas of enquiry, including what we now call science, we must be content with probability. There is one area of enquiry of great concern to us where Locke feels that this epistemological moral needs to be developed at length, and this of course is religion. That Jesus is the Messiah or that the dead shall rise again are propositions which cannot be known but must be believed. The shrinking of the province of knowledge in the strict sense is thus the theme that connects the first and second halves of book 4.

Locke's great successor Immanuel Kant famously said that he sought to abolish knowledge in religion to make room for faith. It would not be quite accurate to apply this remark to Locke. As we have seen, he believed that he had succeeded in offering a demonstrative proof of the existence of God; unlike Kant, or even some Scholastics, Locke is committed to the possibility of demonstrating at least one proposition in natural theology. But by the standards of his time Locke was distinctly unorthodox in his readiness to shrink the sphere of what could be strictly known in religion. The most striking evidence of this is furnished by his attitude towards the issue of personal immortality. For Locke, what constitutes personal survival is something we can know; indeed, he is prepared to state necessary and sufficient conditions for such survival. But that persons will in fact survive their death is something of which we can have no certainty, but which we must believe on the basis of revelation. In his commitment to this position Locke is set apart from the majority of his contemporaries.

To say that Locke seeks to abolish religious knowledge to make room for faith would be a pardonable overstatement; by contrast, to say that his emphasis on faith is motivated by a desire to downgrade the role of reason would be wildly inaccurate. Locke's attitude towards fideism in religion can be easily gauged from his observation on Tertullian's paradox: 'Credo, quia impossibile est: I believe, because it is impossible, might, in a good man, pass for a sally of zeal; but would prove a very ill rule for men to choose their opinions, or religion by' (E 4. 18. 11). Indeed, as I suggested at the beginning of this chapter, Locke seeks to defend the role of reason against two very different sets of enemies. In opposition to both the authoritarian Catholics and individualistic Puritan fanatics, Locke maintains stoutly that reason must be 'our last judge and guide in everything' (E 4. 19. 14).

As a way of approaching Locke's central theses in the philosophy of religion it is helpful to see that he seeks to diagnose a philosophical muddle; the muddle consists in the failure to distinguish between the revealed proposition p and the proposition: it is divinely revealed that p.[9] According to Locke, the revealed proposition p is a matter of divine faith in the sense that it is exempt from rational scrutiny and cannot be doubted: if p is indeed divinely revealed, then there is no role for reason to play in determining its truth-value, for its truth is guaranteed by the fact that it is revealed by God, who cannot lie (E 4. 18. 5). Superficially, such claims may seem hard to reconcile with Locke's insistence that reason must be our last guide in everything, but in reality they are not. So much becomes clear when we turn to his analysis of propositions of the form: it is divinely revealed that p. Such propositions have a very different standing; far from being matters of divine faith which must be accepted, they are subject to critical scrutiny. Reason indeed has an essential role to play in examining their epistemic credentials. Here Locke does not merely argue that we must examine such things as the credibility of the witnesses; he also insists that the content of the supposedly revealed proposition is criterial for determining its status as a divine revelation. Thus if p is in conflict with our knowledge in the strict sense, then we can have no reason to believe that p is divinely revealed; for our rational grounds for believing this (depending on such things as the testimony of witnesses) can never be as epistemically weighty as our grounds for believing the negation of p, where the negation of p is known in the strict sense through the agreement or disagreement of ideas. Thus by conceding that if p is indeed divinely revealed, it must be simply accepted, Locke is giving very little away, for all the emphasis in his account falls on the question whether p is in fact divinely revealed.

In the chapter 'Of Faith and Reason' (4. 18) Locke thus mounts

[9] Cf. N. Wolterstorff, 'Locke's Philosophy of Religion', in Chappell (ed.), *Cambridge Companion to Locke*, 190–2.

a masterly attack on the authoritarian enemies of religion who seek to deny the individual the right to examine the evidence for himself in religious matters. In the fourth edition of the *Essay* Locke complements this attack by a polemic against the enemies of reason within his own individualistic camp; these enemies are the Puritan fanatics or 'enthusiasts' who lay claim to a special kind of certainty which comes directly from God. Locke explains their position with pleasing irony:

Would he not be ridiculous who should require to have it proved to him, that the light shines, and that he sees it? It is its own proof, and can have no other. When the spirit brings light into our minds, it dispels darkness. We see it, as we do that of the sun at noon, and need not the twilight of reason to show it us. This light from heaven is strong, clear, and pure, carries its own demonstration with it, and we may as rationally take a glow-worm to assist us to discover the sun, as to examine the celestial ray by our dim candle, reason. (*E* 4. 19. 8)

The enthusiast's light from heaven is thus supposed to be superior to knowledge in Locke's strict sense and to rational belief that is based on the careful examination of the reliability of witnesses. In the case of conflict between knowledge and private revelation the enthusiasts believe themselves justified in preferring the latter.

In opposition to the enthusiasts Locke returns to his favourite strategy (first seen in the polemic against innate knowledge) of arguing through a dilemma. He challenges his opponents to tell us just what is the proposition which they claim to see with a light from heaven; he thinks that it must either be the religious proposition *p* (e.g. that I am filled with the Holy Spirit) or the proposition that *p* has been divinely revealed. Suppose they say the former. In that case they can be confronted with a further dilemma: either they know that *p* in Locke's sense, in which case revelation is unnecessary, or they merely believe that *p* without strictly knowing it. If they believe *p* without knowing it, they can be challenged about the grounds for their belief. If they respond by saying that they believe that *p* because it has been revealed by God, then they are caught in a circle, for their only ground for believing that *p* is divinely revealed is their assurance that *p*. And the enthusiasts can be convicted of just the same circular reasoning if they embrace the second horn of the initial dilemma—that is, if they choose to claim that what they see with a light from heaven is that the proposition has been divinely revealed to them. Thus, as Locke says, their position comes down to the bald assertion that they are sure because they are sure.

Locke's argument will strike most readers as forceful and conclusive. But if they condescend to engage in argument, the enthusiasts themselves might charge it with begging the question; Locke simply assumes that there can be no supernaturally infused way of knowing which is somehow self-authenticating. But of course the burden of proof in this case lies with the enthusiasts.

Belief and Toleration

Locke is an individualist about knowledge in a conceptual sense: it is of the very nature of knowing that it cannot be done for us by someone else; as we have seen, this implies that even the justification for our knowledge claims cannot cite the authority of others. It is tempting to say that, by contrast, he is an individualist about belief in a normative sense: our beliefs ought to be based on a critical examination of the evidence. We may of course come to believe that p on the grounds that p is asserted by reliable witnesses or authoritative experts, but that is a very different matter; it is still the case that we ought to make up our own minds about the credentials of the witnesses or authorities in question.

The contrast, however, may be a little too simple-minded, for it can be doubted whether Locke is really committed to a normative claim about belief. If we ask: why must I examine the evidence for my beliefs?, the answer may well be: because rationality requires it; it then seems that the 'must' in question is more like a logical 'must' than a normative one. In other words, to be rational essentially involves critically examining the evidence for oneself; anyone who fails to do this fails to satisfy the logical requirements for rationality. However, it seems that we could get a genuine normative requirement if we suppose that, for Locke, we have a duty to be rational. It can be plausibly argued that an obligation to examine the evidence for one's beliefs is logically inherited from the obligation to be rational.

Even if we suppose that Locke is making normative claims in connection with belief, it is important to see just what they commit him to. Descartes notoriously appears to hold that it is possible to

believe at will; at least if I am not having clear and distinct perceptions, I can simply decide to believe that the earth is round. At first
sight, the supposition that Locke is making normative claims about
belief might seem to commit him to a similar position. Consider,
for example, a proposition which there are rational grounds for
accepting but to which, for some reason, I do not assent. Then it
may seem as if Locke would say that I ought to believe the proposition in question, and then on the further plausible assumption that
'ought' implies 'can', he would be committed to holding that it is in
my power to believe the proposition in question. But this reading is
clearly mistaken. Any normative theses which Locke advances in
connection with belief commit him only to the claim that we ought
to undertake a voluntary critical examination of the evidence, and
that claim is consistent with holding that belief itself is not a voluntary action; in other words, it is consistent with holding that any
belief which results from the critical examination of the evidence is
not something over which I have voluntary control.

This result is important, for in the *Letter on Toleration* Locke
deploys this anti-Cartesian thesis about the nature of belief as a key
premiss in a case against religious persecution. Locke there argues
that since belief is not under our voluntary control, it is not the sort
of thing that can be influenced by threats, coercion, or inducements.
Persecution may of course change people's behaviour; it may cause
them to frequent the churches approved by the authorities, but it is
necessarily futile for the purpose of causing them to change their
beliefs (*ET* 68–9, 120–1). In the *Essay*, however, it is less clear how
far he is committed to the anti-voluntarist position on belief. On the
whole, it is this position which seems to predominate. Certainly he
makes some seemingly unequivocal statements. 'As knowledge, is
no more arbitrary than perception: so, I think, assent is no more in
our power than knowledge' (*E* 4. 20. 16). Moreover, Locke insists on
the distinction mentioned above; though we cannot believe at will,
it is in our power to enquire or not to enquire into the grounds for
our beliefs: 'But though we cannot hinder our knowledge, where
the agreement is once perceived; nor our assent where the probability manifestly appears upon due consideration of all the measures
of it: yet *we can hinder both knowledge and assent, by stopping our
enquiry,* and not employing our faculties in the search of any truth'
(*E* 4. 20. 16). The voluntary suspension of enquiry may thus have
an indirect effect on our belief, but to acknowledge this is not of

course to imply that belief is directly under the control of the will. Yet, as in the chapter 'Of Power' (2. 21), where there are tensions over the nature of human freedom, so too in the final chapters of the *Essay* Locke's anti-voluntarist pronouncements about belief are accompanied by some statements of an apparently contrary tendency; for instance, he even remarks that 'assent, suspense, or dissent are often voluntary actions' (*E* 4. 20. 15). On the subject of belief, then, the *Essay* does not yield the sharp contrast with the Cartesian position that it appears to do at first sight. The lack of a sharp contrast is compounded by the fact that Descartes's position on belief is a nuanced one; although he recognizes many cases where we may believe at will, he also insists that clear and distinct perception, or overwhelming evidence, compels assent.

It is the *Letter on Toleration* rather than the *Essay* to which we must turn for an anti-voluntarist theory of belief which is pressed into service of a case for religious liberty. None the less, in reading the final sections of the *Essay* no one can miss Locke's critique of authoritarian societies in which freedom of conscience is denied and critical thinking is actively discouraged (e.g. *E* 4. 20. 4). We can also hardly fail to see how strongly Locke deprecates the habit of mind which tends to accept views without critical scrutiny; indeed, as we have seen, Locke criticizes the Cartesians for returning to authoritarian habits of mind through the use they make of the doctrine of innate knowledge (*E* 4. 20. 8). In its commitment to intellectual toleration and the 'open' society the *Essay* is clearly a forerunner of the Enlightenment. We must now turn to Locke's more overtly political defence of freedom against the authoritarian state.

10

THE EVILS OF ABSOLUTISM

No one can doubt that there is a degree of ideological continuity between the *Essay Concerning Human Understanding* and Locke's mature political theory as expressed in the Second Treatise of Government. In both works he manifestly appears as a champion of freedom against the claims of the authoritarian state. Although the Second Treatise does not directly make the case for religious toleration, it is well to remember that it was designed to forestall the emergence of a regime which would suppress all freedom of conscience in England.[1] But to some readers the two works seem to be very different in philosophical tendency; the Second Treatise appears to be infused by a more dogmatic, less critical spirit than the *Essay*. Even on specific issues the relationship between the two books is problematic; for instance, Locke's position in the Second Treatise is not obviously consistent with the denial of innate moral knowledge which is defended in the *Essay*.

There is some truth in these claims, but it would be wrong to deny that there is any philosophical continuity between the two works. The side of the *Essay* to which Locke's political theory is most obviously linked is what I have called its metaphysics of morals. As we have seen, his discussions of free will and personal identity have a markedly theological cast; they explore the implications of divine justice, as meted out in an afterlife, for the theory of

---

[1] The Second Treatise, together with the First Treatise, was first published in 1690 under the title *Two Treatises of Government*. The First Treatise is a point-by-point refutation of the theories of Sir Robert Filmer; it was published in an incomplete form, since Locke had lost part of the original manuscript. The *Two Treatises* was published anonymously. On the historical background, see T, introd.

human agency and responsibility. In a rather similar way the Second Treatise starts from the assumption that human beings are God's property and proceeds to deploy this assumption as a key premiss in a case against absolutism.[2] No less than his account of personal identity, Locke's political theory in the Second Treatise has proved remarkably fruitful and influential, and, not surprisingly, there are secular arguments as well which appeal to a less religious age than his own. But it is still fair to say that at the very heart of the Second Treatise is a theological argument about the proper function of the state.

From a modern standpoint, far and away the most important champion of absolutism in the seventeenth century was Thomas Hobbes. In his immortal masterpiece *Leviathan* Hobbes famously, or notoriously, argued that in the interest of peace and security people must submit to a sovereign state whose authority over its citizens is absolute in the sense that it is unlimited by any constitutional restrictions whatever. Hobbes's obvious pre-eminence as a theorist of absolutism has led many readers to suppose, rather uncritically, that he must be Locke's chief target. In the last forty years, however, this assumption has been strongly disputed;[3] it is now claimed that not merely the First Treatise but even the Second Treatise makes most sense when read as a polemic against the obscure patriarchalist theory of Filmer. And indeed, although the Second Treatise reaches anti-Hobbesian conclusions about government, it can hardly be said to engage very directly with the arguments of *Leviathan*. Hobbes's own premisses in *Leviathan* are aggressively secular, and for this reason it would be poor strategy on Locke's part to seek to refute Hobbes by laying out a theological case against him. No doubt the Second Treatise makes some shrewd incidental points against *Leviathan*, but it is not a systematic internal critique of that work. Indeed, Locke's relationship to Hobbes, like his relationship to Descartes, is a complicated one which includes elements of overlap as well as opposition. Not merely does Locke share a number of assumptions with Hobbes, but on occasion he also allows himself to be pulled closer to Hobbesian teachings than he would be prepared to admit. What does seem

[2] The theological dimension of the argument of the Second Treatise is emphasized by John Dunn in *The Political Thought of John Locke* (Cambridge, 1969).

[3] This assumption is criticized by Laslett in his introduction to *Locke's Two Treatises of Government*.

fair to say is that the Second Treatise of Government is haunted by the ghost of Thomas Hobbes.

Natural Law

One assumption that Locke shares with Hobbes is a methodological one: the assumption is that the correct way to tackle questions about the grounds and limits of political obligation is by performing a thought-experiment. We must consider individuals like ourselves in abstraction from all political institutions and relationships whatever; the result of this thought-experiment is the so-called state of nature. Any agreements that individuals so situated rationally make to establish a political society are then supposed to be normative for us; they are supposed to illuminate our own political rights and obligations. Just why this should be so is a question well worth asking. In the case of Hobbes the idea seems to be that the absolutist state which such individuals would set up is the only form of political organization which is purpose-built, as it were; it is uniquely adapted to the facts about human nature as analysed by Hobbes. In the case of Locke, who fails to advance a systematic theory of human psychology, the answer is perhaps less clear; his view may be that there are universal moral constraints on the form a legitimate political society may assume, and that these constraints can be best understood by means of the thought-experiment he calls the state of nature.

Locke's theory of the state of nature has two very different, and complementary, sides to it. One side is purely normative: it consists in specifying the jural relationships in which individuals so situated would stand to one another. The other side is purely factual or descriptive: it consists of a hypothesis about how such individuals would behave if there were no government. Obviously these two sides of the state of nature are logically quite distinct from each other; for from the claim that individuals are bearers of certain rights and duties nothing follows about whether they would in fact behave according to these norms. In a later section I shall briefly consider Locke's descriptive account of the state of nature; here, and in the following two sections I shall explore his normative theory. We shall see that in developing both sides of his theory he seeks to put as much distance as possible between himself and Hobbes, but whether the distance between them on either count is as big as it appears is open to question.

Locke effectively begins his normative account by telling the reader that 'the *state of nature* has a law to govern it, which obliges every one: and reason, which is that law, teaches all mankind, who will but consult it, that being all equal and independent, no one ought to harm another in his life, health, liberty or possessions' (*T* II. 6). The concept of natural law is a very old one in political philosophy, going back at least as far as the Stoics. Indeed, the core idea that there are certain duties which are binding on all people at all times and in all places receives perhaps its most memorable expression in an even earlier work, *Antigone*. Here is how Antigone justifies her decision to defy Creon's edict forbidding the burial of her dead brother:

> That order did not come from God. Justice,
> That dwells with the gods below, knows no such law.
> I did not think your edicts strong enough
> To overrule the unwritten unalterable laws
> Of God and heaven, you being only a man.
> They are not of yesterday or today, but everlasting,
> Though where they come from none of us can tell.[4]

The Stoic concept of natural law was subsequently assimilated into the Christian philosophical tradition; medieval philosophers might dispute whether the duties of natural law were binding because they expressed the will of God or were the will of God because they were independently binding. None the less, there was general agreement that in one way or the other natural laws were irreducibly moral laws which enjoyed divine sanction. Hobbes, by contrast, introduces the revolutionary idea that the laws of nature are not irreducibly moral laws at all; rather, they are maxims of prudence by adopting which rational self-interested individuals can increase their chances of staying alive. Hobbes further argues that the laws of nature are not strictly laws until they are commanded by the sovereign or by God;[5] however, whether God has in fact commanded them is not

---

[4] Sophocles, *Antigone*, in *The Theban Plays*, trans. E. F. Watling (Harmondsworth, 1949), 138.

[5] *Leviathan*, 1. 15.

something that can be known by natural reason, since there can be no natural knowledge of God.

Locke's own remarks on natural law in the Second Treatise are thin and perfunctory; as he himself acknowledges rather impatiently, it is not his purpose in this work 'to enter . . . into the particulars of the law of nature' (*T* II. 12). But from his early academic lectures to the late *Reasonableness of Christianity* natural law was a topic of intense concern to Locke. As we would expect, the evidence of these writings is that he seeks largely to undo the Hobbesian revolution and return to a more conservative tradition in moral philosophy. Certainly, from first to last Locke seeks to resist the reduction of natural laws to self-interested maxims; one of the early lectures or disputations is entitled: 'Is Every Man's Own Interest the Basis of the Law of Nature? No' (*ELN* 205).[6] In the text of the disputation itself he follows this up by remarking that 'utility is not the basis of the law or the ground of obligation, but the consequence of obedience to it' (*ELN* 215). Locke is sometimes prepared to say that right and convenience go together, but he never suggests that the one is reducible to the other. None the less, in one way, as we shall see, Locke proves to be a Hobbesian about the law of nature in spite of himself.

Locke confronts a cluster of problems concerning the knowledge of natural law. Faced with the claim that there is such a law, a person may reasonably ask how we can know what it prescribes. In the Second Treatise he gestures at an answer by saying that it is 'writ in the hearts of all mankind' (*T* II. 11). By helping himself to the Pauline phrase, Locke seems to be suggesting that we can discover what our duties are under natural law by turning our mental gaze on the contents which have been inscribed on our minds at least since birth; in the early *Essays on the Law of Nature* he himself had used the Pauline phrase in precisely this sense. But in that case Locke's teachings on natural law in the Second Treatise are egregiously inconsistent with his position elsewhere. In the *Essay Concerning Human Understanding*, as we have seen, he argues at length against the doctrine of innate moral knowledge, and in the early lectures on the law of nature he expressly denies that it is innate.

[6] The works published under the title *Essays on the Law of Nature* are in fact more like Scholastic disputations than essays in our sense.

The claim that the law of nature is written in our hearts seems subject to all the objections which Locke and others have raised against nativist theories. As we have seen, Samuel Parker had objected that the appeal to innateness was entirely lacking in epistemic value; from the fact that a proposition is innate in our minds it does not follow that it is true. By a curious irony, in his polemic against innate moral knowledge Locke himself makes a remark which suggests a reply to this objection, although in context of course he has no intention of giving any comfort to his nativist opponent. It is open to the defenders of an innate moral law to say that the issue of falsity does not arise, for what is inscribed on our minds is imperatives such as 'Parents, preserve your children', and such imperatives are not principles or propositions which have a truth-value (*E* 1. 3. 12). This is an interesting reply, although it will not get the Locke of the Second Treatise very far. For it can still be asked how we know that these imperatives are truly laws, and, as we shall see, this is a question which gives Locke a lot of trouble.

It is natural to come to the defence of Locke in the Second Treatise by saying that his quotation from St Paul should not be understood too literally. It is true that, for convenience, Locke helps himself to a phrase which was widely used as a kind of shorthand expression for a theory of innate moral principles, but he is not using the phrase in that way here. All he means to assert is the weaker claim that the law of nature can be known by the use of our natural faculties, and such a claim is obviously consistent, on Lockean principles, with recognizing a role for sense-experience in the acquisition of moral ideas and beliefs. In the early *Essays on the Law of Nature* Locke asks: 'Can the Law of Nature be Known by the Light of Nature?' and answers his own question in the affirmative (*ELN* 123).

The retreat to this weaker claim no doubt represents Locke's best strategy for defending the consistency of his teachings between different works. But the issue of consistency is not the only problem which confronts him; he faces a further difficulty in explaining how, by the use of our natural faculties, we can have knowledge of the natural law *qua* law.[7] In the *Essays on the Law of Nature* Locke is clear that several conditions must be satisfied for knowledge of a law:

---

[7] This problem is emphasized by Leo Strauss in *Natural Right and History* (Chicago, 1953), ch. 5.

First, in order that anyone may understand that he is bound by a law, he must know beforehand that there is a lawmaker, i.e. some superior power to which he is rightly subject. Secondly, it is also necessary to know that there is some will on the part of that superior power with respect to the things to be done by us, that is to say, that the lawmaker, whoever he may prove to be, wishes that we do this but leave off that, and demands of us that the conduct of our life should be in accordance with his will. (*ELN* 151)

Now in the case of natural law, the lawmaker is supposed to be God, and it may seem challenging enough to show that these conditions are in fact satisfied. But the real problem for Locke arises not from the difficulty of proving that God exists or that he has issued certain commands; it arises rather from his concept of law in general.

In the *Essay Concerning Human Understanding* and elsewhere Locke shows himself to be committed to a very definite theory of law. A law, for Locke, is not of course just any command or imperative; nor is it even, as Hobbes thought, just a command issued by a competent authority; rather, it is a command issued by such an authority which has sanctions annexed to it. In the *Essay* Locke is very clear that sanctions are of the essence of law:

Since it would be utterly in vain, to suppose a rule set to the free actions of man, without annexing to it some enforcement of good and evil, to determine his will, we must, wherever we suppose a law, suppose also a reward or punishment annexed to that law. It would be in vain for one intelligent being, to set a rule to the actions of another, if he had it not in his power, to reward the compliance with, and punish deviation from his rule, by some good and evil, that is not the natural product and consequence of the action itself. For that being a natural convenience, or inconvenience, would operate of itself without a law. This, if I mistake not, is the true nature of all *law*, properly so called. (*E* 2. 28. 6)

And in the *Letter on Toleration* Locke observes that 'if no penalties are attached to them, the force of law vanishes' (*ET* 68–9). To know, then, that certain moral rules are strictly laws, we must know that God has annexed punishments and rewards to their breach and observance respectively. But it is just this condition that seems impossible to satisfy on Lockean principles. For here and elsewhere Locke debars himself from the option of saying that the sanctions in question may operate in this life; hangovers, for example, are 'natural inconveniences' attendant on getting drunk, but they are not legal sanctions since 'they would operate without a law'. And though in correspondence he seems to retreat a little,[8] in the *Essay* he appears to hold that in this world there are no other effects which satisfy the conditions for being sanctions required by the natural law. It follows, then, that the sanctions in question are eschatological. But unfortunately Locke teaches that the existence of an afterlife is not something that we can discover by the use of our natural reason. It is not until a late work, *The Reasonableness of Christianity*, that he comes close to recognizing the force of the problem. Here he bemoans the failure of philosophical efforts to demonstrate the content of the law of nature or the grounds of its obligation:

It is true, there is a law of nature, but who is there that ever did, or undertook to give it us all entire, as a law; no more, nor no less, than what was contained in and had the obligation of that law? Whoever made out all the parts of it, put them together, and showed the world their obligation? (*LW* vii. 142)

And Locke goes on to suggest that philosophers' failure with regard to the law of nature may be traced to the difficulty of demonstrating the existence of sanctions:

Those just measures of right and wrong, which necessity had anywhere introduced, the civil laws prescribed, or philosophy recommended, stood [not] on their true foundations. They were looked on as bonds of society and conveniences of common life, and laudable practices. But where was it that their obligation was thoroughly known and allowed, and they received as precepts of a law; of the highest law; the law of nature? That could not be, without a clear knowledge and acknowledgement of the lawmaker, and the great rewards and punishments, for those that would or would not obey him. (*LW* vii. 144)

Even here, however, Locke stops short of conceding that the difficulty of knowing the existence of such sanctions is more than a contingent one.

We are now in a position to see how in their teachings on natural

---

[8] In a letter to his friend James Tyrrell Locke seeks to leave open the possibility that the sanctions of the law of nature may operate in this life. But he does not explain what these might be if they are not the 'natural inconveniences'. See Locke to Tyrrell, 4 Aug. 1690, *CL* iv. 111.

law Hobbes and Locke are not so far apart as they appear to be. Locke regularly insists, in contrast to Hobbes, that self-interest is not the ground of our obligation to obey natural law, and there is no reason to dispute his assertion. But Hobbes had also taught that by natural reason we are unable to discover that the laws of nature are properly laws, and it seems that Locke is logically committed by his principles to agreeing with this assertion; the principles of morality cannot be known to be more than 'bonds of society, and conveniences of common life'. In the Second Treatise of Government Locke suggests that the law of nature is not attended with any epistemological difficulties, but we can see that he is merely whistling in the dark.

Natural Rights

Although he may have difficulty solving some of the epistemological problems it raises, Locke certainly asserts a doctrine of natural law in the Second Treatise; under such a law we have a duty not to harm other people in their 'life, health, liberty, or possessions' (T II. 6). Many readers of the Second Treatise suppose that they hear in these words the first adumbration of Locke's theory of natural rights. It is a curious fact about the Second Treatise, however, that he rarely speaks in so many words of a natural right to life, liberty, and property. Despite his alleged influence on the American Declaration of Independence, even the attribution of such a doctrine to Locke cannot be simply taken for granted. Perhaps a version of the doctrine may be found in the Second Treatise, but it is a version rather different from what it is often taken to be.

It is easy to suppose that Locke's doctrine of natural law straightforwardly entails a theory of natural rights, but this supposition would be mistaken. We can see that it is a mistake by considering the moral status of animals. One might argue that we have a duty, under natural law, not to treat animals with cruelty, but to recognize such a duty does not logically commit one to the ascription of rights to animals. A medieval philosopher might say that the bearer of rights in this case is not the animal but God; it is he whose rights are violated when a cat, for example, is tortured for pleasure. We have a duty under natural law in respect of animals, but we do not have a duty to them in a sense which would imply that they were bearers of rights.

Such a view of the moral status of animals offers a clue to understanding Locke's position on the moral status of human beings. Suppose we ask: why is it wrong to kill and enslave other people in the state of nature? Locke's answer to this question is clear, for he follows up his account of our duties under natural law with this explanation: 'men being all the workmanship of one omnipotent, and infinitely wise maker; all the servants of one sovereign master, sent into the world by his order and about his business; they are his property, whose workmanship they are, made to last during his, not one another's pleasure' (T II. 6). Human beings, then, are God's property, and we have a duty under natural law not to destroy or vandalize what belongs to God. Our duty not to kill or enslave other people is a special case of our duty to respect God's property rights. From the thesis that we are God's property Locke derives the taboo on suicide; since we belong to God we do not have the right to take our own lives. The taboo on suicide in turn grounds the taboo on self-enslavement. To enter a contract of slavery would be to give another person the right to dispose of us at pleasure, but since we do not have such a right over ourselves, we cannot transfer it to someone else.

The idea that we are God's property thus does important work in Locke's political theory; it provides the only foundation for the taboo on suicide and self-enslavement. But it would perhaps be an exaggeration to say that, for Locke, God alone is the true bearer of rights; after all, Locke famously says that every man has a property in his own person. Here we may take advantage of the fact that property rights may be of different kinds; we might say that though, in respect of human beings, God is the freeholder, we ourselves are the leaseholders, and that for this reason our right to do as we want with ourselves is subject to certain restrictions. In this way Locke's thesis that we are God's property can be reconciled with his further thesis that every man has a property in his own person.

Human beings, then, may be regarded as bearers of natural rights in a derivative sense. But to say this is not of course to say that Locke agrees with Jefferson in regarding such rights as inalienable (a term which Locke never uses in the Second Treatise). To make headway with this question we need to know what is meant by the term 'inalienable'.[9] If an inalienable right is understood in a strong sense as a right which cannot be lost in any way, then Locke appears not to believe that any of our natural rights are inalienable in this sense; certainly he is clear that natural rights to life and liberty can be forfeited by wrongdoing (i.e. by violations of the law of nature). If, however, an inalienable right is understood in a weaker sense as a right which cannot be voluntarily given up, then the position is more complicated, and some distinctions need to be made. The natural rights to life and liberty might be called inalienable, but, as we have seen, they are inalienable only by virtue of the fact that we are not the ultimate bearers of these rights; we have only a kind of leasehold in our persons. By contrast, the natural right to property (see next section) is in one sense not inalienable; a property right is indeed the paradigm of a right which can be transferred (for example, by gift or contract of sale). And there is one further right which we all possess in the state of nature simply by virtue of being human beings which is also not inalienable: this is what Locke calls the right to execute the law of nature. This right to punish offences not only can be renounced; its renunciation in favour of the community is what constitutes the very essence of a political society: 'wherever therefore any number of men are so united into one society, as to quit every one his executive power of the law of nature, and to resign it to the public, there and there only is a *political, or civil society*' (T II. 89). At other times, as we shall see, Locke suggests a rather different criterion; the defining characteristic of political society is that no one is judge in his own case.

The doctrine that it is of the very essence of natural rights to be inalienable is thus not to be found in Locke, whether the strong or the weak sense of the term is at issue. But before we conclude this section it is worth noting that there are two generalizations that can be made about Lockean natural rights. In the first place, they are all claim-rights or entitlements; in other words, they correlate with obligations (under natural law) on the part of other people. In this respect they are to be contrasted with so-called liberty rights. The idea of a liberty right may be easily illustrated. Suppose that you and I are walking down the street and I am the first to notice a $5

---

[9] Here I am indebted to A. J. Simmons, 'Inalienable Rights and Locke's *Treatises*', *Philosophy and Public Affairs*, 12 (1983), 175–204.

bill in the gutter.[10] There is a sense in which I have a right to appropriate the bill, but it would be wrong to say that you are under any obligation to stand idly by and let me enrich myself in this way. Secondly, Lockean natural rights are active in nature; that is, the obligations with which they correlate are simply duties of non-interference. They are thus to be contrasted with the so-called rights of recipience. When, for example, it is claimed that people have a right to a minimum standard of living, what is at issue is clearly a right of recipience; it is being asserted that there is some person or institution (presumably the state) which is under a duty to provide such benefits for people. In the broad context of philosophical development, it is this second characteristic which matters most, for it distinguishes Lockean natural rights from those which are recognized by the socialist tradition. But in the context of his own time it is perhaps the first that is most significant, for it sets Lockean natural rights apart from those which are recognized by Thomas Hobbes.

Property Rights

'God . . . *has given the earth to the children of men*, given it to mankind in common' (*T* II. 25). Locke's famous chapter on property (chapter 5) may seem to be one of his most secular discussions, and certainly its subject is not an obviously spiritual one. But as his initial quotation from the Psalms suggests, even here he avails himself of assumptions about God's purposes for his creatures. And, as we shall see, attention to Locke's theological assumptions helps to dispel some puzzles of interpretation.

Locke's chapter on property stakes out an anti-Hobbesian position, but its agenda is set by the project of responding to Filmer. Filmer had explained the genesis of property rights in terms of God's original grant of dominion to Adam; subsequent owners of property were supposed to be Adam's heirs. Locke of course does not share Filmer's assumption that political philosophy can be done by simply glossing biblical history; as we have seen, he is

[10] Cf. H. L. A. Hart, 'Are there any Natural Rights?', in A. Quinton (ed.), *Political Philosophy* (Oxford, 1967), 57.

committed to the methodological starting-point of the state of nature. But Locke sees that, in terms of his own methodology, he is faced with a serious challenge; he needs to be able to explain how exclusive property rights could legitimately emerge in a state of nature where the initial situation is one of negative communism, that is, one where no one owns anything. Now one of Locke's contemporaries had sought to meet this challenge; Pufendorf had argued that people in a state of nature must obtain the consent of their fellows before the fruits of the earth can be privately appropriated.[11] But Locke rejects Pufendorf's theory as a clumsy solution which would effectively condemn the human race to starvation (*T* II. 28). Locke's task, then, is to find a more satisfactory answer to the challenge that Filmer had thrown down.

In retrospect it is possible to see that Locke's own general theory of appropriation has been foreshadowed in his initial discussion of our moral standing in relation to God. In chapter 5 Locke famously argues that it is labour and labour alone which confers a property right in a previously unowned thing. In terms of this general theory we can see how Locke was justified in claiming that we are God's property; for God mixed his labour with us who were not previously owned by anyone else. Strictly speaking of course, there is a disanalogy between divine labour and human labour. Human beings mix their labour with raw materials which they do not themselves produce but are provided by nature; God, by contrast, creates the human race *ex nihilo*. But this disanalogy does not undermine the case for saying that, on Lockean principles, we belong to God. For Locke has theological warrant for thinking of divine creation as a form of labour; and if refashioning raw materials provided by nature confers a property right, then *a fortiori* creation *ex nihilo* also confers a property right. God's ownership of the human race is thus justified by virtue of the general theory.

Locke offers two main arguments for his labour theory of appropriation. His first argument turns on the key premiss that every man has a property in his own person (*T* II. 27). According to Locke, my ownership of my person extends not just to my body, but also to my labour. It follows, then, that by mixing my labour with a previously unowned object, I mix with it something that I own. My

[11] S. Pufendorf, *De Jure Naturae et Gentium*, 4. 4. 13. For the historical background to Locke's theory of property, see J. Tully, *A Discourse on Property* (Cambridge, 1980).

labour is somehow supposed to seep over into the whole object, which therefore becomes permeated with my ownership: 'Whatsoever then he removes out of the state that nature hath provided, and left it in, he hath mixed his *labour* with, and joined to it something that is his own, and thereby makes it his *property*' (T II. 27). This argument may seem to sit uneasily with the thesis that we are God's property, but, as we have seen, the appearance of inconsistency can be removed by supposing that Locke recognizes different kinds of property rights; even if my self-ownership is only a kind of leasehold, it can be sufficient to found an exclusive property right to those objects with which I mix my labour.

A difficulty with this argument is to see why we should accept that my ownership of my labour comes to permeate the whole object with which I mix it. That there is something questionable about the argument emerges in Locke's discussion of its application to particular cases. Locke famously discusses the case of a man who gathers acorns or apples under a tree and subsequently eats them; in accordance with his principles Locke argues that the first act of gathering, being an instance of labour, conferred a property right to the fruits of the earth. Locke holds that it is uncontroversial that the man has appropriated them; 'no body can deny that the nourishment is his' (T II. 28). But here Locke seems to be guilty of equivocating between two senses of the possessive adjective. We can illustrate the point by means of another example from Lewis Carroll. When the Knave of Hearts steals some tarts and then scoffs the lot, there is a trivial sense in which the nourishment is his; that is, it is he and no one else who derives the benefit. But it hardly follows from this fact that he has a right to it. Of course Locke would deny that the Knave of Hearts has acquired a property right, for the tarts were stolen; Locke's discussion concerns only those cases where the fruits of the earth are previously unowned. But his assertion that the existence of the right is uncontroversial in such cases may still trade on the ambiguity we have noticed.

Later in the chapter Locke seems to make play with an argument from desert. When I mix my labour with an object, I increase its value; thus I am entitled to the object whose value I have thereby increased (T II. 40). A difficulty with this argument is that it depends on a false assumption; it is not universally true that mixing one's labour with an object increases its value. In Nozick's example, if you find some apples and spray toxin on them, then by Locke's criterion you have mixed your labour with these fruits of the earth; but it would hardly be true to say that you have increased their value.[12] One may also wonder why the person is entitled to the object rather than just the value he has added. Presumably the problem is that if I merely own the added value, then there is no concrete object which I own, and for Locke this is counter-intuitive. Of course, if someone else owns a piece of driftwood and I (through agreement) add to its value by turning it into a chair, then I can be compensated for my labour, but this case presupposes property rights whose origin Locke is trying to explain.

Labour, then, for Locke is the basis of property rights, but labour is not, strictly speaking, a sufficient condition for just appropriation; natural law imposes a strict limitation which must be respected if appropriation is to be just:

The same law of nature, that does by this means give us property, does also *bound* that *property too. God has given us all things richly* . . . is the voice of reason confirmed by inspiration. But how far has he given it us? *To enjoy.* As much as anyone can make use of to any advantage of life before it spoils; so much he may by his labour fix a property in. Whatever is beyond this, is more than his share, and belongs to others. Nothing was made by God for man to spoil or destroy. (*T* II. 31).

Since the work of Macpherson it has become usual to suppose that this 'spoilage limitation' is supplemented by another limitation imposed by natural law; we have a duty to leave 'enough and as good' for others (*T* II. 33).[13] Locke does indeed say that if this 'sufficiency limitation' is satisfied, then 'no body could think himself injured' (*T* II. 33). But he nowhere explicitly states that we have a duty under natural law to leave enough and as good for others. Locke, with his eyes fixed mainly on land at this point, seems to think that the satisfaction of this condition is virtually automatic in the state of nature, and that this is why there is no extra duty to honour the sufficiency limitation.

The supposition that, for Locke, natural law imposes the two limitations on what may be justly appropriated has given rise to some mistaken objections. Readers who are in the grip of this sup-

[12] R. Nozick, *Anarchy, State and Utopia* (Oxford, 1974), 175.
[13] C. B. Macpherson, *The Political Theory of Possessive Individualism* (Oxford, 1962), ch. V, esp. 203–20.

position have sometimes been puzzled why he needs the spoilage limitation at all; it has seemed to them that the sufficiency limitation is adequate for his purposes. To see the point of the objection consider his own example of the river. Locke explains: 'No body could think himself injured by the drinking of another man, though he took a good draught, who had a whole river of the same water left him to quench his thirst. And the case of land and water, where there is enough of both, is perfectly the same' (T II. 33). Suppose, then, that instead of drinking the water for refreshment, I choose to splash my friends with it so that it goes to waste; if there is still plenty of water left for you and everyone else, it seems that no one's rights have been violated (my friends were in a playful mood and did not at all resent being splashed). Thus the objection is that the 'spoilage limitation' is simply otiose.

The basic mistake which underlies this objection is a misguidedly anthropocentric conception of natural law. It is true that natural law may impose duties in respect of our behaviour towards our fellow human beings; we have a duty to preserve human life as much as possible and not to harm people in their life, health, liberty, and possessions. But reference to other human beings is not essential to natural law, and even those duties which do involve such a reference seem to derive from a more basic obligation to respect God's rights; as we have seen, Locke justifies his claim that we must respect the moral boundaries of other people by saying that they are God's workmanship, and therefore his property. Thus even if, as in the river example, no human being is injured by my wasteful actions, it does not follow that no moral agent is injured. God has a property right in the river, and this right is violated if I make use of the water in a way that fails to respect his purposes in creating it. The 'spoilage limitation' which natural law imposes derives from the same source as the duty not to harm or destroy innocent human beings. Far from being otiose, it is crucial.

If the preceding analysis is correct, then we are in a position to find fault with a famous and controversial account of Locke's chapter on property. Macpherson not merely popularized the thesis that Locke states two natural-law limitations on what may be justly appropriated; he also propounded the further thesis that these limitations apply only at a primitive stage of the state of nature. After the introduction of money the two limitations are, as it were, transcended. The idea here is that what is morally important, for Locke, is honouring the spirit, rather than the letter, of the two limitations; the spirit in question is supposed to be the principle that no one must be made worse off by individual acts of appropriation. The appearance of money on the scene allows us to honour this principle without observing the limitations themselves. How the 'spoilage limitation' is supposed to be transcended is clear: money is not the sort of commodity that rots or corrupts in the possession of the owner. How the alleged 'sufficiency limitation' is supposed to be transcended requires a more complex explanation. Briefly, the explanation turns on the claim that when land is privately owned and cultivated, it becomes much more productive than it would otherwise be. Thus even though there may not be enough and as good for others, they are not injured by my ownership, since they are the beneficiaries in terms of an improved standard of living. A journeyman or day labourer who receives monetary compensation for his labour is much better off than he would be if land were not in private hands. The larger moral which Macpherson wishes to draw is that Locke has a hidden agenda in this chapter: his real purpose is to justify the accumulation of unlimited amounts of private property.

Even its defenders must admit that this interpretation receives at best very oblique support from the text. But we can see that it is also based on clearly false assumptions. In the first place, as we have seen, Locke never states that there is a duty under natural law to leave enough and as good for others; thus it is simply misguided to seek in Locke's text for an elaborate account of how this limitation is transcended after the invention of money. In relation to property, natural law imposes only the one limitation—the proscription against spoilage—and while there is a sense in which this limitation is transcended after the invention of money, we should remember that it derives from a more general duty to respect God's property rights. And respect for God's property rights involves a respect for his purposes which seems inconsistent with the accumulation of unlimited amounts of capital. It is not for nothing that Locke writes of evil concupiscence and the *amor sceleratus habendi* (criminal love of possession) (*T*. II. 111).

In spite of Locke's strictures against avarice, some readers have felt that he is on the side of those with a great deal to lose, and it is possible to admit that he betrays more sympathy for the propertied classes than perhaps he realizes. None the less, it is no part of

Locke's purpose in the chapter on property to develop an ideology suitable for an emerging capitalist class. Rather, Locke's purpose must be understood, more straightforwardly, in the light of his quarrel with absolutism. Theorists of absolutism of both the Filmerian and Hobbesian kind had argued that private property is a benefit which is enjoyed as a gift from the sovereign; and what the sovereign gave the sovereign could take away.[14] On this point at least Locke is in direct conflict with Hobbes in arguing that fully fledged property rights could be possessed within the state of nature. We carry these rights with us as part of our moral baggage on entering political society, which may not take them away from us without our consent (as mediated, for example, by the votes of our elected representatives). Locke may believe that it is a function of government to protect private property, but this belief of itself hardly qualifies him as an apologist for unfettered capitalism.

The Case against Absolutism

Locke's chapter on property thus prepares the ground for the full-dress case against absolutism which is at the heart of the Second Treatise. To say this of course is not to say that the work is above all a refutation of *Leviathan*, for, as we have seen, the theory of absolutism was not the exclusive property of Hobbes; its exponents included not merely patriarchalists like Filmer but defenders of the divine right of kings who took their stand on Paul's teaching that the powers that be are ordained of God.

Locke's opponents may be regarded as a diverse group, and he perhaps pays a price for mounting such a blanket assault; he ignores some distinctions that mattered to some of his opponents. In the first place, he tends to write as if an absolute state was necessarily a monarchy; and while this assumption may have been shared by some of his opponents, it was not made by Hobbes, who allowed that the sovereign need not be a single person. Further, Locke often bills his polemic as an attack on absolute and arbitrary power, and though on occasion he distinguishes them (*T* II. 139), he generally tends to use the two adjectives in a way that suggests they are virtual

---

[14] This point is well made by D. A. Lloyd Thomas in *Locke on Government* (London, 1995), 91.

synonyms. But not all of his enemies would have accepted such an equation. Some of them would have insisted that while sovereign authority should be absolute it should not be arbitrary; in other words, the monarch should indeed be unlimited by any constitutional restraints, and may be held to account by God alone, but he does not have the right to govern according to whim in defiance of precedent, custom, and reason.

The most fully developed of Locke's arguments against the absolute state seeks to show that it could not be legitimately established by people leaving the state of nature. Concerning the legislative, which he regards as the supreme power in the state, Locke writes:

> It is *not*, nor can possibly be, absolutely *arbitrary* over the lives and fortunes of the people. For it being but the joint power of every member of the society given up to that person, or assembly, which is legislator, it can be no more than those persons had in the state of nature before they entered into society, and gave up to the community. For no body can transfer to another more power than he has in himself; and no body has an absolute arbitrary power over himself, or over any other, to destroy his own life, or to take away the life or property of another. (*T* II. 135)

In this argument Locke's fundamental thesis that human beings are God's property comes to fruition, as it were. Although it is not explicitly formulated here, it is this theological assumption which underlies the premiss that nobody has an absolute arbitrary power (which here means right) 'over himself, or over any other'. This last phrase is important, for Locke sees here, as he sometimes does not, that it is insufficient for his polemical purposes to insist simply on the taboo on suicide. For a defender of absolutism could grant this taboo, while still maintaining that the absolute state is a morally legitimate institution. In other words, Locke's opponent could argue that though we do not have an absolute right over ourselves, in the state of nature we none the less have an absolute right over the lives of others; if we all then transfer this right to the state, there will be no individual over whom it does not have absolute authority.

An apparent difficulty with Locke's argument is his assumption that any authority the state possesses must have been transferred to it by people on leaving the state of nature. It may be objected that this assumption is simply common to all thinkers who seek to found the authority of the state on a contract or on consent, and that it cannot be challenged without also challenging the whole methodology of the 'social contract' tradition. But this objection is mistaken. It is open to the contractarian to argue that the authority of the state derives (at least in some respects) from a renunciation rather than a transference of rights; this authority is none the less founded in consent, since subjects agree that all except those whom they designate as rulers shall give up the rights in question. Hobbes, for example, regards the sovereign right to punish as deriving in this way from the natural right to all things which he ascribes to people in the state of nature. And somewhat similarly, Locke holds that the executive power of the law of nature is renounced in favour of the political society. Thus his opponent could dispute the premiss that if the state is absolute, its authority must have been transferred to it. But this is not a serious difficulty in Locke's argument. For, as we have seen, he denies that anyone has an absolute arbitrary right in the state of nature; thus there is no such right to be renounced in favour of the rulers.

Locke concludes, then, that the absolute state is not a morally legitimate option. A second argument reaches an even stronger conclusion: the absolute state 'which by some men is counted the only government in the world, is indeed *inconsistent with civil society*, and so can be no form of civil government at all' (*T* II. 90). In support of this conclusion Locke appeals to the fact that in the absolute state the monarch is judge in his own case. He concedes that even under absolutism subjects have an appeal to law and judges to decide controversies with their fellow subjects, but he insists that they have no such right of redress against the sovereign himself. Hence the absolute state fails the test for a political society; indeed, its members are still in the state of nature.

At first sight this last thesis may seem to be one to which Locke is not entitled. Locke appears to understand the state of nature here as a condition in which everyone is judge in his own case, and it is not clear how the absolute state satisfies this definition; as he recognizes, even the absolute state leaves room for appeal to impartial judges for the redress of grievances against fellow subjects. The conclusion, then, which it seems that he should draw is that an absolute state is neither fish nor fowl but a kind of hybrid. On the one hand it is not a political society because at least one person is still judge in his own case, and on the other hand it is not a state of nature because at least some people are not judges in their own cases. But reflection suggests that there is a way of defending Locke's actual conclusion. The key point is to see that, despite appearances, there is a sense in which everyone is judge in his own case under absolutism; every subject is in this position in any dispute which arises with the sovereign, and the sovereign is similarly situated with respect to all his or her subjects. But in that case the conception of a state of nature must be rather a weak one; it must be defined as a condition in which everyone is judge in his own case in respect of someone, rather than as a condition in which everyone is judge in his own case in respect of everyone.

Locke's second argument is more coherent than it appears, but it is unlikely to move Hobbes, for he would simply reject the definition of political society to which it appeals. Indeed, neither of the two arguments we have examined would make much impression on Hobbes; the first argument, as we have seen, depends on an axiom of natural theology which would be rejected by Hobbes on the ground that by reason alone we can know nothing of God except that he exists.[15] These reflections are not offered as criticisms of Locke, for we have no reason to believe that Hobbes is the intended target of either argument.

Hobbes is more clearly the target of a third argument. Locke argues that it would be imprudent for people to exchange the state of nature for absolute sovereignty since the proposed remedy is worse than the disease it is supposed to cure. Locke concedes that the state of nature, considered now in its behavioural aspect, is subject to 'inconveniences' (T II. 13) which result from people being judges in their own cases, but he denies that it is a state of war of all against all, as Hobbes claims. With its inconveniences the state of nature is clearly preferable to living under an absolutist regime where people are at the mercy of a sovereign with vast power who is subject to no constitutional restraints. Locke is contemptuous of anyone who can think this a good bargain:

As if when men quitting the state of nature entered into society, they agreed that all of them but one, should be under the restraint of laws, but that he should still retain all the liberty of the state of nature, increased with power, and made licentious by impunity. This is to think that men are so foolish that they take care to avoid what mischiefs may be done them

[15] *Leviathan*, 3. 34.

by *polecats*, or *foxes*, but are content, nay think it safety, to be devoured by *lions*. (*T* II. 93)

Of course even this argument turns on a premiss which Hobbes would reject; in his estimate the evils of the state of nature are far worse than the mischiefs which polecats may cause. But inasmuch as it appeals to considerations of rational self-interest, it challenges Hobbes on his chosen turf.

It is sometimes objected that Locke muddies the waters by giving two very different and inconsistent accounts of the state of nature, considered as a hypothesis about human behaviour outside government.[16] In chapter 3 of the Second Treatise he seeks to put as much distance as possible between himself and Hobbes by emphasizing that the state of nature is not a state of war; indeed in places he emphasizes this theme so strongly that even the polecats and the foxes seem to be temporarily forgotten. The state of nature appears to be a place where people respect the rights and duties under natural law which define the condition in its normative aspect:

And here we have the plain *difference between the state of nature, and the state of war*, which however some men have confounded, are as far distant, as a state of peace, good will, mutual assistance, and preservation, and a state of enmity, malice, violence, and mutual destruction are one from another. Men living together according to reason, without a common superior on earth, with authority to judge between them, is *properly the state of nature*. (*T* II. 19)

In chapter 9, by contrast, Locke has a different agenda; here he seeks to explain what impels people to leave the state of nature at all, and in explaining this, he appears to paint a much less favourable picture of life in these circumstances: the state of nature is an 'ill condition' (*T* II. 127) which is 'full of fears and continual dangers' (*T* II. 123). On the whole Locke diagnoses the source of the evil in moral backsliding: people know what their duties are under natural law, but out of self-love fail to perform them. But there is also a hint of the idea that the law of nature may not be as easy to know as he had earlier suggested.

It is tempting to suppose, then, that Locke is in two kinds of trouble here. Not merely is he guilty of inconsistency in his account of the state of nature in its behavioural dimension; he is also in

[16] Macpherson, *Possessive Individualism*, 238–47.

danger of undermining his prudential argument against Hobbes. For if the state of nature is as 'nasty', or almost as 'nasty', as Hobbes insists, then perhaps it would be rational after all to exchange it for the security of absolute sovereignty. But these criticisms are premature. Locke can in fact be defended against both these charges, though perhaps with unequal success.

In the first place, the charge of inconsistency should be viewed with some scepticism. It is perfectly proper for Locke in different contexts to emphasize alternately the assets and liabilities of the state of nature, provided he is clear throughout that it has these two sides to it. And it is plausible to maintain that this condition is satisfied. Thus the fact that in the early chapters he dwells on the assets and in the later chapters on the liabilities is not sufficient grounds for convicting him of inconsistency. And even in the early chapters Locke is not blind to the defects of the state of nature; indeed he describes them in a way that is of a piece with his later account. The fundamental evil of the state of nature which he stresses in chapter 9 is its insecurity; and insecurity is a theme that is at least announced in chapter 3. Even when we enjoy periods of peace, there is always the danger that the state of nature will topple over into the state of war; for there is no provision for preventing the escalation of minor disputes into major conflicts. It is worth noting that the peace of the state of nature could be precarious even if its inhabitants were unaware of the fact; they might be in a psychological state like that of drivers who are unaware of a precipice at the side of the road. Indeed here we might find one way of contrasting the Hobbesian and Lockean accounts. The Hobbesian state of nature is inhabited by people of a paranoid disposition; they are constantly aware of the danger of outbreaks of conflict. The Lockean state of nature is no less objectively insecure, but it is inhabited by people of a less fearful frame of mind.

It may still be objected that in places Locke not merely overlooks the liabilities of the state of nature; he implies or indeed asserts that it has no liabilities. As we have seen, he holds that men living together according to reason is properly the state of nature. But this claim can perhaps be defended in the light of his theological commitments. To say that people living in peace with one another according to reason is properly the state of nature is to say that they thereby live according to God's purposes. Locke does not mean to imply that the state of nature has no serious inconveniences or that it may not degenerate into a state of war; rather, he wishes to emphasize that it has the potential to be a condition in which God's intentions for the human race are fulfilled.

The charge of inconsistency can thus to some extent be rebutted. But perhaps the most important point to be made in Locke's defence is that even if it could be sustained, it would not damage his prudential argument against absolutism. Locke may appear uncertain whether the state of nature is really preferable to absolute sovereignty, but he is clear throughout that limited government— government which protects natural rights—is preferable to either; such a form of government offers all the alleged advantages of absolute sovereignty with none of its disadvantages. Thus it would not be rational for people to choose absolute sovereignty when limited government, the best option of all, is within their grasp. The fact, if it is one, that the state of nature and absolute sovereignty dispute for second place in Locke's mind is thus of no consequence.

We can now see that the real issue between Hobbes and Locke is not whether the state of nature is nasty but whether limited government offers a genuine stable alternative. Hobbes advances ingenious arguments to show that it does not: the options of absolute sovereignty and the state of nature are not merely exclusive but also exhaustive. But the experience of modern western democracies tends to suggest that his arguments must be unsound; on this issue it is Locke, not Hobbes, who has been vindicated by history.

Consent and the Limits of Obligation

Everyone knows that Locke's main purpose in the Second Treatise is to argue that we are under no obligation to obey tyrannical regimes. But it is misleading to say that Locke seeks to defend a right of rebellion against tyrants. For it is important to Locke to argue that it is not the subjects who can be convicted of rebellion; it is rather their absolute and arbitrary rulers. Making play with Latin etymology, Locke claims that 'those who set up force again in opposition to the laws, do *rebellare*, that is, bring back again the state of war, and are properly rebels' (*T* II. 226).

Locke's claim that it is absolute and arbitrary rulers who are the rebels may strike us as Orwellian Newspeak, but it is important to see how it is justified by a central strand in his thinking. For Locke holds that those who seek to exercise absolute and arbitrary power are guilty of failing to respect God's property rights; by violating their duties under natural law, they thereby put themselves into a state of war with their people: 'Whenever the *legislators endeavour to take away, and destroy the property of the people*, or to reduce them to slavery under arbitrary power, they put themselves into a state of war with the people, who are thereupon absolved from any farther obedience, and are left to the common refuge, which God has provided for all men, against force and violence' (T II. 222). Now, according to Locke, those who violate natural law and bring back the state of war forfeit their (derivative) natural rights to life and liberty. Thus absolute, arbitrary rulers lose their moral standing and may be treated like any beast of prey (T II. 16).

Locke's thesis that such rulers bring back the state of war may seem difficult to reconcile with his earlier thesis that absolute monarchs are in a state of nature with their people. For he seems to think that the state of nature and the state of war are conditions which logically exclude each other. It is tempting to suppose that this is one of those rare occasions when Locke wishes to distinguish between absolute and arbitrary rule; one might say, then, that it is arbitrary rule which marks a return to the state of war. But this attempt at a solution will not work, for in crucial passages he speaks alternately of arbitrary and absolute power (T II. 222). The answer, I think, is that when Locke says that absolute monarchs are in a state of nature with their subjects, he is thinking in the abstract of a morally misguided set of constitutional arrangements; when he says that absolute monarchs put themselves in a state of war with their people, he is thinking of the actual exercise of a falsely pretended authority.

Locke, then, is not accurately described as vindicating a right of rebellion, but he is certainly arguing that we have no obligation to obey tyrannical rulers. Moreover, we may do more than engage in civil disobedience; we have the right to 'appeal to heaven'—that is, resort to arms—against such rulers. But at this point we are faced by a puzzle concerning the overall coherence of Locke's central argument in the Second Treatise. For he notoriously introduces a doctrine of tacit consent which is not only attended with internal difficulties but has also appeared hard to reconcile with his thesis that we have no obligation to obey tyrants.

Locke introduces his doctrine of tacit consent in the following, rather natural way. In accordance with his principle that people are naturally free and equal, he argues that no one can be under political obligation except through his own consent (T II. 95). For Locke, consent is required not just to establish a legitimate political society in the first place; it is required to place any human being under an obligation to obey an existing government. But Locke wants to hold that people can be obliged to obey governments to which they have not given their express consent through such acts as taking an oath of allegiance. And he is not a modern democrat who believes that if governments are to be founded on consent, then all mature citizens must have a legal right to vote in elections. To fill the gap in the argument that his principles create for him, Locke appeals to the notion of tacit consent, and tacit consent, it turns out, is given by merely residing in the territories of a government:

> I say, that every man, that hath any possession, or enjoyment, of any part of the dominions of any government, doth thereby give his *tacit consent*, and is as far forth obliged to obedience to the laws of that government, during such enjoyment, as any one under it; whether this his possession be of land, to him and his heirs for ever, or a lodging only for a week; or whether it be barely travelling freely on the highway; and in effect, it reaches as far as the very being of anyone within the territories of that government. (T II. 119)

Locke is clear that tacit consent does not make a person a full member of a political society, but he seems to insist that it does generate an obligation.

Readers who have heard of Locke's reputation as a defender of government by consent are apt to be surprised and disappointed by this doctrine; and some may even feel that the whole notion of tacit consent is a bogus one. But this last reaction would be unjustified. Locke is correct to hold that there are circumstances in which silence is a sign of consent, and it can be shown that this principle is one on which we rely in everyday life in order to legitimate decisions. As John Simmons observes, if Chairman Jones announces a change of time in the departmental meeting and asks for objections, his colleagues would normally be said to have consented if they remain silent.[17] But as Simmons also observes, if silence is to count as an expression of consent, there must be agreed ways of indicating dissent, and these must be reasonable at least in the sense that complying with them does not involve consequences which are very detrimental to the potential dissenter. Locke's doctrine of tacit consent seems to violate this condition, for on his principles the only way of indicating dissent from a regime appears to be emigration.

Perhaps the underlying reason for dissatisfaction with Locke's doctrine of tacit consent is that he seems to mischaracterize his own position. If we consider Locke's examples of tacit consent, we may feel that they really illustrate a different basis of political obligation. The examples he describes are all cases where people enjoy certain benefits from government; even someone who barely travels freely on the highway enjoys the benefits of police protection and, let us suppose, well-paved roads. But in that case it seems as if Locke is implicitly appealing to a principle of fairness or gratitude; people who receive benefits have a moral duty to give something back—in this case, obedience to the laws. Whether this principle is regarded as morally compelling tends to differ from person to person.

More striking perhaps, in the context of the work as a whole, is the issue whether Locke's doctrine of tacit consent is consistent with his other commitments. He appears to say not merely that silence is a sign of consent but that such consent obliges people to obey any government whatever in whose territories they reside. It follows, then, that residence obliges people to obey even tyrannical governments. If this is his position, it is blatantly inconsistent with his basic goal in the Second Treatise of Government. Locke would not wish to say, as we have seen, that he defends a right of rebellion against tyranny, but he certainly wishes to say that people are under no obligation to obey it.

The difficulty can be met by clarifying the role which consent plays in Locke's political thought. It has often been said, loosely, that for Locke consent is the sole ground of our obligation to obey the state. But this claim is misleading if it is taken to imply that he regards consent as a sufficient condition of political obligation. This reading may be encouraged by his discussion of residence in para-

[17] A. J. Simmons, 'Tacit Consent and Political Obligation', *Philosophy and Public Affairs*, 5 (1976), 274–91.

graph 119, but if we turn to his more general statements about consent, we see that it does not capture his position. In paragraph 95 Locke is careful to say that consent is only a necessary condition of obligation: 'Men being, as has been said, by nature, all free, equal and independent, no one can be put out of this estate, and subjected to the political power of another, without his own *consent*.' To have a claim on the allegiance of the people a government must not only have their consent, whether given expressly or tacitly; it must also protect their natural rights to life, liberty, and property; in Locke's terms, it must keep its trust with the people.[18] If a government satisfies both these conditions, they have a duty to obey it.

Not surprisingly, then, Locke is not committed by his doctrine of tacit consent to the absurd thesis that people have a duty to obey tyrannical governments. But there is one further problem of consistency for Locke's teaching about consent, which arises in his chapter 'Of Conquest' (chapter 16). Locke wishes to argue that the Greeks who live under Turkish occupation have the right to 'free themselves from the usurpation or tyranny which the sword hath brought in upon them' (*T* II. 192). But Locke justifies this intuitive claim in a way that seems troublesome; he appeals to the fact that the Greeks have not given their consent to Turkish rule. Of course, if the Greeks have not consented, it does indeed follow on Lockean principles that they are under no obligation to obey the Turks. But what is at issue is whether Locke can consistently maintain that the Greeks have not given their tacit consent, for they reside in territories which the Turks administer, and residence, as we have seen, is a sign of consent. It seems, then, that he should adopt a different strategy for defending the right of the Greeks to cast off the Turkish yoke; he should say that although consent has been given, no obligation thereby arises because of the moral iniquity of Turkish rule.

There are two ways, I believe, in which Locke could defend the consistency of his actual position. One defence, in particular, stays close to his text. For Locke, residence counts as an expression of consent only if the form of government was originally established with the free consent of its citizens; it is this condition which is not

---

[18] This solution to the problem is similar to that proposed by Simmons, ibid. Simmons, however, is prepared to say that consent is the ground of political obligation, even while recognizing that it is only a necessary condition.

satisfied in the present case. As he suggests, the ancestors of seventeenth-century Greeks 'had a government forced upon them against their free consents' (T II. 192). Secondly, Locke implicitly at least recognizes that if silence is to count as a sign of consent, there must be some agreed means of indicating dissent. It is true that his theory here is not very satisfactory, for he appears to believe that emigration may satisfy the demands of this principle. But unsatisfactory as it is, Locke's position may be adequate for his present purposes, for perhaps the Turks do not even allow the Greeks a right of emigration. If that is the case, and there is no other means for indicating dissent, then the Greeks will indeed not have consented, and hence will have no duty to obey the Turkish regime.

Locke's championing of the rights of subject peoples against their oppressors leaves little mystery about the source of the subsequent appeal of his political thought. The *Two Treatises of Government* was first published in 1690, and the century ahead was to culminate in two revolutions which were undertaken by people who were in varying degrees imbued with Lockean principles. As we have seen, the philosophical fit between Locke's two greatest books may be problematic, but there can be little doubt about their ideological continuity. The *Essay Concerning Human Understanding* opens with a polemic against a doctrine which gave aid and comfort to the friends of dogmatism; it closes with a book which attacks the enemies of reason and toleration in religion. The Second Treatise of Government begins by asserting the freedom and equality of people in a state of nature, and it ends by defending the right of oppressed peoples to 'appeal to heaven' against tyranny. It is hardly surprising if in the following century the name of Locke became inextricably linked with the cause of freedom.

Bibliography

Editions

(See also works cited in the List of Abbreviations.)

An Early Draft of Locke's Essay, ed. R. I. Aaron and J. Gibb (Oxford, 1936).

John Locke: Two Tracts on Government, ed. P. Abrams (Cambridge, 1967).

John Locke: Drafts for the Essay Concerning Human Understanding *and Other Philosophical Writings*, ed. P. H. Nidditch and G. A. J. Rogers (Oxford, 1990).

John Locke: Some Thoughts Concerning Education, ed. J. W. and J. S. Yolton (Oxford, 1989).

Biography

CRANSTON, M., *John Locke: A Biography* (London, 1957).

FOX BOURNE, H. R., *Life of John Locke*, 2 vols. (London, 1876).

General Surveys of Locke's Philosophy

AARON, R. I., *John Locke*, 3rd edn. (Oxford, 1971).

ASHCRAFT, R. (ed.), *John Locke: Critical Assessments*, 4 vols. (London, 1991).

CHAPPELL, V. (ed.), *The Cambridge Companion to Locke* (Cambridge, 1994).

DUNN, J., *Locke* (Oxford, 1984).

MABBOTT, J. D., *John Locke* (London, 1973).

MARTIN, C. B., and ARMSTRONG, D. M. (eds.), *Locke and Berkeley: A Collection of Critical Essays* (London, 1968).

O' CONNOR, D. J., *John Locke* (London, 1952).

ROGERS, G. A. J. (ed.), *Locke's Philosophy: Content and Context* (Oxford, 1994).

YOLTON, J. W., *Locke: An Introduction* (Oxford, 1985).

—— (ed.), *John Locke: Problems and Perspectives* (Cambridge, 1969).

General Studies of the *Essay*

AYERS, M. R., *Locke*, 2 vols. (London, 1991).

GIBSON, J., *Locke's Theory of Knowledge and its Historical Relations* (Cambridge, 1917).

JENKINS, J., *Understanding Locke* (Edinburgh, 1983).

LOWE, E. J., *Locke on Human Understanding* (London, 1995).

MACKIE, J. L., *Problems from Locke* (Oxford, 1976).

TIPTON, I. C, (ed.), *Locke on Human Understanding* (Oxford, 1977).

WOOLHOUSE, R. S., *Locke's Philosophy of Science and Knowledge* (Oxford, 1971).

—— *Locke* (Brighton, 1983).

YOLTON, J. W., *Locke and the Compass of Human Understanding* (Cambridge, 1970).

Studies of Individual Topics in the *Essay*

The Theory of Ideas

BARNES, J., 'Mr Locke's Darling Notion', *Philosophical Quarterly*, 22 (1972), 193–214.

BENNETT, J., *Locke, Berkeley, Hume: Central Themes* (Oxford, 1971), ch. 1.

CHAPPELL, V., 'Locke's Theory of Ideas', in Chappell (ed.), *Cambridge Companion to Locke*, 26–55.

GREENLEE, D., 'Locke and the Controversy over Innate Ideas', *Journal of the History of Ideas*, 33 (1972), 251–64.

STEWART, M. A., 'Locke's Mental Atomism and the Classification of Ideas', *Locke Newsletter*, 10 (1979), 53–82; 11 (1980), 25–62.

YOLTON, J. W., *Perceptual Acquaintance from Descartes to Reid* (Minneapolis, 1984), ch. 5.

The Philosophy of Matter

ALEXANDER, P., *Ideas, Qualities, and Corpuscles: Locke and Boyle on the External World* (Cambridge, 1985).

AYERS, M. R., 'The Ideas of Power and Substance in Locke's Philosophy', *Philosophical Quarterly*, 25 (1975), 1–27; repr. in Tipton (ed.), *Locke on Human Understanding*, 77–104.

—— 'Mechanism, Superaddition, and the Proof of God's Existence in Locke's *Essay*', *Philosophical Review*, 90 (1981), 210–51.

BENNETT, J., *Locke, Berkeley, Hume: Central Themes* (Oxford, 1971), chs. 3–4.

—— 'Substratum', *History of Philosophy Quarterly*, 4 (1987), 197–215.

MANDELBAUM, M., *Philosophy, Science and Sense Perception* (Baltimore, 1964), ch. 1.

MCCANN, E., 'Locke's Philosophy of Body', in Chappell (ed.), *Cambridge Companion to Locke*, 56–88.

WILSON, M. D., 'Superadded Properties: The Limits of Mechanism in Locke', *American Philosophical Quarterly*, 16 (1979), 143–50.

Personal Identity and the Mind–Body Problem

ALLISON, H. E., 'Locke's Theory of Personal Identity: A Re-Examination', *Journal of the History of Ideas*, 27 (1966), 41–58; repr. in Tipton (ed.), *Locke on Human Understanding*, 105–22.

ALSTON, W., and BENNETT, J., 'Locke on People and Substances', *Philosophical Review*, 97 (1988), 25–46.

BENNETT, J., 'Locke's Philosophy of Mind', in Chappell (ed.), *Cambridge Companion to Locke*, 89–114.

FLEW, A., 'Locke and the Problem of Personal Identity', *Philosophy*, 26 (1951), 53–68; repr. in Martin and Armstrong (eds.), *Locke and Berkeley*, 155–78.

HELM, P., 'Did Locke Capitulate to Molyneux?', *Journal of the History of Ideas*, 42 (1981), 669–71.

THIEL, U., *Lockes Theorie der personalen Identität* (Bonn, 1983).

Freedom and Volition

CHAPPELL, V., 'Locke on the Freedom of the Will', in Rogers (ed.), *Locke's Philosophy*, 101–21.

Classification and Language

AARSLEFF, H., *From Locke to Saussure: Essays in the Study of Language and Intellectual History* (London, 1982).

ASHWORTH, E. J., ' "Do Words Signify Ideas or Things?" The Scholastic Sources of Locke's Theory of Language', *Journal of the History of Philosophy*, 19 (1981), 299–326.

—— 'Locke on Language', *Canadian Journal of Philosophy*, 14 (1984), 45–73.

GUYER, P., 'Locke's Philosophy of Language', in Chappell (ed.), *Cambridge Companion to Locke*, 115–45.

HACKING, I., *Why does Language Matter to Philosophy?* (Cambridge, 1975), ch. 5.

KRETZMANN, N., 'The Main Thesis of Locke's Semantic Theory', *Philosophical Review*, 77 (1968), 175–96; repr. in Tipton (ed.), *Locke on Human Understanding*, 123–40.

LOSONSKY, M., 'Locke on Meaning and Signification,' in Rogers (ed.), *Locke's Philosophy*, 123–41.

MACKIE, J. L., 'Locke's Anticipation of Kripke', *Analysis*, 34 (1974), 177–90.

Knowledge and Faith

LAUDAN, L., 'The Nature and Sources of Locke's Views on Hypotheses', *Journal of the History of Ideas*, 28 (1967), 211–23; repr. in Tipton (ed.), *Locke on Human Understanding*, 149–62.

PASSMORE, J., 'Locke and the Ethics of Belief', in A. Kenny (ed.), *Rationalism, Empiricism, and Idealism* (Oxford, 1986), 23–46.

WOLTERSTORFF, N., 'Locke's Philosophy of Religion', in Chappell (ed.), *Cambridge Companion to Locke*, 172–98.

—— *John Locke and the Ethics of Belief* (Cambridge, 1996).

WOOLHOUSE, R. S., 'Locke's Theory of Knowledge', in Chappell (ed.), *Cambridge Companion to Locke*, 146–71.

WOOZLEY, A. D., 'Some Remarks on Locke's Account of Knowledge', *Locke Newsletter* 3 (1972), 7–17; repr. in Tipton (ed.), *Locke on Human Understanding*, 141–8.

Moral and Political Philosophy

ASHCRAFT, R., *Revolutionary Politics and Locke's* Two Treatises of Government (Princeton, 1986).

COLMAN, J., *John Locke's Moral Philosophy* (Edinburgh, 1983).

DUNN, J., *The Political Thought of John Locke* (Cambridge, 1969).

LAMPRECHT, S., *The Moral and Political Philosophy of John Locke* (New York, 1962).

LLOYD THOMAS, D. A., *Locke on Government* (London, 1995).

MACPHERSON, C. B., *The Political Theory of Possessive Individualism: Hobbes to Locke* (Oxford, 1962), ch. 5.

SCHNEEWIND, J. B., 'Locke's Moral Philosophy', in Chappell (ed.), *Cambridge Companion to Locke*, 199–225.

SIMMONS, A. J., 'Tacit Consent and Political Obligation', *Philosophy and Public Affairs*, 5 (1976), 274–91.

—— 'Inalienable Rights and Locke's *Treatises*', *Philosophy and Public Affairs*, 12 (1983), 175–204.

—— *The Lockean Theory of Rights* (Princeton, 1992).

STRAUSS, L., *Natural Right and History* (Chicago, 1953), ch. 5.

TULLY, J., *A Discourse on Property: John Locke and his Adversaries* (Cambridge, 1980).

Comparative Studies

ALEXANDER, P., 'Boyle and Locke on Primary and Secondary Qualities', *Ratio*, 16 (1974), 51–67; repr. in Tipton (ed.), *Locke on Human Understanding*, 62–76.

AYERS, M. R., 'Locke versus Aristotle on Natural Kinds', *Journal of Philosophy*, 78 (1981), 247–72.

CURLEY, E. M., 'Locke, Boyle, and the Distinction between Primary and Secondary Qualities', *Philosophical Review*, 81 (1972), 438–64.

—— 'Leibniz on Locke on Personal Identity', in M. Hooker (ed.), *Leibniz: Critical and Interpretive Essays* (Minneapolis, 1982), 302–26.

JOLLEY, N., *Leibniz and Locke: A Study of the* New Essays on Human Understanding (Oxford, 1984).

PHEMISTER, P., 'Locke, Sergeant, and Scientific Method', in T. Sorell (ed.), *The Rise of Modern Philosophy* (Oxford, 1993), 231–49.

ROGERS, G. A. J., 'Locke's *Essay* and Newton's *Principia*', *Journal of the History of Ideas*, 39 (1978), 217–32.

SCHOULS, P. A., *The Imposition of Method: A Study of Descartes and Locke* (Oxford, 1980).

WIGGINS, D., 'Locke, Butler, and the Stream of Consciousness; and Men as a Natural Kind', *Philosophy*, 51 (1976), 131–58; repr. in A. Rorty (ed.), *The Identities of Persons* (Berkeley and Los Angeles, 1976), 139–73.

WILSON, M. D., 'Leibniz and Locke on "First Truths"', *Journal of the History of Ideas*, 28 (1967), 347–66.

YOLTON, J. W., *John Locke and the Way of Ideas* (Oxford, 1956).

Index

Printed in the United States
40324LVS00002BA/95